GREATER EXPECTATIONS

Children
Reading Writing

Edited by
Eve Bearne

CASSELL

Cassell plc
Wellington House   215 Park Avenue South
125 Strand   New York
London WC2R 0BB   NY 10003

© Eve Bearne and the contributors 1995

First published 1995

British Library Cataloguing-in-Publication Data
A catalogue record for this book is available from the British Library.

ISBN 0–304–33168–6 (hardback)
     0–304–33170–8 (paperback)

Typeset by York House Typographic Ltd, London W13
Printed and bound in Great Britain by Redwood Books, Trowbridge, Wiltshire

Contents

List of Contributors

Holly Anderson was a nursery teacher for eighteen years before working as an advisory teacher and now as Senior Lecturer in Language and Professional Education at Homerton College, Cambridge. Her interests include early years education, particularly writing development. She has written a number of articles based on her work with teachers and children and is currently involved in a collaborative research project with Norway, looking at writing in the early years in both countries.

Eve Bearne has taught English and drama in schools and colleges for thirty years. She was Project Officer for the National Writing Project and co-editor of a number of their publications. She is author of several books about language and literacy and co-editor of a range of books about children and literature. She is a part-time Senior Lecturer at Homerton College, Cambridge and spends the rest of her time writing and researching into aspects of literacy.

Claire Escott is a primary school teacher in Dorset. Her interest in children's language developed during her time studying at Homerton College, Cambridge, and, more recently, she has been looking at ways of developing children's experience of using information texts.

Ian Eyres was a primary class teacher and language specialist for thirteen years. His particular areas of interest are drama, writing and bilingualism. He is currently a peripatetic language and curriculum development teacher with Cambridgeshire's Multicultural Education Service.

Peter Fifield qualified as an archaeologist before deciding to train as a teacher. He has worked in comprehensive schools and special education for some years. His work is mainly concerned with the humanities and he is currently developing ways of extending access to the curriculum for children who experience a range of medical, physical and learning difficulties.

Mike Millroy is a junior school Deputy Head working in Essex, whose interest in classroom research started while taking an Advanced Diploma course at the Cambridge Institute of Education and continued with his involvement in the Essex Reading Project. His work on the use of reading journals was initially inspired by the work of Anne Thomas of the Centre for Language in Primary Education and, thereafter, by the children in his classroom.

Angela Ridley studied drama and English at Homerton College, Cambridge and now teaches in a primary school in Royston, Hertfordshire. She is interested in the ways in which stereotypical notions are socially transferred and how classroom approaches to examine such influences might be developed.

Rachel Sparks Linfield is a Senior Lecturer in Primary Science and Co-ordinator for professional studies at Homerton College, Cambridge. As both a teacher and a lecturer Rachel has carried out research into her own practice and children's ideas in different curriculum areas. Recent publications include a pack on teaching science and drama at Key Stage 1: *Science Through Stories* with Lesley Hendy, and a range of articles about science in magazines and journals.

Sarah Theaker teaches in a Cambridge junior school. Her love of story and storytelling has flourished since her first foray into *The Secret Garden* and she is now hoping to develop this interest through an MA in Children's Literature.

Janet Towlson is an early years teacher. She first began to look carefully at children's literacy when she was involved with the Language in the National Curriculum project in Essex, looking at young children's home uses of writing. Currently working with 4-year-olds, Janet is committed to finding ways to help children become more powerful speakers, listeners, readers and writers.

Mary Waterson worked in primary and secondary schools for many years. For the past twenty years she has been particularly involved in the education of Traveller children. She was, for some time, Field Officer for the Advisory Council for the Education of Romany and other Travellers (ACERT) and was awarded one of the Other Book Awards for *Gypsy Family*, published in 1978.

David Whitley is a Senior Lecturer in English at Homerton College, Cambridge. Before this he worked for a number of years with emotionally disturbed children. His research interests include children's use of media texts, medieval literature and the history of the fable which he has written about in *Voices Off*, to be published by Cassell in 1996.

Introduction

Greater Expectations:
Reflections of Difference

This is a book about expectations – and surprises. The teachers whose work makes up the book all began with some expectations – often quite high – of what children could achieve. They were all surprised. One of the reasons for these unexpected consequences was a genuine urge to find out. Their robust enquiries and investigations into children reading and writing in classrooms meant that their own practice had to be carefully scrutinized, both by themselves and the children they worked with. And such rigour led them to some unlooked-for discoveries. This kind of courage carries its own rewards in the new knowledge established by their work. It makes clear the importance of practical enquiry to the development and extension of educational theory. Certainly, the turbulence of the last decades of this century means that teachers have to hold firmly on to the rocks of their embedded theories. The whirlwind of curriculum change promoted by government and the gusts of new literacies and developed technologies have blown away much of the ground cover, so that the contours of theory can be seen more clearly. They can be recognized and made explicit, and this is what teachers are increasingly able to do.

But, of course, this is not a book simply about teachers and their theories; it is about children and classrooms, about reading and writing. After all, teachers' continuing endeavours are to help children 'get better at it' – whatever that 'it' might be. All of the questions that teachers continually ask themselves, all of their informal and formal enquiries and investigations into their classroom work, have that one end in sight – to help raise children's standards of attainment. That is what educational theory is supposed to be all about. It should feed into classroom work and grow from it. There has to be an exchange between practice and reflection if theory is genuinely going to assist teachers in pushing outwards the boundaries surrounding children's learning. This all sounds very serious – and indeed it is – but on the way, and in the teachers' accounts in this book, there is a good deal of pleasure. Children's voices echo through the pages, invigorating us and reminding us of why it is important to hold on to firm ground while storms are raging. So much of what goes for educational debate is more about pride than progress, division rather than integration. It is good to remember that it is the children who both justify and challenge any changes we might want to make in teaching, by forcing us to make clear what our aims and intentions really are. Leila, one of the children in this book, asks Mary Waterson, 'Why are we doing this?' There cannot be a more important question, and it is a question worth asking about this book. Why have the teachers whose work is represented here done it – and why in this way? Why have they carefully documented their own classroom concerns about reading and writing? And why have they looked at the two together and not concentrated on either reading or writing? After all, the National Curriculum requires that these two Attainment Targets are separately assessed and reported. Part of the answer lies in the fact that fragmentation of language – even describing language as 'English' – impoverishes. It also narrows. While dutifully following National Curriculum requirements, many teachers – not least the writers of this book – have become aware that children's best interests are not always served by trying to promote and describe their progress in reading, writing, speaking and listening separately.

One clear example can be seen in the ways in which current concerns about children's standards of reading have tended to narrow perspectives. The debate between protagonists of different methods for developing reading, particularly in the early stages of children's school careers, and the arguments over which lists of books should be included in the National Curriculum, have tended to neglect some equally important areas which are significant in consideration of a full reading curriculum and children's developing literacy. Recent reports by Her Majesty's Inspectorate, and now by OFSTED, have themselves stressed the importance of extending the range of children whose reading is already fluent.[1] If the debate stays within the limited areas of early reading and mainly concentrates on fiction, then the possibility of extending competence and encouraging a wider range of reading strategies is immediately limited. Similarly, overanxiety about method can lead to teaching strategies which do not allow space for the teacher to discover what children already know or for children to put school versions of literacy alongside their existing knowledge of texts drawn from their home and community cultures. In adopting more expansive than restrictive practices, the school curriculum can provide important spaces. Lissa Paul quotes the moving and elegant curriculum description given by Madeline Grumet in her book *Bitter Milk*: 'A curriculum designed for my child is a conversation that leaves space for her responses, that is transformed by her questions. It needn't replicate her language or mine, but must be made accessible to our interpretation and translation.'[2] The space referred to here is gendered space, but Madeline Grumet provides us with an equally eloquent plea for space for race, class and cultural difference. Conversation leads to exchanges of views and allows space for different positions in constructing theories about literacy and schooling.

Fragmentation or Integrity?

It is natural that there should be concern over those children who are struggling to acquire literacy. If literacy matters, so does non-literacy – crucially to those children who are described as 'failing'. And difficulties with reading and writing have their impact on the whole of learning. Language is so fundamentally tied to growth of knowledge in all areas of the curriculum that to try to teach and assess children's language development by separating reading from writing can lead not only to frustration and concern about the nature and validity of assessments but, most importantly, to the danger of fragmenting children's learning. The outcome of narrowing practice can so easily become restricted expectations, with obvious implications for future learning. It is more important to see how difference and integrity can go hand in hand. By integrating, rather than fragmenting, approaches to reading and writing, attention can be given to individuals – those who need to be given opportunities to go faster and further and those whose progress is a cause for concern, as well as all those in between – while taking a wider view. This view sees reading and writing as firmly related, and worthy of careful scrutiny in order to establish a clear view of what constitutes a vigorous literacy environment.

This book, then, is also about literacy. It seeks to make explicit the significance of the interrelationships between reading and writing – and, of course, deals with speaking and listening too. Literacy draws strongly on spoken and heard language, and home language is the bridge which helps children to move into the symbolic systems of reading and writing which they meet in school. So there is a continuing thread of reference to the language communities of the children and to the wider cultural and social implications of literacy. Further than this, though, this is a book about critical literacy – critical in two senses. First, and perhaps more usually, literacy is seen as critical throughout the separate chapters because it matters. It may be too strong to describe literacy as at crisis point, but it has certainly come to matter very much in the public areas of media exposure. Assertions and counter-assertions, passionately felt and argued, have become a regular feature of news coverage. Allegations about falling standards and notions of teacher accountability and parents' rights in relation to literacy have become familiar political weapons, and literacy has come to be described in the language of crisis. Since this vehemence is a social and cultural reality, literacy needs to be viewed critically. It needs to be carefully and thoughtfully examined and theorized. It certainly does matter – to any nation and its children; to all the nation and all its children. In the literate futures of the children lies the principled potential of the nation.

In her remarkable book *Always Coming Home* the continually intriguing writer Ursula Le Guin creates a future people called the Kesh. In a conversation about the community's archives, the archivist explains that they find it 'safer' to give information than to keep it:

Giving involves a good deal of discrimination; as a business it requires a more disciplined intelligence than keeping, perhaps. Disciplined people come here ... historians, learned people, scribes and reciters and writers, they're always here ... going through the books, copying out what they want, annotating. Books no-one reads go; books people read go after a while. But they all go. Books are mortal. They die. A book is an act; it takes places in time, not just in space. It is not information, but relation.[3]

This is tough to digest and, as might be expected from Le Guin, shakes established ideas. But in pointing to the idea of literacy and literate outcomes as processes to be experienced, to be placed in relation to other literacy events and practices, rather than seen as unchanging objects of study or unquestioning reverence, she certainly does offer a new perspective on the values attached to literacy in society now. The book also offers a sideways look at what might be worth considering (critically) about the literacies of the future

– those which will be in the hands of the children presently in our classrooms.

Literacies and Representations

Critical literacy in its wider, theoretical sense is reflected in the everyday
practice of the classroom. Le Guin rattles complacency or even proper
reverence for what can be written down and kept, and forces a re-
examination of the texts we present to, and expect from, the children we seek
to serve through education. The destabilizing effect of the archivist's view
foreshadows what we know about the times we are moving into and the shifts
in perceptions of what will count as valid and valuable literacy. We are now
educating children not just for one kind of literacy but for a range of *literacies*
or 'notations' as Margaret Meek puts it:

we must extend our notions of literacy, the uses and functions by which it is
described, to include the images and *notations* which are common, current and
important in our world beyond language in print. Representations of the world can
be read in other places than books.[4]

In that case, the argues, although the children themselves might outstrip
adults in their speedy use of new technologies, teachers need ways to help
children describe and frame what they already know. It is becoming daily
more and more evident that children have recourse to, and sometimes
sophisticated knowledge of, a wide range of texts besides printed books.
Other forms of popular literacy are newspapers, advertisements, computer
games, comics, films, pop videos, television news coverage with graphs, maps,
inserts and computer graphics, magazines, letters, computer printouts and
street literacy. We can add to these the increasing attention given in school to
children's own writing, picture books and visual texts – maps, charts and
diagrams. Children will need to learn how to put all of these elements of
literacy, as well as the more traditional forms, into a critical frame. The
sudden and proliferated range of texts and 'representations of the world'
means that it is even more critical for children to be able to exert discrimination and choice over the literacies which surround them. To be able to read
behind the images, through the notations or between the lines takes on greater
urgency; at times of crisis it becomes imperative to read and write texts with
the eyes of a critic. There is no better way to learn how to read critically and

attentively than learning how to write carefully and with conscious attention to constructing the text.

Children's Knowledge about Texts

Not only must children be able to read their own and others' representations of the world sharply and analytically, but so must teachers. Recent curriculum initiatives have drawn attention to the importance of being able to recognize and describe development in children's writing in terms of the technical and organizational features of texts. This goes hand in hand with identifying a young writer's increasing ability to use writing to serve particular and chosen intentions and to reach specific and varied readerships (or audiences).[5] Not only must children's implicit knowledge of texts be brought into the open, but, crucially, teachers' own understandings need to be made explicit in order to help them forge their own views of how best to tackle the classroom demands of helping children to energize their experience of an increasingly complex range of texts. What, for example, can a teacher make of this text written by Peter, a monolingual English 7-year-old whom I met in a suburban school on a snowy day:

First of all I spotted the intricate and detailed symbolic script. Then I noticed that the 'translation' followed left to right then right to left directionality. When I asked Peter about his writing he explained that this was 'snowman language'; he pointed out that it was 'like Arabic' and showed me how the direction of the text moved across the page and back again. When I asked him how he knew about 'Arabic' he said that his mum had told him, but that he had also seen it on television. It is worth thinking not only about what this reveals about Peter's knowledge of text, both at sentence level and larger organizational structures, but also about what it tells us about a 7-year-old's 'reading' of the spoken texts of home and the television as offering information which he might not otherwise have encountered. Then, of course, it is worth reflecting on the astounding cognitive (and pedagogic) implications of this fragment of text from a child described by his teacher as of average ability and who certainly was not showing the same level of confidence or performance as many of his peers.

When children write they are likely to draw on any models which are available in their literacy environment. The forms and formats of various texts – visual and print – will influence the ways they write, both in and out of school. These assertions may seem rather obvious, but it is easy to forget just how powerfully children can draw on and combine a variety of forms. Often, as in Peter's case, there are reflections of several other texts woven together through the agency of the writer's own communicative intentions. Andrew's account of how disaster came to the world (see p. 8) shows very clearly how varied these intertextual resources can be.

One of the most obvious sources which Andrew is drawing on is, of course, the Pandora story which his teacher, Cath Farrow, had read to the class.[6] But if you wanted to list the range of texts which he has interwoven you might find biblical reflections (both Old and New Testaments) as well as classical myth, not just in the references in the content, but in the cadences of the narrative itself – 'there will be death and life', for example, and, perhaps, in the figure of Judas kneeling far right. There are references to wildlife informational text – 'dig a big set under the ground' – and to medical knowledge of how germs and diseases are spread. There is the clear influence of comic book texts where sound and movement are represented graphically and, we think, to a poem by James Stephens about a half dog half cat. Andrew knows how traditional stories begin and end and has a strong sense of the storyteller's art, the pauses and rhythms of a told story combined with the literary dignity of 'the disaster came causing chaos'. No doubt there is a great deal more that might be drawn from this piece. What it very clearly shows is that in a first draft a young writer can powerfully control and shape images presented through a wide range of visual and verbal media.

Disaster came to the
Wold

One Peaceful
Summer day long
long ago there lived
a man called Judus and
One night Jupitr sent a messenger
(Mercury) there he said there will
be a great storm. because
Some one had offended
the smashed the box of
satisfactory. There will be death
and life so shelter
yourself. Dig a big
pit under the ground.
There will be snow and
frost, and insects that
spread germs and disisses!
So spread the news. It will
come in four days time.
Here is a box. Do not
open the it until the
disaster disaster comes! then Mercury
Went. The chaos disaster came
causing caos. So Judus
opend the box.

and oll jumped the five
Thurropuss, half dog half
cat.

The Thurropuss said, I
the Thurropuss, I have hope
in to me trust me I have a
very big blow it to they
went to the top of the set. Thano
going down to the set.
Thurropuss went and blew
the storm away but the
germs and disieses were
still on the earth.

Both of these, very brief, examples from Peter and Andrew suggest strongly that children's comprehension of texts might well be deeper and more sophisticated than could be discovered from traditional exercises to test understanding. Their comprehension extends beyond the meanings of texts they have met and drawn on, to a wide knowledge of the ways in which texts are constructed to make different meanings clear. I happened on Peter's piece by good fortune; I was in the right place at the right time and did not have any other demands on my time, so I had the chance to notice his snowman writing. It is chilling to speculate how many similarly revealing pieces have gone out with the rubbish at the end of a school day. Andrew's Thurropuss work was just one of a range he had been working on. In both cases it would have been quite possible to miss what their texts had to say. Once we know what each of these young writers (and readers) knows about and can do with texts, there is no turning back. The implication is, of course, that greater teacher awareness of children's reading and writing behaviours and knowledge, including image and pictorial reading, can lead to more ambitious ways of extending children's literacy. When teachers read children's writing with a more sharpened sense of how writing reflects reading, they are in a better position to move literacy forward.

What Can Be Expected

This book begins, then, with a close look at the exact relationship between reading and writing as evidenced in the classroom. How do the two interact with each other and how can teachers use the interdependence to raise children's levels of achievement? In offering some possible ways forward, the whole area of language is analysed, including the essential role of talking and listening in promoting literacy. This wide view of texts of all kinds moves to a tighter focus in the second part of the book. Here, the details of close and attentive reading and careful, planned text construction can be seen operating in a range of classrooms. The third part of the book puts together those close features of reading and writing with the wider cultural interpretations which texts involve, suggesting how children's classroom literacy can build on their sometimes unexpected and often neglected knowledge of other literacies. Finally, the postscript indicates the practical ways in which teachers' greater expectations of young reader-writers can be used to help them make even greater progress in reading and writing.

By making space and hearing, or by taking time and seeing what children know and can do about and with texts, even very small insights can lead to significant discoveries. One important space is the open door between the classroom and children's families and literacy communities. Then there are the historical spaces of time which children are able to encompass; the spaces between different views about how best to teach reading and writing; the imaginative spaces inside children's heads; and the seemingly infinite spaces they can create for storing knowledge of texts.

A theme which returns throughout the different chapters concerns greater expectations: put simply, the recurring motif is *the more you expect, the more children show they can do.* The implications for the teachers whose classrooms are represented here seem to be threefold: *now I know they can do this, I can expect even more* or *I'd never have expected they knew about that at their age.* Or, occasionally, and perhaps most excitingly, *I'd expected them to come up with one set of ideas and they presented me with something quite different....* The accounts are narratives of sometimes hard but always enlightening journeys. And, as in all good stories, the element of surprise – 'and suddenly . . .' – often takes the narrative, and the hearer/reader, 'away from the norm'[7] in unexpected directions.

Notes and References

1. Department of Education and Science reports by HMI (1989, 1990) *The Teaching and Learning of Reading in Primary Schools.* London: DES. OFSTED (1993) *Boys and English.* London: DfE.

2. Paul, L. (1993) Gender wars. In M. Barrs and S. Pidgeon (eds) *Reading the Difference: Gender and Reading in the Primary School*, p. 79. London: Centre for Language in Primary Education.

3. Le Guin, U. (1993) *Always Coming Home*, p. 334. Glasgow: Harper Collins.

4. Meek, M. (1992) Literacy: redescribing reading. In K. Kimberley, M. Meek and J. Miller (eds) *New Readings: Contributions to an Understanding of Literacy*, p. 233. London: A&C Black.

5. Both the National Writing Project and the Language in the National Curriculum (LINC) Project have made significant contributions to theories of text construction.

6. More of Andrew's work and the environment in which it was encouraged can be seen in Bearne, E. and Farrow, C. (1988) *Writing Policy in Action: the Middle Years.* Milton Keynes: Open University Press.

7. Meek, M. (1988) *How Texts Teach What Readers Learn*, p. 12. Stroud: Thimble Press.

Part One
Taking on the Texts

A significant marker of developing literacy is an increasing awareness of the different text types available to a writer. This gives adults the responsibility of finding ways for young readers to get into dialogue with the texts they read, questioning them, finding points of contact and using them as examples of possible ways to make their own texts. This means not only putting developing writers in the position of trying out different forms and formats for themselves, but also providing models and examples in a broad reading curriculum. However, just providing examples and opportunities is not enough. If young readers and writers are genuinely to develop repertoires of available texts, there needs to be careful, planned and systematic intervention to help them on the way. This opening section looks at how teachers can encourage children to take on the texts, to read actively and to write in different ways by using their reading experiences drawn from both outside the classroom and within it. Although they deal with different age ranges, the chapters in this section all identify the importance of providing a wide range of reading experiences, opportunities to write in a variety of forms and formats and systematic provision of ways to reflect on the process of putting texts together.

Questions about what children read, what they write, and how best to help them gain awareness of text construction signal an attention to text which inevitably leads to a wider debate about genre. The central questions seem to be: *what genres of writing should children be exposed to and be able to use?; at what stage in their education?* and *how should these genres be taught?* Lack of attention to the forms of writing, according to some theorists, has led to unhelpful classroom practice concerning reading and writing. The argument is that teachers need to have greater familiarity with generic structures. A recent report on the teaching of English in the UK highlights the immediate need for schools to 'help teachers acquire more knowledge and expertise in relation to knowledge about language – its structures, functions and variations'.[1] The three chapters in this part of the book examine just that need, giving some possible answers to those questions about genre. By paying careful attention to the ways texts are constructed and encouraging even very young children to make their own, 'Taking on the Texts' moves genre theory into the everyday practicalities of children reading and writing in classrooms.

J. R. Martin, the Australian linguist, outlining his own research, comments that in trying to help young writers extend their reading and writing repertoire, 'Teachers do not really understand what is wrong and so cannot help.'[2] He points out that genres are developed historically and take on particular significance according to the ways they are perceived as cultural artefacts, so that some kinds of text become more valued than others. Gunther Kress, another Australian linguist, now working in the UK, explains that the stability and repeatability of social situations leads to 'a marked conventionality' which becomes so habitual that texts which have been constructed for specific social and cultural purposes become fixed and 'seem simply natural', making their constructedness unnoticeable.[3] Text types, or genres, are social constructs.

Because certain kinds of texts become more highly valued in particular societies, some linguists argue that children should be explicitly taught how to construct specific types of text. This raises some critical issues about literacy. It is not enough, they urge, for children simply to be able to read and write; they need to have access to understanding – and being able to make – the most power-related texts that exist within the society or culture they inhabit. Not to have this facility puts the individual in a powerless position in relation to the most culturally valued genres, and so it is important to teach children ways to tackle specific text structures.

In outlining just how these structures might be taught, attempts have been made to define just what 'genre' implies in an educational theory about texts. Some have suggested that 'A genre is characterised by having a *schematic structure* – a distinctive beginning, middle and end.'[4] However, John Dixon and Lesley Stratta, in response to Gunther Kress, point out that:

if each individual genre is characterised by its schematic structure, this implies that every example of a given species is structurally identical. That seems to fly in the face of the facts – and would certainly have to be demonstrated by a massive analysis for all the 'dozens' of genres that are currently proposed.[5]

They go on to say that 'the idea of a distinctive "beginning, middle and end" seems an extremely vague way of characterising "structures"'.[5] They agree that genre is to do with historically developed forms, and, indeed, agree about the need for young reader-writers to develop versatility in handling different text types. There is no dispute about the link between literacy and power, but Dixon and Stratta represent educationists who argue that rather than 'teaching' different forms or genres, we should help developing writers to identify the range of texts which they might want to use to make their own meanings clear. This latter view would question the fixed nature of genres anyway, pointing out that many texts are made up of several generic elements. Women's magazines, or children's comics, are examples of general categories which might hold within them a whole variety of genre forms. Similarly, a poem might encapsulate a political argument or a picture book reflect issues of social responsibility.

While this point of view agrees that young writers need experience and facility with a range of genres, it argues that to adopt an inflexible view of genre might prevent close attention being paid to the important contribution that children's own experience (which is often expressed through narratives of different kinds) brings to classroom work with texts. When children 'take on' new texts they use the narrative structures of their pre-school experience (see Part Three for a fuller examination of this). The examples of children's texts in this part of the book bear this out; their literacy (and other) experience, viewed through the prism of narrative, reveals important areas for analysis. Claire Escott begins by examining the ways in which children's narrative reading is reflected in their writing. Holly Anderson uses a well-loved picture book for children first of all to scrutinize the structures of the text, and then to make their own, while David Whitley acknowledges children's existing knowledge of traditional stories as a powerful model for writing, revealing significant insights about the ways in which gender influences ways of reading and writing narratives.

In offering a critical view of narrative in schools, J. R. Martin's study identifies an apparently widespread use of 'recount of experience' types of classroom writing, pointing out that although narrative is 'the main type of writing encouraged in schools . . . only a minority of children learn to write successful narrative by the end of Year 6'.[6] It is wise to take his observations seriously. Narrative should be seen as more than simply 'recount of experience' – or, as it is often described, 'do it then write about it'. There is no doubt that this kind of routine, purposeless activity stultifies any writing. However, as Claire Escott points out in the opening chapter of this book, to equate those valuable forms of narrative which are so important to learning, with this kind of pointless classroom task, is too simplistic a way of looking at children, writing and classrooms and misses the important ways in which narrative can be used purposefully.

A further, and centrally important, thread which Holly Anderson takes up in her work with very young readers and writers is the view that narrative carries within it the seeds of other, non-narrative forms of writing and that teachers should pay close attention to just what narrative offers to children's learning as a whole. Her study questions the division of narrative from other kinds of writing and suggests that the way to help developing writers and readers grasp issues of genre is to start from meaning or content, and then relate these to form, rather than attempting to teach forms or genres first. Much of the debate is to do with whether the features of particular forms or genres can be identified and 'taught' or whether 'genre' implies a more complex and shifting picture of text types. This is likely to remain a hot issue for some time. What *is* important, as Holly Anderson shows, is to help children get their own meanings clear, to encourage them to examine and talk about texts in detail as well as offering them chances to read and practise writing in a wide variety of text types.

There is no doubt that even very young children know a lot about different text types and the ways that they are put together. One important intervention by teachers is to help developing writers look carefully at their own texts, to identify and make explicit that knowledge – to bring out in the open what they know about how we organize language to make meaning. This implies not only the kinds of close attention to text described in Holly Anderson's chapter, but teachers' increased awareness and use of the textual knowledge children bring into school with them. As Claire Escott points out, often children's understanding of literacy in the home 'is divorced from their understanding of it in school' (p. 35). If children are to 'take on the texts' then they will need experience of examining the larger structures of lengthy texts as well as looking at details at sentence level. Further to these close kinds of scrutiny, David Whitley argues that there needs to be attention paid to the content of children's reading and writing.

Narrative as a Starting Point

Since narrative is such a central feature of the debates about genre, this section begins with Claire Escott's examination of narratives by six young writers in Years 5 and 6. Focusing on narrative is not only a particularly useful way of identifying what children know about texts of many kinds, including non-narrative texts, but also a valuable means of promoting and extending that knowledge. Gordon Wells asserts that 'stories provide a major route to understanding'.[7] He goes on to say: 'Constructing stories in the mind ... is one of the most fundamental means of making meaning; as such it is an activity that pervades all aspects of learning'[8] and argues that stories provide mental frameworks for other kinds of learning:

in listening to stories read aloud [children] not only extend the range of experience they are able to understand but also begin to assimilate the more powerful and more abstract mode of representing experience that is made available by written language.[9]

Harold Rosen also points to the ways in which story leads to other learning: 'Inside every narrative there stalk the ghosts of non-narrative discourse ... inside every non-narrative discourse there stalk the ghosts of narrative.'[10] He goes on to emphasize that narrative 'is an explicit resource in *all* intellectual activity'.[10]

Our own everyday experience of narrative shows that we can organize narrative texts to explain, persuade, argue, entertain and so on. If I am soon to meet someone in rather stressful circumstances where I want to convince them of something, I might well use narrative to prepare myself – to rehearse the scenario of what I want to say. Similarly, many people can remember constructing a story in their heads and trying it out first before using it to explain or justify to an adult why they were doing something nefarious! Even very young children do this and their storymaking can often be seen as making hypotheses as they explore the possible worlds of 'what if'. Their play reveals 'what if Teddy could speak' or their narratives begin from, for example, 'what if I could fly to the moon'. Imaginative play is, after all, hypothesis – trying out ideas to see how far they can take us.

When children play with narrative they are making experimental guesses about the world; predicting and exploring imagination to see how it matches with the real world they inhabit. It is always worth trying to establish just what kinds of literacy awareness young writers have so that they can be helped to make that knowledge explicit.

Issues of Content

One of the problems of an approach to text which concentrates mainly on form or genre is that, in arguing the relative merits of different ways of approaching text structures, it runs the risk of not dealing adequately with the *content* of any piece of writing. It is a familiar experience for a teacher to come across a piece written in an acceptable form – say a persuasive piece – which is technically accurate, but which either makes no sense or includes some aspects which are worrying. Wayne Booth, the American writer, believes that young writers should be 'nourished with narrative'. He points out: 'Who I am now can best be seen by the stories I can now tell. Who I am to become will best be seen in the stories I can learn to tell.'[11] If, as he suggests, narratives have a profound effect on us as developing readers and writers, this has implications for how teachers deal with the content of narratives which are presented to young readers as possible models for their own writing. Similarly, it has implications for the ways in which we receive and discuss texts produced by developing writers.

As David Whitley discovered, teachers can learn a great deal by thoughtful analysis of the narratives that young writers produce. In his examination of gender and children's use of traditional stories, he brings together many of the threads of this first section. If young writers are to become more attentive to the kinds of texts they can produce, and if they are to develop awareness of the ways in which different texts are organized, then one crucial factor is the teacher's role. His work indicates strongly that intervention does not just imply those face-to-face encounters in the classroom, but includes planning, provision of materials, experiences, vocabulary and challenge. Opening up questions of active literacy means more than just providing the experiences of different genres or text types; it requires 'new knowledge' about young reader-writers getting to grips with a range of texts to examine their construction and uses. The three studies in this section suggest ways in which this can be put into practice.

References

1. OFSTED (1993) *English Key Stages 1, 2, 3 and 4 Fourth Year 1992–3: the Implementation of the Curricular Requirements of the Education Reform Act.* London: Office for Standards in Education.

2. Martin, J. R. (1984) Types of writing in infant and primary school. In *Proceedings of Macarthur Institute of Higher Education Reading Language Symposium 5: Reading, Writing and Spelling*, p. 6. Sydney University Extension Program and Dept. of Linguistics.

3. Kress, G. and Knapp, P. (1992) Genre in a social theory of language. *English in Education* 26 (2), 10.

4. Christie, F. *et al.* (1984) *Language Studies: Children Writing Study Guide*. Geelong: Deakin University Press.

5. Stratta, L. and Dixon, J. (1992) The National Curriculum in English: does genre theory have anything to offer? *English in Education* 26 (2), 20.

6. Martin, J. R. and Rothery, J. (1986) What a functional approach can show teachers. In B. Couture (ed.) *Functional Approaches to Writing: Research Perspectives*, p. 254. London: Frances Pinter.

7. Wells, G. (1986) *The Meaning Makers: Children Learning Language and Using Language to Learn*, p. 206. London: Hodder and Stoughton.

8. Wells, G. (1986) *The Meaning Makers: Children Learning Language and Using Language to Learn*, p. 194. London: Hodder and Stoughton.

9. Wells, G. (1986) *The Meaning Makers: Children Learning Language and Using Language to Learn*, p. 200. London: Hodder and Stoughton.

10. Rosen, H. (1985) *Stories and Meanings*, p. 12. Sheffield: NATE Publications.

11. Booth, W. (1984) The nurture of narrative. Paper presented at *A Telling Exchange*, University of London, Institute of Education.

Chapter 1

Bridging the Gap
Making Links between Children's Reading and Writing

Claire Escott

When reading and writing are seen as linked, rather than separate, language modes, a new dynamic is set up. This suggests more than a straightforward relationship; it signals a far more active and complex set of interrelationships. Of course, as they read, readers take in understanding of text forms which give them good models for possible ways to write. However, any text entering the consciousness of the reader meets other texts. What we read intermingles with all that we have read and heard previously, all those texts drawn from earlier experience, and becomes transmuted by our interpretation of the text – an interpretation shaped by personal and cultural factors. Then, when it comes to the writing of texts, there is a further element of interpretation which is influenced by the nature of the writing task, the intentions of the writer and the needs of the reader. In this opening chapter, Claire Escott unpicks some of those complexities and places cultural experiences of texts within the classroom context. By examining the narratives of six 10- and 11-year-olds in a Cambridgeshire primary school, by discovering their perceptions about reading and writing, she points to some of the crucial factors involved in helping children develop 'confidence and a critical eye'.

Every time any one of us puts pen to paper to write, we do so, whether consciously or not, with the expectation that what we have written will later be read. If we have just written a shopping list, the reader may simply be ourselves; if we have written a book, the audience will be much wider than that. But the essential point is that writing is meant to be *read*; it is intended for an audience, whether that audience seems insignificant or important. If we understand this, then the two processes of reading and writing become inextricably linked, with important implications for the teaching of both in the primary classroom. The material that children read may affect what they write and, equally importantly, gaps or deficiencies in children's reading experiences might restrict their ability.

The English National Curriculum contains two separate Attainment Targets for Reading and Writing, but the Programme of Study for Writing acknowledges the links between them in some important ways. It proposes that children should be given opportunities to read examples of all types of writing, and purposeful opportunities to produce their own examples of writing of these various types. In terms of more imaginative writing, the document proposes the following: '[Pupils should] be helped to increase their control of story form, through their experience of the stories they have read and heard.'[1] As such, the National Curriculum leaves open the possibility of teaching reading and writing so as to extend children's experiences in both areas by building on the links between them. Since many children's reading experiences consist largely of stories, and much of the writing they are asked to do is in story form, it is worth considering the stories that children write in rather more detail in order to suggest some ways in which reading choices affect writing outcomes.

The Value of Stories

Hilary Minns[2] undertook a study of five children, examining their literacy experiences both at home, when they were of pre-school age, and in school. Her observations about the children's experiences of storytelling before they even arrive in the reception class are particular revealing. Community and cultural traditions, learned within the context of the family, are of central importance to the child's experiences of literacy. The vast majority of children, from whatever social or ethnic background they may come, have encountered stories whilst still of pre-school age. These stories may have been in the form of picture books, or part of an oral tradition existing within the child's culture, but they will all have provided children with some sense of story.

To show that the reading and writing of stories in the classroom is of vital importance to the child's development, it is necessary to be clear about what we see to be the value of stories. What do they contribute to the child's experience? Stories offer children the chance to consider representations of the world and its values. Applebee suggests that in this way stories help children to acquire expectations without the pressure of having to separate the world from make-believe. Though they eventually come to understand that some of this world is only fiction, this understanding will cause them to reject only specific characters and events: 'the recurrent patterns of values, the stable expectations about the roles and relationships which are part of their culture will remain.'[3]

The stories which children tell or write themselves also make an important contribution to the child's attempts to make sense of the world. If they tell stories about themselves, they are creating a sense of their own personal history and identity. Stories which are the product of their imagination allow them to consider, with the safety of distancing that fiction allows, new circumstances and possibilities. They allow children to enter a world in which they are in control of the situations and the destinies of the characters they create. In creating their own fictions children are able to find a powerful medium of self-expression.

Given these thoughts on the value of stories, it is easy to see the need for teachers to consider how best to release the child's imagination within the classroom context. To do this it is necessary to understand the process from the child's point of view, and to know what influences the child's attempts to write. Once this is understood, we can begin to see a way forward which will enable us to give every child the opportunity to write effectively – not only in the imaginative sense, but for a variety of other purposes as well. A child's view of reading, and perception of what he or she is asked to do in writing, can reveal important and sometimes startling evidence.

In the Classroom: Children's Views of Reading and Writing

Much has been said about the apparent limitations of reading schemes and the undoubted advantages of allowing children access from a very early age to the full range of literature available to them. This is an argument which takes as its central issue the question of *how* children learn to read. But it is important to set aside the complexities of the academic debate and to consider how *children themselves* view reading. A small study, undertaken with six children in Years 5 and 6, yielded some significant reflections. It began with an interview about reading. What do they see to be its purpose?

One of the questions forming part of the reading interviews asked the children why they thought it was important to be able to read. Gavin's response was representative of five of the children:

So you can read worksheets in class.

Only Lisa gave a different answer altogether:

Because it's a lot of fun reading. It can put some new ideas in your imagination.

What is interesting about Gavin's response is that earlier on in the interview he had talked of enjoying reading stories because 'they're exciting. Sometimes they have adventures in them.' At home he has lots of books and spends time reading them. Yet in the classroom, reading takes on a purely functional purpose; evidently there is a wide gap between his understanding of literacy at home and in the classroom.

Similar results emerged when I talked with the children about writing. When we discussed the difficulties encountered, and the improvements that could be made to a first draft, the majority of the children responded with references to the technicalities of their writing, not its creative content. For example:

[I find it difficult] if you're trying to do your best writing and you make a mistake. You either have to start again, and you don't do it as well 'cause you're really annoyed, or you have to get a sticky label and ruin it altogether. (Owen)

[If I did it again] I would do the writing better – make it bigger. (Guy)

For these children, the emphasis of writing activities in the classroom appeared to be on its technical skills. Yet they had powerful imaginations – as their writing showed. It seems, however, that for the majority of them this imaginative input was incidental to their writing – in Frank Smith's terms they saw the task of writing as one of transcription rather than composition.[4] The problems with spelling and punctuation, and the handwriting difficulties which the children referred to in their interviews, were all evident in their writing. But there was evidence too of an awareness (to varying degrees) of the demands of storywriting. I decided that examination of this aspect of the writing process would offer insights into how teachers might use and extend children's reading experiences to help them write.

Exposing children to a classroom which has a rich literacy environment – one in which reading is a highly valued activity, where their own writing is placed within a reading environment, and in which children learn to read their own and others' texts critically – will allow them to learn to read the writing of others, which will inform their own writing, thus greatly extending their own capabilities.

An Analysis of Children's Writing: Six Brief Case Studies

In order to find ways of creating this literacy environment, some under-standing of the ways in which children write is helpful. What follows is an analysis of the writing of the six children in an attempt to show what influenced them in their writing, the kinds of problems they encountered and the notions they possessed about the concept of storywriting.

All of the children had recently written a book about a rubbish dump to link with the subject of waste, which formed part of their class project for that term. These books form the basis of the analysis, but examples of other work are also referred to.

Lisa (aged 9) proved by her reading and writing interviews, and by her own writing, the rich capacity of her imagination. She quite clearly saw reading as an opportunity to indulge and extend that imagination; unlike all the other children, she made no reference to the more functional purposes of reading. Lisa was the only child of the six who still regularly had a story read to her at bedtime; she talked of the 'beautiful tales', such as *Coral Island*, *Black Beauty* and *Tom Sawyer* which her father read to her. Evidently, then, Lisa brings from home a rich background of stories – and both her interviews showed her mind to be full of possible stories.

What, then, of Lisa's own writing? Her book, *A Trip in the Dump* (Figure 1.1) opens as follows:

One day I was walking across the bridge when some big bullies started chasing me. They chased me deep into the dump where they left me.

She begins, then, in conventional story form with the words 'One day'. She knows, too, that the language of books and stories has its own register, and is able to exploit that in her own writing: the bullies chased her 'deep into the dump' – not a colloquial phrase, but one that belongs comfortably in the storytelling genre.

This opening paragraph is preceded by what seems to be a chapter heading (although if this is the case, the book presumably contains only one chapter

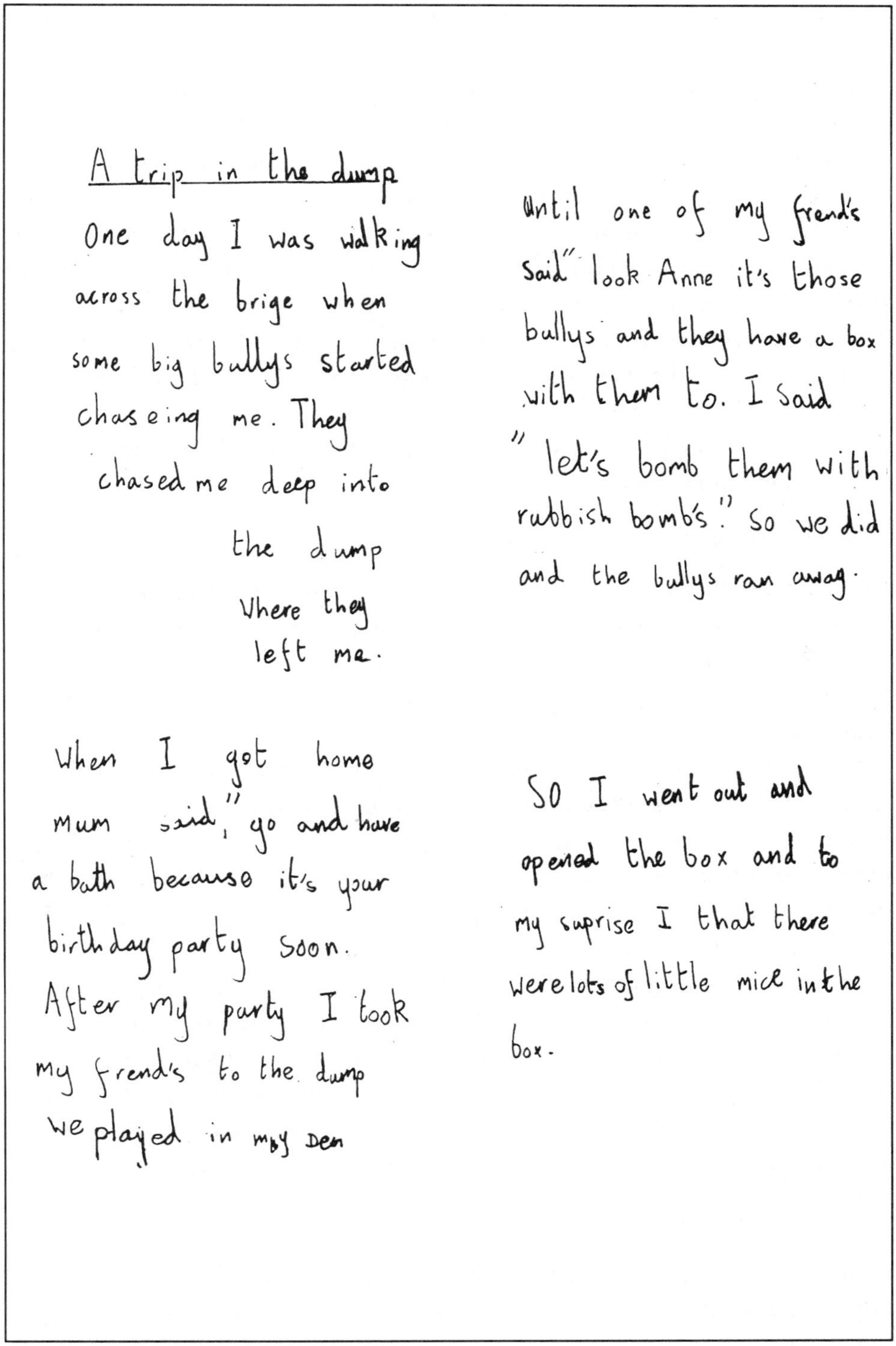

A trip in the dump

One day I was walking across the brige when some big bullys started chaseing me. They chased me deep into the dump Where they left me.

When I got home mum said," go and have a bath because it's your birthday party soon. After my party I took my frend's to the dump we played in my Den

Until one of my frend's said" look Anne it's those bullys and they have a box with them to. I said " let's bomb them with rubbish bombs." So we did and the bullys ran away.

So I went out and opened the box and to my suprise I that there were lots of little mice in the box.

Figure 1.1 Sample of Lisa's writing.

for there are no further headings), showing that Lisa has at least some understanding of the format of books and their division into chapters.

When Lisa was asked to read the opening of another child's book, and suggest how she would develop and conclude the story if it were her own, she spontaneously outlined a coherent structure and plot (albeit a predictable one) which satisfactorily resolved the story for the reader. Thus it is perhaps surprising that Lisa has problems in sustaining the promising beginning to her own story. The book contains a number of incidents, leading eventually to the discovery of mice in the dump, but there is no real sense that these incidents are linked, and the story does not reach any kind of satisfactory resolution. Given that she had a mind so full of imaginative stories, and an obvious love of reading, Lisa's case presents some interesting questions.

Owen (aged 10) had a very different view of reading. He suggested that he was a good reader because

I speak clearly, don't go too fast and don't mumble.

Undoubtedly this was a comment on reading as he saw it in the classroom context. His class had a period of quiet reading every day, during which time one reading group read aloud to the class teacher. It seems that, as a result, Owen believes reading aloud to be an important element in his success as a reader.

Owen placed little value on the reading and writing of stories, regarding the task of writing up science experiments as 'more important' in school, and preferring at home to watch films rather than read books (although he is a member of his local library and borrows books from there). Above all he likes war and science fiction, and for him the action and excitement of these films are the elements which constitute a good story.

Owen's writing, given almost any theme as a starting point, reflects his reading and film interests extensively. His book about the rubbish dump is a science fiction story containing 'battle mansions', lasers and guns (Figure 1.2), and throughout there is evidence of a vivid imagination fuelled almost exclusively by the television programmes and films he watches. His language at times captures the story-telling register in the same way that Lisa's does:

It was a cold, dark misty night

forms the opening of his book. But there are also the visual images and sound effects of his film and television viewing, evident, for example, in the following extract:

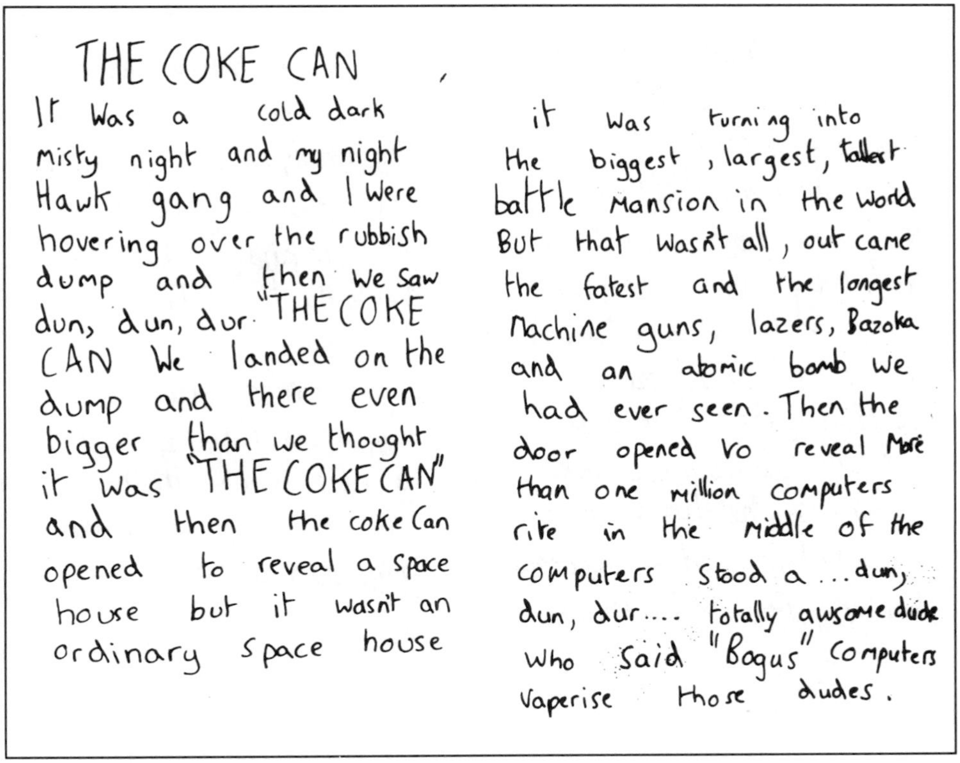

> **THE COKE CAN** ,
>
> It Was a cold dark misty night and my night Hawk gang and I Were hovering over the rubbish dump and then We Saw dun, dun, dur "THE COKE CAN We landed on the dump and there even bigger than we thought it Was "THE COKE CAN" and then the coke Can opened to reveal a space house but it wasn't an ordinary Space house
>
> it Was turning into the biggest, largest, tallest battle Mansion in the World But that Wasn't all, out came the fatest and the longest Machine guns, lazers, Bazoka and an atomic bomb We had ever seen. Then the door opened Vo reveal More than one million computers rite in the middle of the computers Stood a ...dun, dun, dur.... totally awsome dude Who said "Bogus" Computers Vaperise those dudes.

Figure 1.2 Sample of Owen's writing.

Then the door opened to reveal more than one million computers. Right in the middle of the computers stood a ... dun, dun, dur ... totally awesome dude, who said, 'Bogus computers, vaporise those dudes.'

Owen's book succeeds in sustaining excitement throughout, and is shaped into a coherent story. He is undoubtedly stuck within one genre in his writing (although he is obviously comfortable with the genre, and writes competently within it), presenting an interesting challenge for the teacher who wishes to broaden his horizons.

Owen does have a clear understanding both of audience and of story structure. Asked to comment on another child's story, he offered constructive criticisms and articulately explained his own reasons for not liking the story, whilst acknowledging its good qualities and accepting that it might appeal to other readers. In both his own book, and in his response to his classmate's story, Owen showed an understanding of the need for the author of a story to write with the intention of interesting the reader – an important step towards understanding about readership.

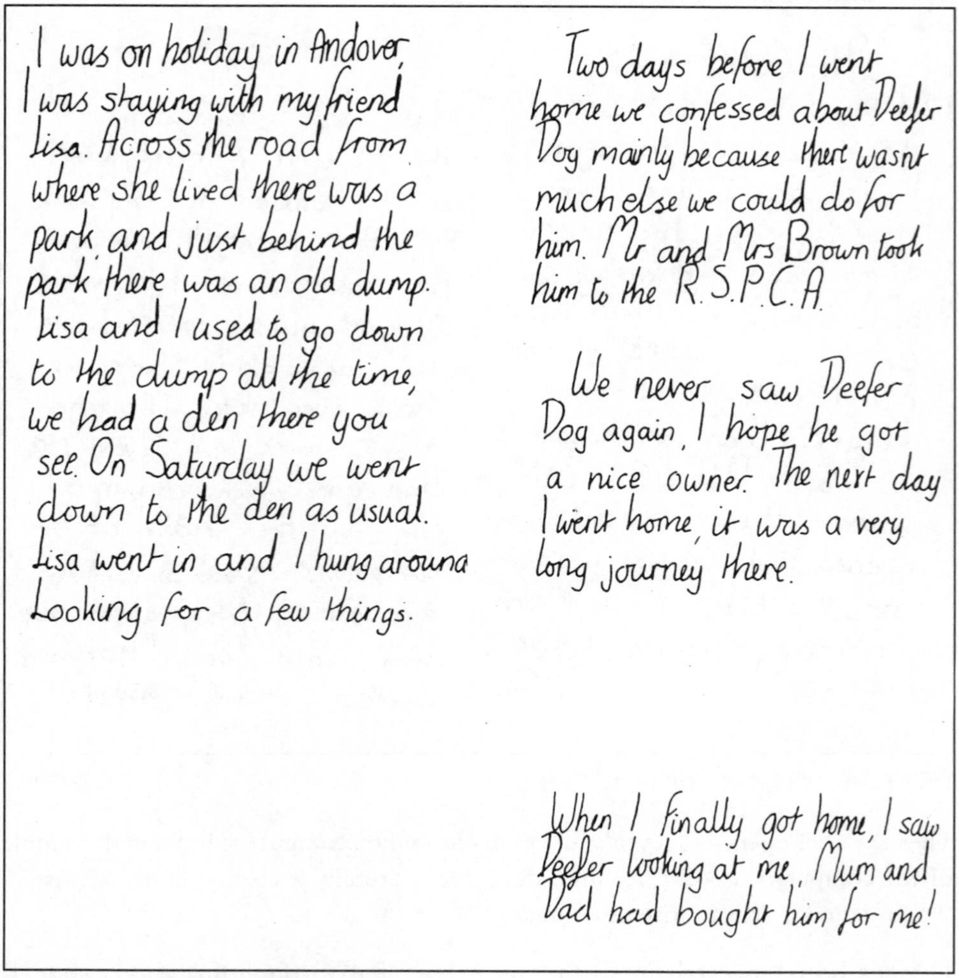

> I was on holiday in Andover,
> I was staying with my friend
> Lisa. Across the road from
> where she lived there was a
> park, and just behind the
> park there was an old dump.
> Lisa and I used to go down
> to the dump all the time,
> we had a den there you
> see. On Saturday we went
> down to the den as usual.
> Lisa went in and I hung around
> Looking for a few things.

> Two days before I went
> home we confessed about Deefer
> Dog mainly because there wasnt
> much else we could do for
> him. Mr and Mrs Brown took
> him to the R.S.P.C.A.

> We never saw Deefer
> Dog again, I hope he got
> a nice owner. The next day
> I went home, it was a very
> long journey there.

> When I finally got home, I saw
> Deefer looking at me, Mum and
> Dad had bought him for me!

Figure 1.3 Sample of Carol's writing.

Carol (aged 10) saw herself as a good reader because she was in the top reading group, and again saw reading as important in terms of being able to read worksheets in class. She was very reserved about her reading interests; basically she enjoys stories about dogs, and listed several titles to illustrate this interest.

Of the six pieces of work, Carol's book (Figure 1.3) was the one which showed the most awareness of stories and their conventions. Shaped coherently, it was a story that belonged to the 'little girl' genre in which two girls find a dog and look after it secretly until their parents find out and take the dog to the RSPCA. At this point it looks almost as if Carol will subvert the genre by giving us a sad ending, but on the last page the resolution is of the conventional 'happy ever after' type.

The writing throughout shows an understanding of the language of books, characterized particularly by the number of alternatives she uses for the word 'said':

Lisa came running. 'Look Lisa,' I said, 'What is it?'

   'It's a puppy,' cried Lisa. 'Isn't it sweet. I wonder who it belongs to.'

   'I don't know,' I replied. 'Shall we keep him in our den?'

   'Yeh!' exclaimed Lisa, 'He can live here. It's quite sheltered from the wind and rain, and we can bring him food.'

Commenting on Owen's action-packed, science fiction story, Carol was reserved and offered little criticism, adverse or otherwise. Perhaps, unlike Owen, she found it difficult to comment on stories which were outside the genre with which she was most comfortable and familiar.

Gavin (aged 9), like Lisa, enjoys stories because 'they're exciting. Sometimes they have adventures in them.' He has lots of books at home and enjoys reading them in his spare time. Why, then, did he feel it was important to be able to read? Here he differed from Lisa, referring only to reading in its classroom context:

If you get a worksheet and you've got to read it through and put in the missing answers, and you can't read it, you won't get anywhere.

Like Owen, Gavin watches a lot of television and enjoys science fiction and cartoons; both these influences are evident in his story (Figure 1.4), which is televisual throughout the narrative and has pictures which are especially reminiscent of cartoons.

Other writing that Gavin produced, like his book about the dump, showed an admirable grasp of the conventions of dialogue, as well as a number of expressions we would describe as part of the storytelling register. He described how he draws both from books he has read and television programmes he has watched when he writes his own stories.

Interestingly, when Gavin was asked to describe what his book was about he gave an outline that suggested a well-constructed story. Read in isolation, however, the written story would lead us to conclude that Gavin found storyline quite difficult. Though the elements of the story he describes in his verbal explanation are all evident in the book itself, and whilst the effect of his reading and television choices on his writing can be clearly seen, the finished product does not have the coherence of the verbal outline.

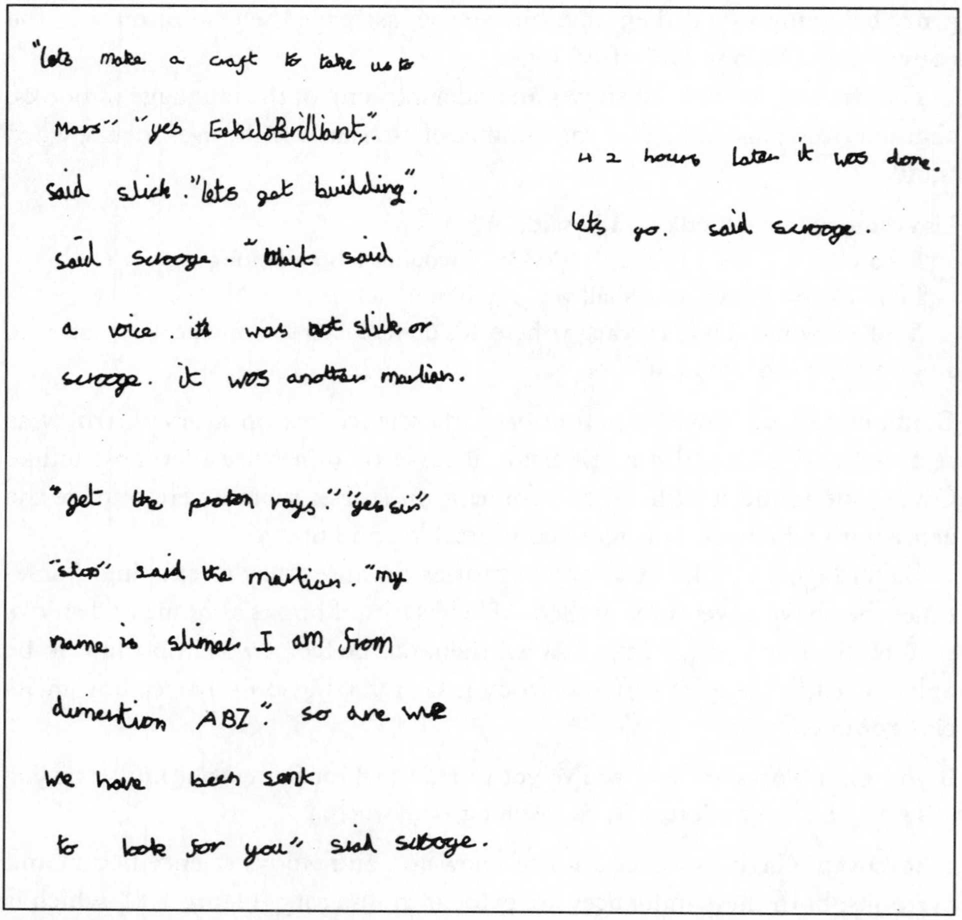

"lets make a craft to take us to

Mars" "yes EekdoBrilliant".

said slick ."lets get building".

said scrooge . "that said

a voice . it was not slick or

scrooge . it was another martian.

"get the proton rays ." "yes sir"

"stop" said the martian . "my

name is slimac. I am from

dimention ABZ". so are we

we have been sent

to look for you" siad scrooge.

4 2 hours later it was done.

lets go . said scrooge .

Figure 1.4 Sample of Gavin's writing.

Christine (aged 10) could only recall reading the 'Just William' stories when she was asked about the kinds of books she liked to read, but her own writing suggests a much wider experience than this. In her book about the dump (Figure 1.5), her main character, Charles, is described as 'a bit of a scamp. He had ginger hair, lots of freckles and rather big ears that stuck out' – quite evidently the stuff of Blyton and Crompton. But there is also a reference to a 'little white rabbit', reminiscent of *Alice in Wonderland*, whilst an incident involving bottles of methylated spirit and washing-up liquid reminds us of Roald Dahl's *George's Marvellous Medicine*. In a poem she wrote called 'Bedtime', Christine's use of the idea of a midnight feast was typical of the genre of school stories.

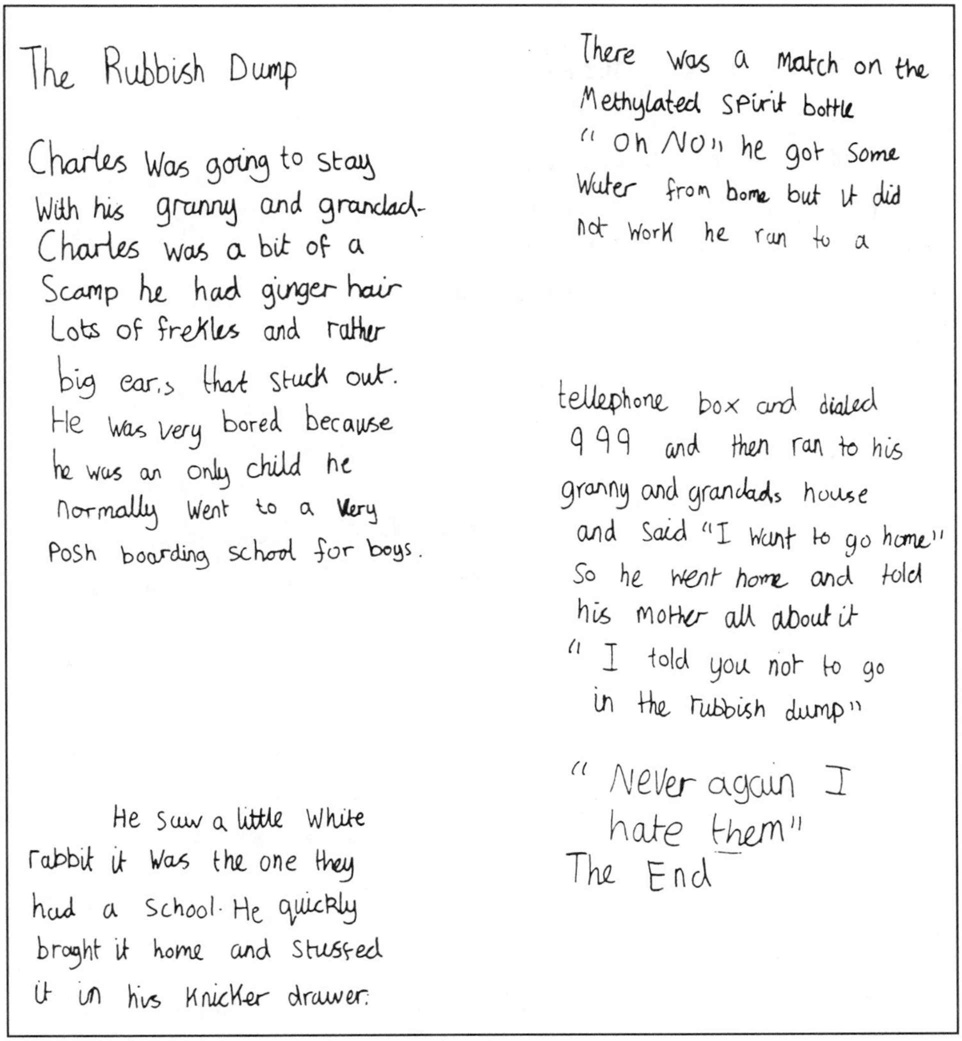

The Rubbish Dump

Charles Was going to stay
With his granny and grandad-
Charles was a bit of a
Scamp he had ginger hair
Lots of frekles and rather
big ear,s that stuck out.
He was very bored because
he was an only child he
normally Went to a Very
Posh boarding school for boys.

He saw a little White
rabbit it Was the one they
had a School. He quickly
broght it home and Stussed
it in his Knicker drawer.

There was a match on the
Methylated spirit bottle
"Oh No" he got Some
Water from bome but it did
not Work he ran to a

tellephone box and dialed
999 and then ran to his
granny and grandads house
and Said "I Want to go home"
So he went home and told
his mother all about it
"I told you not to go
in the rubbish dump"

"Never again I
hate them"
The End

Figure 1.5 Sample of Christine's writing.

Christine's writing, then, appears to draw on a variety of sources, and she writes using a mixture of 'book language' and her own spoken voice. However, her book itself makes no real sense, and suggests that she lacks understanding about the shaping of a story. Yet in talking generally about stories, Christine talked of making them interesting for the reader by cutting out long descriptions and concentrating on the action of the story; she understands, then, something about notions of readership. Perhaps she just finds this difficult to translate into her own writing.

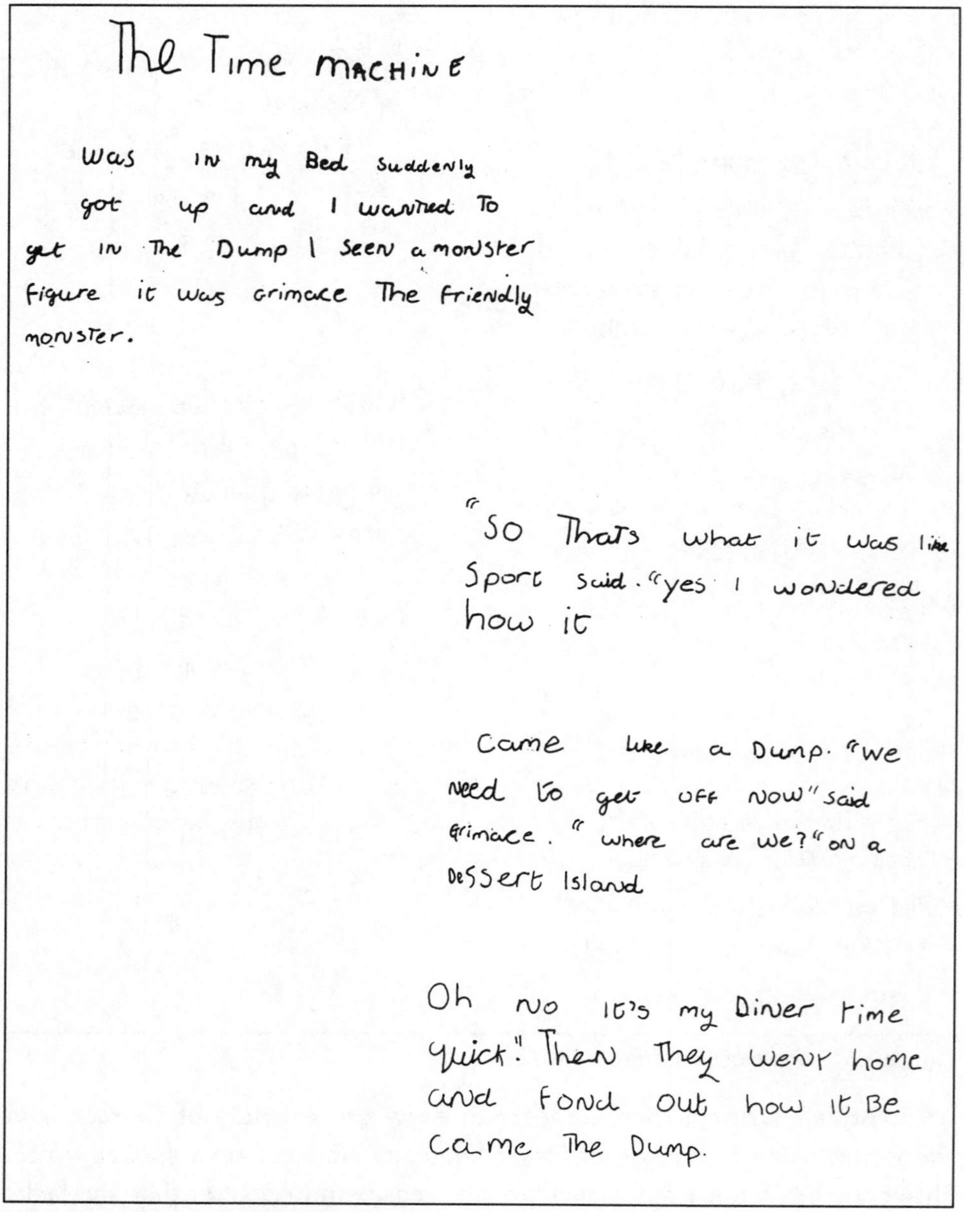

The Time machine

Was   in   my   Bed   suddenly
got   up   and   I   wanted   To
get   in   The   Dump   I   seen   a monster
figure   it   was   crimace   The   friendly
monster.

"So   Thats   what   it   was   like
Sport   said. "yes   I   wondered
how   it

came   like   a   Dump. "we
need   to   get   off   now" said
Grimace. "   where   are   we?" on a
Dessert   Island

Oh   no   it's   my   Diner   time
quick." Then   They   went   home
and   fond   Out   how   it   Be
came   The   Dump.

Figure 1.6 Sample of Guy's writing.

Finally, Guy (aged 10) revealed that his reading experience derived mainly from comics, and this is very evident in both his writing (Figure 1.6) and its illustrations (not shown here). All of his writing is very visual, and often contains vivid sound effects; the train in a poem he wrote on evacuation pulled away from the station with a 'wooooowh' – followed by the customary exclamation mark of the comic-book genre. His illustrations, too, drew extensively from this cartoon-strip influence.

In terms of storyline, Guy shows little understanding. His book contains some story elements, including descriptions of several incidents, but neither the book itself nor his verbal outline suggests any logical sequencing of these events. In addition to this, the pictures in Guy's book seemed to bear little relation to the text accompanying them – another storybook convention which he seemed to be unaware of.

One further point of interest concerning Guy's own writing emerges from his poem about evacuation. Here Guy portrays vividly the feelings of a boy about to be evacuated during World War II. There is no understanding of how to structure a poem, but its content is simple and emotive:

I was frightened for my dad ...

We were off. All the kids were cheering.
But I was crying. A boy was crying as well because
He was frightened for his mum.

Although not part of this particular study, another child in the same class – Darren – wrote a similarly moving poem on the same subject, showing an admirable command of both language and poetic form. Darren's poem is especially interesting, because nothing else he wrote (despite his being of generally high ability) came even close to matching the quality of this poem:

He feels dismal and alone in a vast
Unfriendly world.
He is nervous and scared.
Anxious to go and abandoned
He feels like crying
But bottles it up.

Guy and Darren were children from army families who had shared the experience of seeing their fathers go away to fight in the Gulf War, and it seems sensible to suggest that they were drawing on intensely personal experiences in the writing of these poems. This raises issues about the importance of recognizing and building on the children's own experience in their writing – a point to be discussed later.

Broadening the Analysis: What Do These Children Tell Us?

It can be seen that children's writing can be used as a mirror of their reading experiences. It is important to help children see that reading is about more than identifying words on a page, and to recognize what it is that children take from texts that they read and bring to texts that they write. Furthermore, the case studies have shown that children draw from more than just book texts in their writing. Though they may be unaware of it, material from sources such as the classroom, media texts, computer games and their own experiences is evident in the imaginative texts that children produce.

Of course, to attempt to draw general conclusions from the evidence above alone would mean making far too many assumptions, not least that this random cross-section of pupils from one class could be a representative sample of children. Obviously this is somewhat unlikely and the analysis needs to be broadened. Conclusions can then be drawn in two areas: the children's understanding of the concept of story, and their views on reading and writing.

Applebee suggests that every time we encounter a new story we assimilate it with our past experiences of stories.[5] This past experience has contributed to our expectations about characters, patterns of behaviour, suitable endings, and so forth. Since every story we encounter will be different, our understanding is altered and expanded by the new characters and situations we meet; these will be accommodated into our existing experience.

Applebee points to six common conventions of stories: beginning with a title or a formal opening phrase, such as 'Once upon a time'; ending with a formal closing – for example, 'the end' or 'they all lived happily ever after'; the use of consistent past tense; the acceptance of 'make-believe' characters and events; the possibility of incorporating certain conventional or 'stock' character types and situations; the use of the register of language common to storytelling.

The above analysis referred briefly to the use of some of these conventions in the children's work. This can be taken further, bearing the following assertion in mind:

The extent to which these conventions are recognised and used by children can be taken, to a certain extent, as an indication of the degree to which stories have begun the long march from the child's initial recognition that a story is in some way different from other uses of language, to the final firmly established recognition of story as a mode of communication.[6]

All six children whose case studies have been considered used at least some of these conventions in their stories. All of them used the past tense, and there are examples of stock characters and situations which show evidence of the children's reading experiences: Christine's 'Enid Blyton' character (Charles); Carol's story firmly set within the genre of 'little girl' stories; and both Gavin's and Owen's heroes who triumph against the odds over their opposition. These conventions can only have become part of their understanding of the concept of story through the books they have read and heard.

Of course, the extent to which children are able to exploit these conventions in their own writing will differ depending on the child. For example, take the use of a formal ending. We know from our adult texts that such endings are rarely of the explicit types that Applebee suggests, yet we do still expect them to offer some kind of resolution to the events and themes explored throughout the novel. In her book, despite the difficulties she had with maintaining a storyline, Christine concludes with the words 'The End'. She has not resolved her story; she simply concludes the narrative with a full stop. But she knows enough about books to recognize the need for some sort of definite indication that she has reached a conclusion; hence her formal ending. The reader knows that the book is finished whether or not the ending satisfies.

On the other hand, Carol's book contains no formal phrase to signify the end in the way that Christine's does. But we know we have reached the end just the same. Carol knows that the text itself must lead to a conclusion and successfully achieves this. She might well have finished with the words 'and they all lived happily ever after', but she relies on readers to draw on the implications of the text to assume this for themselves. This suggests that her understanding of the possibilities of narrative is more sophisticated than Christine's, but it is a tentative conclusion that warrants further investigation.

All the children had drawn from their reading experiences to some extent, although with differing degrees of proficiency. In basic terms, the narratives of the majority of the stories consist of a chain of events with a central focus – a character or situation – around which the events take place. Each incident develops from the previous one, and at the same time elaborates a new aspect of the theme or situation. In terms of this understanding of narrative, Carol, and to a lesser extent Owen, achieved the greatest success with their own stories.

With what Applebee describes as a 'focused chain', there is still a story in which all the incidents are linked to, for instance, a central character. But the overall narrative does not necessarily have any coherence. Lisa, Gavin and Christine all had a central focus in their stories, and all related a series of events. The events were linked to the central character, but were simply a chain of events which did not ultimately constitute a storyline.

Guy's story falls into Applebee's category of 'unfocused chain narratives', in which a series of incidents are related, but with no specific focus to link them: 'The result is a story which . . . has much of the structure of a narrative, but which as a whole loses its point and direction.'[7]

In all three of these categories the children have grasped something about the conventions of narrative from their reading experiences. In order to increase their proficiency and their confidence, such experiences must be extended.

A further aspect referred to in the above analysis was the children's awareness of the register of language in storytelling. Through their experience of stories children will gradually come to realize that the language of storytelling has its own register – hence the evidence of 'book language' in children's stories.

Even from this small study, leaving aside the children's success with the overall structure of the narrative, it is clear that the children who showed some awareness of the register of language common to storytelling were the ones who read most extensively. Owen – whose main experience was of films – adopted many more televisual conventions than anything else in his narrative, and Guy, who employed almost no 'book language' at all, was the child who appeared from his interviews to have the most limited range of reading experiences.

It might be argued from the above conclusions that the ability to exploit fictional narrative (or any other kind of narrative for that matter) results largely from the child's experiences of reading narratives written for the same purpose. However, a rich background of stories alone will not automatically enable children to successfully produce their own stories. Lisa, despite possessing an imagination fuelled by the books she had read and heard, found maintaining a storyline very difficult. Her interviews suggested that she saw stories – both those by herself and those by others – as a way of combining her imagination and her own real-life experiences. Gavin also possessed a good deal of knowledge about the value of stories, and showed evidence of a vivid imagination – but he too encountered problems in writing his own stories.

What is it that causes these children problems when they are asked to create their own narratives?

The fact is that we do not need to teach children to be imaginative (the above children's stories all proved that), because it is a natural function of their brains. The books they read undoubtedly feed into their imaginations and influence their subsequent writing, but this is not enough. As Smith points out: 'They do need to learn the conventions by which creativity can become manifest in composition; they need to discover what can be done with written language.'[8] Smith goes on to suggest that the difficulties children have in telling stories may have nothing to do with a lack of something to say. They may simply be uncertain of how to link episodes, or of the conventions of ordering sentences and paragraphs. We accept that children are influenced by the *content* of what they read – and that they use it in their own writing. To some extent they also use the *conventions*. Could they not, then, be taught to 'read like a writer'[9] so that they might learn to fully exploit these conventions, and consequently produce more effective pieces of their own writing?

Children need to see themselves as both readers and writers, and that both these modes of language have a valuable purpose. Yet as noted earlier, with the exception of Lisa, the children saw both reading and writing as largely classroom tasks and nothing more. And if they did assign reading some importance in the home, they saw its purpose in the classroom context as something quite different.

This is an issue of vital importance. *It seems likely that, for some children at least, their understanding of literacy in the home is divorced from their understanding of it in school.* Every child brings with them to school some literacy experiences from home. This cannot be ignored if a positive view of literacy is to be encouraged.

At home the child may well have experienced reading in an intimate, one-to-one context. In school, reading is a classroom activity organized for a large group of children – a very different context. Some children will adapt easily to this change, but undoubtedly others will become confused as they try to match what they have learned about reading outside school with what is now expected of them in class. Furthermore, if reading is given a purely functional purpose, then this consequently devalues the importance of stories. Such a devaluation provides little motivation for the children to write their own stories.

Some Implications for the Classroom

Reading Resources

One of the major implications of the above conclusions concerns the range of reading material made available to children in school. This can be related to the earlier comments about the value of stories, and children's experiences of them before they first come to school. In selecting books for children to choose from in school, it is crucial to acknowledge what children may have brought with them from their home culture, either as part of an oral tradition or because they have been read to from an early age.

The books offered must validate both their own experiences and the stories which they tell themselves. They must offer the opportunity to deal, at a distance, with such complex themes as conflict, death, and family relationships – themes they will want to explore in their own writing at some point.

One final issue needs to be raised in relation to the reading material made available. In any written text a relationship is assumed between the writer and the reader. It is the writer's task to successfully gauge what this relationship will be and to write accordingly, and this factor will have implications for the types of writing which are available to be read in school. Sometimes authors try, and fail, to create a rapport with young readers. This will result in children reading books in a language which appears unusual and remote to them; such material must be avoided if texts are to be meaningful.

If, as seems clear, children draw on the models of texts offered to them, the kinds of texts they should be encouraged to use must be 'multilayered'; that is, they must allow the reader to make sense of them on any personal plane, whatever sophistication or knowledge they may possess.

Few would deny the need for a rich diet of quality reading material in the classroom, or that the successful reader does not simply recognize words on a page but reads instead with the understanding that it is the meaning beyond the words which is important. However, the ways in which children's reading choices can be used (both their own independent choices, and the ones they are encouraged to make through the material offered) to successfully affect their writing outcomes need to be considered.

Above all, children need opportunities to place their own writing in a reading context. In this way they sense that their texts are worthwhile, and they are able to see themselves both as readers who are also writers, and as writers who are also readers.

Children as Critical Readers

To do this, children need to become critical readers and writers of their own and others' writing. It is this issue which, above all others, demonstrates the vital links between reading and writing. Even as adults, faced with the task of writing something in a genre with which we are unfamiliar, we tend to look for guidance to the work of other writers in the same genre. Children need to learn reading behaviours which enable them to read their own and others' texts critically, and to use the writing of others to inform what they write themselves. If children are subconsciously influenced by what they have read, helping them to become conscious of what they already know and then seeking to extend this knowledge can only serve to help them exploit further the possibilities of the written word.

All schools place some value on the process of drafting. But it is all too easy to assume that children know and understand this importance too. All six children studied above placed little or no value on the drafting process. For them, the first draft was simply something to be checked by the teacher for spelling mistakes before a final neat copy was made. None of the children said they would change anything about their story if they wrote it again (except Guy, who said he would make the writing bigger!).

The problem was by no means a school which did not value drafting, so it seems fair to suggest that the children did not know how to read their own written texts or those of others critically, and were thus unsure of how to make valuable improvements to their first drafts. How can the process of drafting be assigned greater value?

A vital issue is that of readership, since it is this which places all forms of writing in a meaningful context. If children can be helped to understand the notion of audience, they will have a basis from which to start critically analysing their own writing and that of others; if we know that we are writing for a specific audience, we can consider whether the content and structure of our writing are appropriate for them.

The common ground between the reader and the writer is the message contained within the writing – this is what makes writing into reading material. This vital purpose of writing will be lost on children if their most common purpose for writing is to produce something that is intended only to be read and marked by the class teacher. To fully understand notions of readership, children need to be motivated to write by being given a task that involves the need for genuine communication between the writer and the reader.

The question 'who is the reader?' is one that determines the format, content and level of formality of what is written, and thus cannot be ignored if writing is to be purposeful. Once the child knows and understands about readership, further questions can be asked of a reading text, whether written by themselves or someone else, which relate to that understanding. Is the content appropriately interesting, informative and imaginative? Is the narrative coherently structured and organized into paragraphs/chapters, and so on? Is the mode of language appropriate to the purpose/audience – is the intended message clear to the reader?

To produce writing that effectively communicates a message to the reader, the child needs to read the texts of others in the same critical way. And this is yet another reason for ensuring that they are encouraged to make reading choices which will give them rich experiences of different kinds of texts – and that when we discuss with children what they have read, we ask questions of them which draw their attention to these important aspects.

An understanding that behind every printed text lies a real author who, like them, faced a blank sheet of paper at the outset can be a difficult concept for children to grasp. The visit of a professional author to the school is an invaluable way to help demystify the writing process for them. If the children read the author's books prior to the visit and are encouraged to formulate questions about the writing process – how and why certain decisions about content were made, how the book actually came to be written (ideal for demonstrating the value of drafting), and so on – they will be in a position to draw not only from the content of their reading experiences in their writing, but also from an understanding of the process which underlies it.

In encouraging children to become authors of texts for children younger than themselves, we can make it possible for children to engage in the same task as a professional adult writer writing for children. It requires the examination of other published books aimed at the same market for ideas and an investigation of the interests and preferences of the audience, as well as the need to write with a specific audience in mind, drafting and redrafting until the content is fully appropriate. Such experience of creating texts provides an opportunity for children to demonstrate their understanding of how to use written language.

Margaret Wallen makes some relevant points with regard to this idea of children writing for real audiences.[10] If the audience is genuine, then the response to the writing becomes more than just a teacher's tick – it is an authentic response from a real reader: 'the writer can begin to feel the power to influence and persuade, to give pleasure or even to invite criticism'.[11]

Above all, such genuine writing opportunities place writing in an entirely new context. Children are no longer writing to tell their teacher something that teacher already knows, or simply writing a story because they have been told to. Instead, the writing has real authority; if children recognize this they can write with a renewed sense of purpose.

There is a further issue to consider in helping children read texts critically: the role the teacher plays in their development. In this respect, the comments we make – both verbally and in writing – about the children's work can make a valuable contribution. Of course, technical errors cannot be ignored, but we need also to help the children develop a critically analytical approach to the drafting process. Therefore, even as the children draft their work, our own comments should reflect this. Alongside the correction of technical errors we should seek to value any self-appraisal the child has made in relation to the piece of work, and to suggest areas in which further objective analysis might be made. Furthermore, our comments should be instrumental in extending the child's critical vocabulary.

Although the kinds of writing considered so far have been almost entirely imaginative, it is important to note that many of the conclusions drawn can be applied to writing right across the curriculum. The National Curriculum for English demands that value be assigned to writing tasks of other kinds and in other curriculum areas. Thus, the same principles as those already outlined can be extended across the curriculum. The rich diet of literature offered to children should contain examples of writing written for a range of different purposes, both fiction and non-fiction. The development of appropriate reading behaviours will enable children to read these texts in a critical way which will subsequently inform their own attempts to write.

The ways in which teachers can help children to develop their writing competence, the kinds of influences which might enable them to become successful readers and writers, and the valuable links between these two modes of language have now been outlined. Even so, the demands made of children in their writing activities must not be so prescriptive that they are no longer given opportunities to express themselves freely.

Writing Opportunities in the Classroom

Most writing opportunities in the classroom are teacher-initiated, and a natural reaction when a child appears to be experiencing difficulties or uncertainties with the task set is to respond by being prescriptive about style or format, which instead causes further constraints.

A possible solution to this problem may be to allow children as much freedom as possible at the drafting stage of their writing, whilst ensuring that they do not lose sight of *why* they are writing. If this is so, the child will be in a position to freely express thoughts on paper, simply with some ideas about relevant content in mind. In the subsequent reworkings, an awareness of audience can begin to influence the final shaping of the piece in terms of content, structure and format. Again, greater experience of reading – and reading critically – will lead to a better understanding of the many varied purposes of writing. Teachers may well find that they can afford to be less prescriptive about style and format as children draw on their reading experience to make such choices for themselves, and develop the ability to adopt the style and format appropriate to the piece.

If children are given power over written language, allowing them to explore and create new worlds and possibilities, then we must ensure that we give them opportunities to write what is vital and meaningful to them; the texts they produce must consist of what they want to say.

This point can be illustrated by returning to one of the children considered earlier. Lisa, despite her rich literacy background, and her obvious love of books, encountered quite substantial difficulties in writing her own story. It might be concluded from this that she needs to develop the kinds of critical reading techniques outlined above – but there is more to it than this. When asked where she got her ideas for the incidents in her book, Lisa flicked through the pages and assigned every single incident in the book to a certain experience in her own life. It was almost as if she had used the book to relate a series of incidents which had meaning for her; they had no real relation to each other, apart from the fact that she was central to each of them, and the existence of the rubbish dump was entirely incidental. Perhaps she wanted to write autobiography, and was thus sidetracked from the demands of the story she had been asked to write; it did not offer a meaningful context for her to express herself.

It has become quite clear that stories can be used effectively in classroom writing activities, and children use the *patterning* of stories they know to write about their own concerns (with varying levels of success). These individual choices which they make with regard to *content* are what prevent them from being restricted by the form. In other words, Lisa was not restricted by the request to produce a story, but simply by the required subject matter. Of course it would be impossible to make every writing task in the classroom meaningful to the same extent for every child. But there must be occasions on which we give the children enough freedom to fully exploit the powerful medium of expression which is available to them in the form of narrative.

If it is true that children's difficulties in storytelling arise more from uncertainties about sequencing episodes and making effective use of the techniques of ordering sentences and paragraphs than from their lack of something to say, then the ways in which reading in the classroom is followed up are important. It cannot be enough simply to assume that they are making sense of the many conventions of narrative, just because they are making sense of its content. Opportunities to talk and write about what they have read must also be opportunities to explore more than just the content of the incidents in the book. They must be times when we help them to grapple with some of the more complex issues of readership, registers of language and narrative structures. We must ask questions of them which help, for instance, to identify ways in which the incidents in the book were connected, and how they developed the overall theme or storyline. We must, suggests Meek, ask questions which encourage them to interpret and interrogate the text – 'Do I believe that?', 'Do I like these people?', and so on.[12] And we must go on asking these questions until they have gained the competence to ask them independently.

Such an understanding of how texts work will enhance their development in two major ways. First, they will be free to examine unexpected words and phrases, and characters and situations in the texts they read. Furthermore, they will come to ask the same questions of the texts they write themselves, and in this way will find themselves able to write more effectively.

Conclusion

Children's reading choices and experiences can and do affect their writing outcomes. By asking questions of their reading texts, they come to understand how such texts are structured and the kinds of conventions they contain. Writing for a real audience, and understanding that in doing this they share a common purpose with every writer, will help them to understand the important relationship between reader and writer.

However, there is no magical process by which such concepts and conventions seep into the child's consciousness. Teachers must assist children in their choices of literature, seeking always to find what is meaningful for them, whilst aiming also to give them rich variety. If they can be helped to develop ways of approaching all kinds of texts, including their own, with confidence and a critical eye, they will achieve greater success in both reading and writing.

References

1. Department of Education and Science and the Welsh Office (1990) *English in the National Curriculum*, p. 37. London: HMSO.

2. Minns, H. (1990) *Read It to Me Now!* London: Virago Educational.

3. Applebee, A. (1978) *The Child's Concept of Story*, p. 52. Chicago: University of Chicago Press.

4. Smith, F. (1982) *Writing and the Writer*. London: Heinemann.

5. Applebee, A. (1978) *The Child's Concept of Story*. Chicago: University of Chicago Press.

6. Applebee, A. (1978) *The Child's Concept of Story*, p. 36. Chicago: University of Chicago Press.

7. Applebee, A. (1978) *The Child's Concept of Story*, p. 64. Chicago: University of Chicago Press.

8. Smith, F. (1982) *Writing and the Writer*, p. 192. London: Heinemann.

9. Smith, F. (1982) *Writing and the Writer*, p. 179. London: Heinemann.

10. Wallen, M. (1989) Why do children need audiences for their writing? In National Writing Project *Audiences for Writing*. Kingston upon Thames: Nelson.

11. Wallen, M. (1989) Why do children need audiences for their writing? In National Writing Project *Audiences for Writing*, p. 1. Kingston upon Thames: Nelson.

12. Meek, M. (1990) What do we know about reading that helps us teach? In R. Carter (ed.) *Knowledge about Language and the Curriculum: the LINC Reader*, p. 150. London: Hodder and Stoughton.

Chapter 2

About as Big as the Library
Using Quality Texts in the Development of Children as Readers and Writers

Holly Anderson

One important area of teacher intervention in promoting confident literacy is to help children develop the capacity to make decisions about writing. What is important – and what lies behind many statements about empowering writers – is that the writer should have had sufficient experience of texts and practice in putting them together to be able to develop some independence. This will rely to a large extent on how teachers deal with the early stages of writing in the classroom and how they help young writers to establish some autonomy over the process of composing texts. Working with two infant teachers, Holly Anderson started with a strong model for writing and a great favourite – The Very Hungry Caterpillar *by Eric Carle. By looking closely at this quality text, the teachers hoped to offer children ways of understanding the process of writing. In taking a rigorous approach to narrative, they found that children as young as 6 could discuss structure and content and identify grammatical features. This chapter adds an important new dimension to the analysis of the relationship between reading and writing – the central binding thread of talk. By reflecting on text construction through talk, these children drew on a range of spoken and written models as they became powerful makers of their own texts.*

How to encourage infants to redraft work at text rather than technical level? That was the brief I was given by a teacher of Year 1 and Year 2 children. I had been working with Julie Fuller and her vertically grouped class of

5-, 6- and 7-year-olds in my role as an advisory language teacher. A group of teachers wanted to explore ways in which they could give children more independence in writing. The junior teachers in the group had set up 'response partners' in their classrooms and were investigating with the children what made a good response partner.[1]

The infant teachers in the group, partly driven by forthcoming National Curriculum tests and the need for the children to write unaided so that the spelling levels could be assessed, wanted to look at how to support and encourage children to 'have a go' for themselves without relying on the teacher to supply the correct spelling of words. This was working well, and the teachers had found that careful planning and organization had given children both the structure to build on and the freedom to write for themselves. The children were gaining confidence in their writing, and ideas flowed freely without being constrained by the need to stop to check the correct spelling of a word. If the writing was to be read by others, the children became used to going to a number of sources to check their spellings, and peers, wordbanks, dictionaries and the class teacher were all seen as resources.

The teachers were pleased with this increased independence. It enabled them to see what the children understood and, perhaps more importantly, were ready to be taught. They felt they were able to target their teaching more effectively to meet the needs of the children, but now wanted to consider another important part of the writing process: how to give children opportunities to plan and redraft their work. I wanted the children to think about the choices an author has, to be aware that the writer decides, controls and thus can change the content of a piece of work, in the hope that this would give them a greater understanding of the writing process. I planned to use a well-loved story and ask the children whether they would have made the same choices as the author, getting them to alter the text in any way they chose. Although this did not tackle the very nub of redrafting – the considered choices that an author makes to ensure that the writing best reflects her or his intentions – I nevertheless felt that it would be a step towards the children understanding that ideas, words and sentences are not static; that they are planned for, and can be altered, as the work progresses.

This chapter is an account of my work with the children, and shows the way in which, by choosing a book with obvious literary merit, the children were supported in their development as both readers and writers.

Learning about How Writing Works

Most children see adults writing for functional purposes, e.g. lists, notes, letters and cards, which frequently do not need to be redrafted or crafted. Until work done by the National Writing Project highlighted the way in which children's experiences of functional and environmental print could be extended to their writing experiences in the classroom, most children in school were encouraged to do 'storywriting'. Whilst it is true that 'narrative is a primary act of mind',[2] it is still the case that many children reach the final years of primary school without having control over what is, in fact, a complex and highly structured genre. Martin, in his work on genre theory in Australian schools, found that most children by the end of primary schooling were writing observation or recount rather than true narrative.[3] Because teachers themselves were unfamiliar with genre theory they were often unable to intervene constructively to help children understand the differences between a 'bed to bed' story, in which a number of events are listed in chronological order, and narrative which contains tension and resolution.

In many infant schools in the UK, children are encouraged to write for a variety of purposes, with opportunities for both functional writing and the more traditional writing such as 'news' and 'storywriting'. When appropriate, this writing can be read by other children in the class as well as by the child who wrote it, and so children become readers of each other's work, and writers for a real and known audience. The National Curriculum reflects this broad writing diet, encouraging the practice of including children's own writing as part of the class reading resources. By Level 2 (which is meant to reflect the ability of the average child in the second year of full-time education), children have to show that they are capable of 'using complete sentences, coherently sequencing a chronological account, writing a story containing the rudiments of story structure and producing non-chronological writing'.[4] At Level 3, which, because of the cyclical nature of language, many infants are working within even if they have not achieved all the strands included in that level, similar demands are made on the range of types of writing, but in addition children are expected to revise and redraft, 'paying attention to meaning and clarity as well as checking for matters such as correct and consistent use of tenses and pronouns'.[4] When children reach the end of Key Stage 1, aged between 6 and 7, they are tested in a number of areas of the curriculum. Writing is one of these areas, and all children have had to write a story as part of the Standard Assessment Task for writing. To achieve Level 3 they therefore have to demonstrate the ability to revise and redraft. Some infant teachers have expressed scepticism at encouraging redrafting, feeling that infant children are too young to rework a piece of writing. However, the National Curriculum expects children at Level 3 to be able to redraft writing, and the teachers I was working with wanted to introduce redrafting as part of the writing process from the beginning.

How can we show children the way in which writers of narrative craft, shape and redraft their work? Children see plenty of functional writing in action but rarely see a story being worked. 'Teacher as model' is one way in, and *Shared Reading, Shared Writing*[5] has a wealth of sound ideas to encourage collaboration, for example with the teacher acting as scribe. This has two important purposes: first, to show children how ideas are gleaned, refined and reworked; and second, to help them achieve, with support, things which alone they would not be capable of doing.[6]

Learning about How Writers Use Language

I wanted to find a way to enable children to begin to understand how authors of published work also go through these processes, how they choose their subject and the language they use in order to create a particular impression from a particular viewpoint. Writing is not static, but an interaction between author and reader, and I wanted to work with the children in order to make this explicit.[7] Don Holdaway states the importance to the development of the child as a reader of sharing a well-known and well-loved text and so eventually I decided to look at how, by enabling the children to rewrite *The Very Hungry Caterpillar* by Eric Carle, their development as both readers and writers would be enhanced.[8] What follows is a description and an analysis of the activity.

The children were from a class spanning Years 1 and 2 and so their ages ranged from 5 to almost 7. This meant that their reading development also covered a wide range and, although I wanted to work with children across the age and ability range, I started by taking a group of Year 2 children who were all confident writers to see the possibilities and to provide a model from which the other children could be supported. We discussed *The Very Hungry Caterpillar* as a group and I read it to them before we looked at the text, which I had written large enough for the whole group to see. How would they have written the story had they been Eric Carle? Would they have chosen the same words, and used the same phrases? The children sat silently for a moment, and, as a teacher, I was tempted to intervene (how quick we are to rush in), but my hesitation paid off because eventually one child volunteered: 'It starts at nighttime; you could say, "One night" . . . ' and so we were off. From then on an avalanche of ideas flooded from the children as I struggled, as scribe, to keep pace. As can be seen from Figure 2.1, redrafting took place in a variety of ways:

- at phrase level: 'in the light of the moon' became 'one dark cloudy night'
- at word level: 'pop!' became 'crack!'
- the text was extended: 'he was a beautiful butterfly' became 'she was a very beautiful colourful butterfly'
- alteration was consistently sustained at both sequential and semantic/syntactic level. The days of the week, once changed, had to follow in order. The sex change given to the caterpillar meant that all pronouns had to be altered, not just all the 'he's' to 'she's', but 'himself' and 'his' to 'herself' and 'her'.

The children chose a variety of parts of speech in their alterations:

- nouns: 'oranges' became 'peaches'
- noun phrases: 'one slice of Swiss cheese' became 'one tin of cat food'
- adjectives: 'big' became 'enormous', which also meant that the children had to alter the determiner 'a' to 'an'
- adjectives could be easily added to extend the text, so 'three plums' became 'three squidgy plums'
- adverbs were added to verbs: 'started' became 'scrambled about'
- adverbial phrases: 'more than two weeks' became 'about a month'

A Closer Look at Language

All this provided a wealth of opportunities for the children to reflect on the way language works, and be given a metalanguage through which to do that. One of the decisions a teacher makes when looking closely at text with children is how much new terminology to introduce; much depends on the context, the interest and the capabilities of the children. I began to use terms (all required by the National Curriculum to be introduced to children through

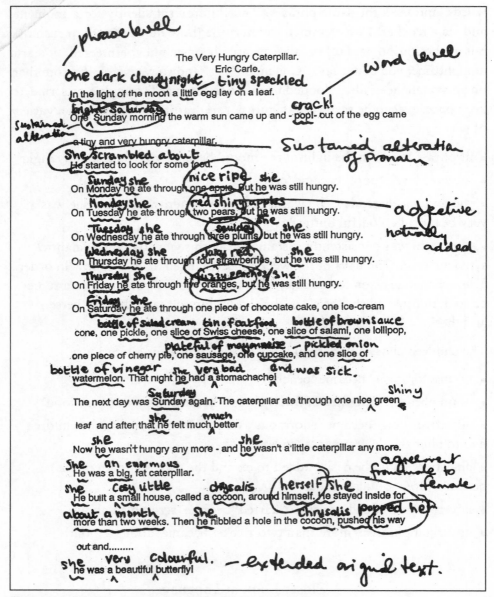

The Very Hungry Caterpillar.
Eric Carle.

phrase level

One dark cloudy night — tiny speckled

word level

In the light of the moon a little egg lay on a leaf.

crack!

bright Saturday   One Sunday morning the warm sun came up and - pop! - out of the egg came

sustained alteration

a tiny and very hungry caterpillar.

She scrambled about   *Sustained alteration of pronoun*

He started to look for some food.

Sunday she   nice ripe   she
On Monday he ate through one apple. But he was still hungry.

Monday she   red shiny apples
On Tuesday he ate through two pears, but he was still hungry.   *adjective*

Tuesday she   squidgy she   *naturally added*
On Wednesday he ate through three plums, but he was still hungry.

Wednesday she   juicy red   she
On Thursday he ate through four strawberries, but he was still hungry.

Thursday she   fuzzy peaches/she
On Friday he ate through five oranges, but he was still hungry.

Friday she
On Saturday he ate through one piece of chocolate cake, one ice-cream

bottle of salad cream   tin of cat food   bottle of brown sauce
cone, one pickle, one slice of Swiss cheese, one slice of salami, one lollipop,

plateful of mayonnaise   - pickled onion
one piece of cherry pie, one sausage, one cupcake, and one slice of

bottle of vinegar   she very bad   and was sick.
watermelon. That night he had a stomachache!

Saturday
The next day was Sunday again. The caterpillar ate through one nice green   shiny

she   much
leaf and after that he felt much better.

she   she
Now he wasn't hungry any more - and he wasn't a little caterpillar any more.

She   an enormous
He was a big, fat caterpillar.

she   cosy little   chrysalis   herself she   *agreement from male to female*
He built a small house, called a cocoon, around himself. He stayed inside for

about a month   she   Chrysalis popped her
more than two weeks. Then he nibbled a hole in the cocoon, pushed his way

out and.........

she   very   colourful.   — *extended original text.*
he was a beautiful butterfly!

Figure 2.1 *The Very Hungry Caterpillar*: The children's version

the contexts of their own writing) such as 'adjective', 'pronoun', 'noun' and 'verb'. I even, at one point, introduced the notion of 'tense' as we debated whether to have the story happening in the present. Although the children were unable to explain their reasons for keeping the status quo, it was apparent that they implicitly knew that most fiction is written in the past tense and so found it difficult to shift to a more unusual format.

The group finally published their own version of *The Very Hungry Caterpillar* which, placed alongside the original version, has become one of the most frequently read and borrowed books in the class collection.

In participating in this activity, the children had been given an insight into the way an author might think about, and reject, ideas for a story. They saw how changes can be made within the process of writing; the techniques that a skilled writer might use to indicate additions or alterations. These had been my original intentions, but the activity provided scope for much more. The opportunity to use metalanguage firmly within a meaningful context was very important, and could have been extended in a number of ways; for example, older children could have tried to alter the narrative from past to simple present, or present continuous, to see what effects would be created in the overall structure of the text. With these children I felt it had been sufficient to use a number of terms in context. Their interest was caught by the idea of using onomatopoeia (a term I also then used) and words such as 'squidgy' and 'juicy' were added. We also discussed alliteration which, although they decided not to include 'plump purple plums' in their final version, provided scope for follow-up work in their topic on 'minibeasts', where they wrote alliterative menus for various creatures, e.g. 'snails sip slimy soup, sweetcorn and swedes'.

Phonemic awareness was revealed by the textual alterations the children made, and they became aware of the composition of words such as 'he' which can be easily altered to 'she' by the addition of a single letter.[9] Incidentally, although we did not discuss it in depth, the children were interested to see that whereas 'himself' became 'herself' it was 'his' not 'him' which became 'her', an indication of the way in which the syntax of standard English is not as logical as one might suppose! In order to make these alterations consistent the children had to scan the text to find all the words that needed to be changed and, as shown above, these were not necessarily the same words each time, so the children really had to call upon their implicit knowledge of the way our language works in order to do this.

It is obvious, I think, how capable these children aged 6 and 7 were of understanding and using their mother tongue. I was surprised, and pleased, to realize just what sophisticated language users they were. But I also wanted to see how well this activity would transfer to a different group of children, so I took another group to see how they would use the support of a well-loved, well-written text to help them create their own story.

Learning to Use Language

Again, I used *The Very Hungry Caterpillar*, but this time I decided to offer additional support and, at the same time, give the children more independence and control over their work, so I gave each child a copy of the text. At first we worked in a similar way to that previously described, looking at and discussing the book together before reading it. I then showed them the draft version of the first group's alterations (this was before it had been finally published for class use) and asked them to discuss how they would have rewritten the story, referring them to the photocopied versions they each had in front of them. Apart from two boys, both reluctant writers, all the children wanted to work alone, perhaps because each child had an individual copy of the text. I agreed to this, and was therefore given an opportunity to look at the way each child approached the task.

Robert (Figure 2.2) was happy to write on his own, although he wanted me to help him spell words he did not have access to in the original text. As can be seen from the illustration, he is a child who wants to produce work which is both accurate and neat. With another activity I might try to free him from a sense of failure when trying out new ideas and taking risks, but in this situation, especially not knowing the children as well as a class teacher would, I felt it was important to give him security and so complied with his requests.

Gillian (Figure 2.3) needed help to get going but then happily made her own alterations. I felt that her rather rapid progression through the narrative towards a resolution may have been because she was planning ahead to minimize the writing involved in her final version. However, when she saw how quick it was to redraft the text which I had put into the computer, I think she may have regretted her decision; especially when she saw the sense of achievement other children felt when they 'wrote' and then obtained such long stories!

Anthony and Jamie (Figure 2.4) were most happy to work in a pair, with me acting as scribe. Neither was fond of the physical act of writing, but, as can be seen from their ideas, this did not stop them from being able to use language in a powerful and imaginative way when composing. At first they were rather hesitant to include the line 'That night he was sick', presumably wondering whether that came under the auspices of a 'rude' topic, which all children know to avoid when with adults, fearing for our delicate constitutions. However, once they had checked that I was not shocked they extended

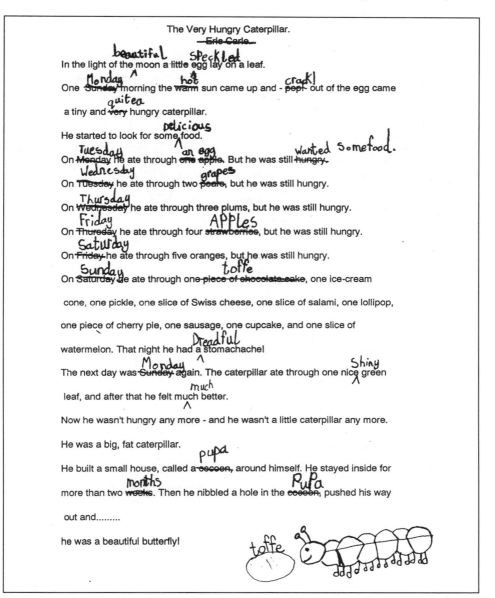

Figure 2.2 *The Very Hungry Caterpillar*: Robert's version

and qualified the statement to 'and nearly died', before going on to paint an even more vivid picture of the effects of the caterpillar's overindulgence and recuperation. I felt, somehow, that they both were able to draw on personal experiences, giving a sense of realism to the narrative! The fact that I was able to scribe their ideas meant pressure was lifted from the physical act of writing and thus they showed their understanding of the

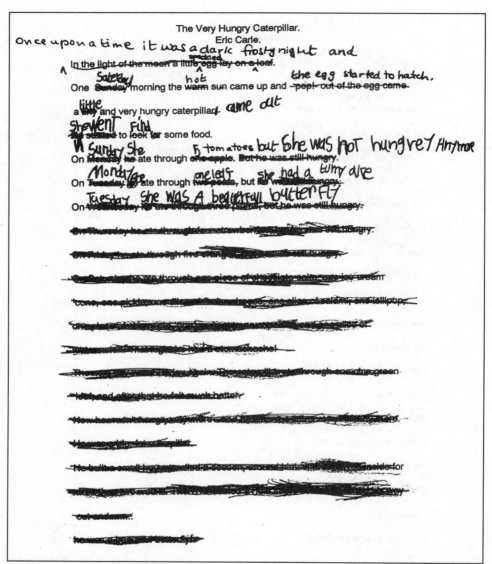

The Very Hungry Caterpillar.
Eric Carle.

Once upon a time it was a dark frosty night and

In the light of the moon a little egg lay on a leaf.
                          speckled

One Sunday morning the warm sun came up and pop! out of the egg came
    Saterday   hot   the egg started to hatch.

a tiny and very hungry caterpillar came out
   little

She went Find
and started to look for some food.

On Sunday She ate through one apple. But he was still hungry.
   5 tomatoes but She was hot hungrey Anymor

On Monday ate ate through one leaf, but she had a tummy ake
   Tuesday
On Tuesday She was A beautiful butterfly

Figure 2.3 *The Very Hungry Caterpillar*: Gillian's version

structures of written, as opposed to spoken, language, using both adjectival and adverbial phrases ('about as big as the library' and 'he felt so strong that he could smash a table down') to qualify statements.

Gillian and Robert, by having to concentrate on the technical as well as compositional skills of writing, made far fewer alterations, but both showed they were capable of extracting information from a text and reforming it with semantic consistency. Each used the original text as well as incorporating ideas from the first group's redrafting, but this is in keeping with the way in

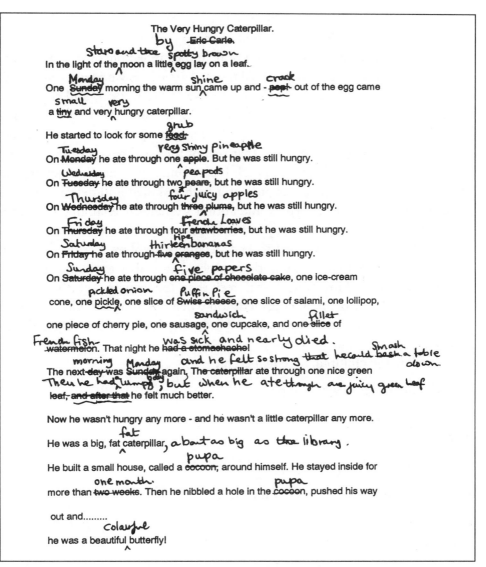

Figure 2.4 *The Very Hungry Caterpillar*: Anthony and Jamie's version

which we all select from within our experiences in order to create the effect
which we want to achieve. Each of the children, as groups, pairs or individuals, built on and made decisions about the original text in order to have
ownership of their final piece of writing. Their sense of achievement was
obvious and I feel had a profound effect on how they saw themselves as
writers. For example, see how firmly Robert replaces Eric Carle's name with
his own in order to establish authorship. These children realized that they
were authors, and could make decisions about their writing in the same way

that a published author can. The printouts on the computer once they had done their final redrafts added weight to this.

So I had achieved my original intention, and by reflecting on and analysing the work I realized that I had achieved more. As teachers we need to ensure we have time for both the children and ourselves to reflect on, and thus learn from, both our achievements and our so-called failures. If reflection is not a part of the teaching and learning cycle, then many opportunities are missed.

I realized, as mentioned earlier, that one of the weaknesses of the activity was that it did not touch upon quality. Redrafting is not merely changing for the sake of change; rather, it is part of a highly skilled and delicate process which includes audience, purpose and author's intention, enabling the author to come as close as possible to the effect that he or she wants to achieve. Moving children from the 'bed to bed' recounts involves a realization that some events have more weight than others, and also that longer is not necessarily better. However, I still feel that the benefits of the activity described make it worthy of consideration when planning for ways in which we can as teachers build on, and extend, the development of children's language.

As readers the children were helped to:

- read a quality text with support

- have attention drawn to directionality/sequencing/words/phrases/sentences

- scrutinize words and patterns within words

- scan text for words/chunks of meaning

- have links between words highlighted ('-day' 's/he') but at no time was meaning sacrificed for analysis at word/phrase level.

As writers the children were helped to:

- appreciate that writing is not 'in tablets of stone'

- work with peers collaboratively, either on group/pair or on individual pieces of writing

- have control over text and work at their own level

- reconstruct writing without emphasis on physical skill

- work on a whole text to see the overall shape of discourse

- use technical terminology in context, thus aquiring a metalanguage

- see and work within a good model for narrative structure

It was Marie Clay who said that '[children] know more about writing when they control more spoken registers and read a wide variety of texts'.[10] Children should be entitled to read (and be read to from) the widest variety of good-quality literature. There are many wonderful books for children either written in or translated into English, and our classrooms should be full of them to help children become sophisticated and discriminating readers. But language development is interdependent, so in order to choose the most appropriate style and vocabulary when writing, children need to have heard powerful models within the different genres of written language, making access to quality texts even more vital. By discussing Eric Carle's book the children had an opportunity to talk about how written language works, thus learning through language, learning to use language, and learning about language.[11]

I should like to conclude by thanking Julie Fuller and Jenny Beadle, whose talents as classroom teachers gave me the opportunity to do this work with their children. The title was chosen partly as a dedication to two boys who, although reluctant writers, were able to create dynamic text, and partly because I feel it captures the spirit of the piece – that without access to libraries full of quality books, children will not have such rich experiences to assist them in their development as writers.

Notes and References

1. This is a way to encourage peer involvement and support in writing at both content and secretarial level and is described more fully in the National Writing Project (1989) *Responding to and Assessing Writing*. Kingston upon Thames: Nelson/National Writing Project.

2. Hardy, B. (1977) Narrative as a primary act of mind. In M. Meek *et al.* (eds) *The Cool Web*. London: The Bodley Head.

3. Martin, J. R. and Rothery, J. (1986) What a functional approach to writing can show teachers about 'good writing'. In B. Couture (ed.) *Functional Approaches to Writing: Research Perspectives*. London: Frances Pinter.

4. Department of Education and Science and the Welsh Office (1990) *English in the National Curriculum*. London: HMSO.

5. Barrs, M. *et al.* (1990) *Shared Reading, Shared Writing*. London: Centre for Language in Primary Education.

6. Vygotsky, L. (1978) *Mind and Society*, p. 85. Boston: Harvard University Press. Vygotsky identified 'the zone of proximal development', highlighting that a child will, with support, achieve today what tomorrow will be achieved independently.

7. For a more detailed exploration of this see: Jones, N. (1990) Reader, writer, text. In R. Carter (ed.) *Knowledge about Language and the Curriculum: the LINC Reader*, pp. 154–67. London: Hodder and Stoughton.

8. Holdaway, D. (1979) *The Foundations of Literacy*. Ashton: Scholastic.

9. Pressure to highlight the teaching of phonics often gives the impression that it is the most important cueing strategy for children when learning to read. It is worth noting just how phonemic awareness is embedded within a whole language approach which uses 'real books'. For detailed accounts of this see: Campbell, R. (1992) *Reading Real Books*. Milton Keynes: Open University Press; Mills, H., O'Keefe, T. and Stephens, D. (1992) *Looking Closely: Exploring the Role of Phonics in One Whole Language Classroom*. Illinois: National Council of Teachers of English.

10. Clay, M. (1983) Getting a theory of writing. In B. Kroll and G. Wells (eds) *Explorations in the Development of Writing*, p. 275. London: John Wiley and Sons.

11. Other case studies showing children using these three aspects of knowledge about language are in: Bain, R., Fitzgerald, B. and Taylor, M. (eds) (1992) *Looking into Language: Classroom Approaches to Knowledge about Language*. London: Hodder and Stoughton.

Chapter 3

Bringing Out the Beast in Them
Reflections on Gender and Children's Use of Traditional Stories

David Whitley

The reading curriculum of any school will often include traditional stories as essential elements in a full range of narratives. There is an implicit assumption, perhaps because they have stood the test of time, that these stories are good for us. They provide moral messages and important cultural witness which seems automatically to find a place in the provision of reading material in classrooms. And, indeed, they are still popular. However, their necessary appearance tends to prevent any careful analysis of just what they do offer – precisely what is the nature of the messages they bring? In his work with a class of 10- and 11-year-olds in a newly built suburban school, David Whitley examines how traditional stories help children to 'scale time' as well as offering teachers some valuable evidence about how young writers use stories firmly embedded in the culture to articulate their own contemporary cultural experience – in this case expressed in gendered identification. David Whitley found that the traditional genre of the beast fable engendered 'pressures in contrary directions'. While working within one model, with a long history of repetition and duration, the young writers worked against its grain by drawing on their own gendered understandings and making their new narratives with the more overtly gendered texts of today. And in doing this, they showed sturdy reclamation of an old form for new and assertive meanings.

What do children make of some of the relatively stable forms in which important traditional narratives have existed? By 'traditional narrative' I mean forms such as fairy tale, folk tale and animal fable, which have been reproduced throughout long periods of history with substantial variations but relatively little change in the deep structure of the stories. What do children make of these forms? That is, how do they understand them? But, as importantly, how do they make these stories again, transform them under the pressure of their own experience and knowledge of the world?

These stable narrative forms have long been held to have particular value and appropriateness for children's development. Yet their universal, seemingly timeless, appeal also provokes more troubled thoughts for those working with children in the modern world. For the universality of these stories often turns out, on closer scrutiny, to be rather partial, resting as it often does on stereotyped patterns of human behaviour and identity which have come, particularly in their gendered inflections, to be increasingly challenged.[1] There is a need, clearly, for us to understand in more detail what the significance of these forms is in working with children and to attend closely, in particular, to what children voice in relation to them. What follows is offered in this spirit – a small contribution to a large, and I think urgent, question.

I want to concentrate here on one of the traditional forms in which I have come to be particularly interested – the 'beast fable' – and to discuss some issues arising from work I was recently able to do with a class of Year 5 and 6 primary school children. The starting point for this work comprised medieval versions of the beast fable, and one of the questions I had hoped to explore was what children might make of the specific historical contexts within which these 'universal' tales were produced. With this in mind I began by trying to establish with the children some sense that these stories had a particular history of which they could feel themselves to be a part. I talked with them a little about Aesop, whose name was familiar to many of them, and also about two medieval writers, Chaucer and Henryson, who had created their versions of Aesop's stories more than five hundred years ago. I told them that Henryson had lived in Scotland and that Chaucer's story was one of a series he had written to be told by an imaginary group of pilgrims travelling to Canterbury together. I wanted to build up a sense of the pastness of the narratives as giving them a rather special feeling but also to embed the notion, when they came to write their own stories, that they would be joining a series of writers who had rewritten tales whose origins could be traced back to an obscure Greek slave living two and a half thousand years ago.

Connecting Past and Present

Part of the magic of these stories is the way they enable us to scale time with a powerful sense of connectedness. And indeed, when the children came to write their own stories, one of them responded directly to this sense of pastness by framing his tale in a perspective that offered a vista over a similarly momentous passage of time. 'Four hundred years ago a fox went out hunting for his prey,' he began impressively, making this everyday event sing out with the significance of its having been remembered across the chasm of history which separates us from the medieval world.

Working with this sense of pastness, then, I followed up a brief discussion of Aesop and the origins of beast fables by relating to them Chaucer's version of the story of the cock Chaunticleer and his narrow escape from the jaws of the fox who flatters him to the hilt in order to trick and eat him. This is the tale which Chaucer allocates to the Nun's Priest in his *Canterbury Tales*: I read them a somewhat simplified prose version written by Selina Hastings.[2] After I had read it we talked for a while about their response to the story and then tried to identify features in it which might characterize what they thought beast fables were like. They were quickly able to identify some features they felt might be important and generally applicable. They felt that the animals in these stories had some human characteristics (most crucially, they were able to talk) although at times they also behaved and moved like the natural animals they represented. They recognized that these stories were often accompanied by a moral and were very sharp in discerning what the moral of the stories I read to them might be. Interestingly, although they seemed very familiar with the convention of extracting a singular moral statement from the tales they had heard, very few wished to use this kind of resolution for the tales they constructed themselves. Though the tales they wrote were, as I shall show later, often very 'Aesopic' in tone, the children seemed to have no active use for the moralizing tradition that so often accompanied the historical versions of these tales. In this sense, as in several others, they had made their own narratives 'modern'.

I had started this project seeking tentative answers to some very broad questions, but I did not have any clear sense of what the outcomes might be. I was particularly interested in the gender implications of writing, however, and aware – though less so than I have subsequently become! – that traditional genres often construe sexual identity in very conservative modes. Janet White puts the case rather more forthrightly when she observes that 'the ready availability of scenarios filled with anthropomorphised animals provides a quick and easy route into some of the most traditional sex-stereotype images encountered by young children, whether as readers or television viewers'.[3] With this in mind I had wanted to offer some experiences of medieval writing which showed something of the range of possibilities that could be explored in this mode. Animal stories in their traditional forms may tend to be male dominated but that they offer potential in different directions is suggested by the fact that both Marie de France and Aphra Behn, two of the very earliest examples in Europe of women forging a reputation for themselves through writing, should have made major contributions to the development of the beast fable form.[4] In retrospect I should perhaps have used one of the stories of these women to offer as an example to the children. In fact the second example that I chose was by another male author, the late-fifteenth-century Scottish writer Robert Henryson. But his adaptation of Aesop's story of the town mouse and the country mouse is very engaging and does, I think, reveal something of the range of possibilities for gender identification available in this genre of writing, even in its traditional contexts.

Aesop's story, you may remember, is very brief. It concerns two field-mice who are friends. Invited by his rural counterpart to dine in the country one day, the town mouse pours scorn on the meagre offerings his friend is able to put together for the meal. A return match is arranged in the town so that the urban mouse can demonstrate to his friend what good living is all about. However, their meal is repeatedly disturbed by humans entering the larder where they are dining and the country mouse decides, rather sententiously, that he prefers 'a simple life with peace and quiet' to 'faring luxuriously and being haunted by fear'.

Henryson's version keeps the essential structure of Aesop's tale, but greatly extends and enhances its details. The comparison between urban and rural life is far more developed and the social identities of the two mice are embellished with the kind of detail ordinarily the preserve of the satirist, rather than the fabulist. The drama of the larder meal is enhanced by the addition of a cat to the human interventions. But perhaps most distinctively, the two mice are attributed female identity, the bond between them being changed to that of sisters, rather than male friends. And indeed the relationship between the sisters becomes almost as important as the judgement on their respective ways of life in this retelling. A brief extract (my own rather heavy prose version of the original Scots dialect verse) will give something of the flavour of the humorous and affectionate artistry that has gone into the depiction of the sisters' emotional closeness and rivalry.

One day the town mouse took it into her head to visit her rural sister whom she had not seen for a long time. She made the hazardous journey alone, scampering over roads and along ditches, creeping under briars, between mossy stones and up slippery banks till at last, when she thought she was near, she called:

'Come out, come out, dear sister! Cry "peep" once, if you can hear me.' The country mouse, recognizing her sister's voice, came scampering out joyfully at once and hugged her in her little arms. They kissed and laughed together, as mice will when they are alone. When the initial pleasure of meeting had lessened somewhat, they teetered off to the country mouse's home. This was indeed a frail and humble dwelling. It was made of moss and fern, woven together to provide the thin walls of a tiny chamber tucked into the hollow under a stone. The entrance was so narrow they had to squeeze through, one after another. Inside it was dark and, to tell the truth, a little damp; but the country mouse soon set to work to make her sister feel at home. She brought out some of her favourite foods; a few nuts, dried peas and some candle wax she'd pilfered from the farm. This hospitality did not impress the town mouse however, who became rather scornful. Puffing out her little chest in pride she said:

'Sister, is this your daily food?'

'Why not?', replied the other, 'This is good fare, is it not?'

'Upon my soul. I think it not, sister,' said the town mouse. 'Why this is a pitiful meal!'

'Now shame on you sister! This is the fare our mother gave us when we were growing up together. You didn't scorn our way of life then, even if we were poor and had no property.'

'My dear sister, please, you'll have to excuse me. I cannot make do with food as coarse as this. I'm used to tender morsels and my stomach simply will not take it. These withered nuts and peas will break my teeth before I get them down.'

Making Their Own Stories

Having talked about the Henryson story, and looked at some other Aesop fables that the children themselves had brought in, the children were now ready to write their own versions. We decided we would put these together to form a book of beast fables representing the class's collective achievement. When we started out I had really had no idea what I thought might emerge from the children's writing. I suppose I had assumed, rather naively, that the medieval examples of fables I had offered the class involved a sufficient range of narrative possibilities not to predispose the children to write in any particular way themselves. I was interested in what they might be attracted to and make use of in the historical form of these stories but imagined they would come to them with a free-floating rather than preset sense of what could be made of the genre. In fact, of course, they came to these stories with their own rich and varied experiences of how animals feature in many different kinds of narrative. One rather troubled child fixed on the notion that writing in this genre provided an opportunity to reproduce one of his favourite computer game heroes – Sonic Hedgehog – in a classroom context. Though the narrative itself was rather flat, he took immense care in reproducing the form of Sonic Hedgehog with the most exacting graphic accuracy, to illustrate his story. One of the girls, with a rather more literary imagination, produced a long and complex story in a hybrid genre that mixed beast fable with detective thriller. She used a clever pun on Inspector Morse/Mouse to legitimate this mix. Such inventiveness in response was exciting, though I should perhaps not have been surprised that the children could make such interesting use of their own experiences of animals within story. What came to interest me even more, however, was the degree to which this inventiveness focused particular issues of gender differentiation in relation to the children's narratives.

In some respects this did not conform to expectations. In a study which bears some similarities to my own, for instance, children in a third-year junior class were invited to produce their own versions of Homer's *Odyssey* after listening to several episodes of a radio version devised for 9- to 11-year-olds.[5] The writer here compared girls' and boys' writing in three broad categories:

- those dealing with emotions (affective)

- those concerning authority, control or personal ascendancy (power related)

- those concerning physical force or bloodthirstiness (violence related)

The second category – power-related issues – appeared to have engaged both girls and boys strongly (though the theme occurred rather more frequently in the boys' writing). But the other two categories produced stark contrasts. This brief quantitative survey found that 'the girls wrote about emotions on a total of forty-two occasions, while the boys wrote about them on only five occasions'. And in the third category – violence-related themes – the distribution was skewed nearly as much in the other direction: 'the girls wrote about physical force and bloodthirstiness on four occasions and the boys on eighteen occasions'.

By comparison, it was clear in the work that the children produced for me on beast fables that there were some differences, at least in relation to the third category of violence. A striking feature of nearly all the stories the children wrote was the degree to which they seemed to be responding to what I would – rather sententiously – describe as the 'existential' quality of the fables inspired by Aesop. Whereas modern stories for children involving animals come in a variety of forms, often focusing on predominately social themes such as an animal/child's first day in school or responses to a new baby in the family, Aesopic fables tend to present a stark world in which issues of survival, of life and death, are central. The girls in the class were not, by and large, drawn towards the more sentimental, wholly anthropomorphized genres of modern animal stories where animals are dressed up to enact essentially human social situations. The raw, existential quality of life-and-death struggle was largely retained by both sexes in the class. Perhaps even more interestingly, the girls' writing showed clear tendencies to resist sentimental resolutions to the plots they had set in motion.

Characteristic of this tendency was a story about two squirrels written by Sally. As in the Henryson fable the squirrels were depicted as female and, it is implied, they are sisters. The plot revolved around the squirrels facing the imminent danger of attack by a fox, an attack which they respond to with a humorous mixture of hysterical alarm and sleepy denial of the reality of the fox's presence. Some influence from Chaucer's story can, perhaps, also be seen here. When they are finally both brought to recognize their dangerous predicament, the alarmist squirrel devises a plan which seems to offer hope of escaping the fox's jaws. But, instead of the happy ending for which the plot seems to be preparing us, the denouement offers a resolution in which the second squirrel, whether through nervousness or ineptitude, fails to carry out her companion's plan to the letter. She is killed, in peremptory fashion, by the fox aggressor. The survivor, called Sarah, is left alone – 'I haven't got any other family', she relates rather pathetically. But the final resolution, offering a stoic recognition that life will continue despite pain and loss, is anything but pathetic: 'For two long weeks Sarah was very upset but eventually got over it and got on with her life. THE END.'

The two aspects that I have indicated to be significant here – writing which both focuses on the threat and consequences of physical violence and resists sentimental resolutions of its themes – are also present in another interesting narrative by one of the girls. Here the story is concise enough to be repeated in full:

The Two Mice

Once upon a time there were two golden brown mice called Sally and Cally. They were sisters but Cally lived with their Dad. Sally lived with their Mum. Their Mum lived miles away from Dad Mouse. Cally has only seen her sister once in her life time, but she still writes letters, but Sally never writes back. Once she wrote back a run away plan. This is what she wrote: [a map giving details of a meeting point for the escape is inserted into the written narrative at this point]. Something terrible went wrong, they did get there, they did meet but a cat came and took Cally. Even if Cally's only seen her sister once, she is my twin sister, so Sally kicked and scratched until the cat bled. The cat let go. Cally started running home and shouted out 'I'll do you a favour one day.'

This brief narrative required an immense amount of effort and concentration from Sonya. I think this shows in what she eventually produced. The story is, in its way, a masterpiece of concision and repays very careful reading. The two sisters (whose identity as twins is suggested by the homophonic pairing of their names even before the story makes this explicit) are carefully distinguished in terms of how they express themselves. Cally is an insistent, perhaps compulsive, verbalizer. Although she has only seen her sister once in her life and has never received a reply to her attempts to communicate, she *still writes letters*. The longing to establish a relationship with her estranged twin is powerfully, and very economically, evoked.

The sister's presence is made manifest in the text through contrast. Sally *does not* write letters: whatever it is she feels is not verbalized. Indeed, her one act of communication in the story is represented in the text not in the form of words but as a map, which is also a plan of action. The story turns on a contrast between the two sisters' modes of expressing commitment to their potential relationship. Where Cally verbalizes her commitment through the medium of her letter writing, Sally's commitment is expressed directly through action, first in the plan that they should run away together, and subsequently through risking her own life to save her sister from the cat. In a sentence whose form suggests the movement of Sally's inner thought (again, it is characteristic that this should not be verbalized in the exterior form of direct speech), we are told that even if the sisters have only seen each other once 'she is my twin sister, so Sally kicked and scratched until the cat bled.'

Violence here is the necessary expression of Sally's commitment to her sister; the detail of the action carried on until blood is drawn is not only vivid, but also provides a dramatically appropriate counterpoint to the strength of the blood bond between the sisters which is being tested here. And just as the supposedly 'boys'' theme of violence is incorporated with such naturalness into the girl's story here, so too the easy resolution of the 'girls'' theme, the successful realization of relationships, is also resisted. For the sisters are not harmoniously united at the end of the story. Cally has received the most telling evidence that her sister reciprocates her own sense of the bond between them. Yet they remain separate; the event which has expressed their potential closeness most fully is consigned to memory, an emotional debt which, Cally suggests, 'one day' will be repaid as action.

Another story (Figure 3.1) shows how the girls' writing discovered both strengths and problematic areas in the beast fable genre. The story here is reproduced in its original form because the illustrations are integral to the narrative. Many of the children were attracted to the notion of imitating medieval scribal conventions which allow marginal illustrations and initial letters to be worked up into beautiful decorative motifs. This story was one of the most successful in incorporating these conventions.

Here again, the issue of violence looms large in the narrative. The writer has centred her narrative on one of the most powerful Aesopic themes, the interdependence of stronger and weaker animals. Indeed, the story seems to take the widest possible perspective on this theme by embedding the central action in a series of vignettes which display the natural world, with stark realism, as essentially a food chain. The thrush eats the snail and would eat the spider; the cat tries to eat the bird; the spider snacks opportunistically on a piece of fly; and so on. What interrupts this natural process is the particular moment when, faced with its own mortality, the stronger animal realizes its need for the weaker as something other than a food item. A recognition of interlocking, rather than conflicting, self-interests is secured, which is anything but sentimental. 'Why should I help you when you tried to kill me?', Henny asks sensibly, and finds her own immediate needs addressed in the reply, 'If you do I will take you home.' The resolution in which this act of mutual self-interest secures an everlasting bond between the creatures, sentimentally anthropomorphized though it is, has to be understood as a rather special bond set off against the remorseless demands of the 'eat and be eaten' world within which it is located.

THE WONDERING SPIDER

enry was a spider but not just any spider Henry loved to explore. This is a story about when Henry got lost in the spinney. Once Henry was walking in the spinney when a gust of wind came and blew her away a mile (well only 50 yards but a mile to her) she landed and noticed there were bits of snail shell being dropped from above. She looked up and saw a big fat thrush sitting on a branch having his mid morning snack. Henry immediately shot under a nearby leaf tripping over her legs as she did. This caught the birds attention and made it drop the snail and fly down. Henry heard the voice of the bird outside saying "you wont get out alive" he paused then said "Im waiting" he felt the gentle padding of the birds feet outside. A cat had got the bird and run of without it. Henry put her leg out to see if it was ok. Then he saw something on his leg so he pulled it in only to find it was a peice of wing from a fly so he ate it. Then he saw a dieing thrush "help me" he said "Im dieing" "why should I" said Henry "you tryed to kill me" "If you do I will take you home" So Henry helped him till he was better. The bird took Henry home and they were best friends forever more. The end

Figure 3.1 The Wondering Spider

This story seems to me to show the value of contexts which encourage girls to take on 'boys'' themes, such as violence, in their writing, and vice versa. The strength of the story is in the way it is able to recognize the prevalence of physical power and need in the world, yet also, through its humane and sentimental ending, to question this. One could speculate, optimistically, that it may be the power of the beast fable genre, in one of its older forms, which has contributed to enabling this girl to explore beyond the conventional gender boundaries of writing for her age group. It is important not to get too starry eyed about this, of course. That the genre engenders pressures in contrary directions is suggested by the difficulty this writer finds in securing a stable gender identity for the hero of her story. Henny starts the story as an adventurous female who 'loved to explore'. Yet half-way through the tale, under the pressure of aggression from the predatory thrush which stalks the entrance to her hiding place, this feminine identity collapses. Just prior to entering the food chain as consumer of the dismembered fly, Henny becomes a 'he'; the male personal pronoun is allocated consistently throughout the second half of the story. Has the theme of aggression, legitimated by the genre, created an unconscious pressure for hero rather than heroine? It is a reminder, at least, that we need to be careful in the way we introduce and work with such material with children.

The story (Figure 3.2) appears, at first sight, to have a similar pattern to that of the boys' stories generally, in that there is no apparent interest in relationships between the mouse and other animals, apart from that involved in the need to escape its predators. But this story, in a subtle, almost poetic way, does evoke feelings even if it eschews the topic of relationships. Indeed, the absence of relationships appears to be the very means of its evoking feelings. At a deep level the subject of the story would seem to be precisely the aloneness and vulnerability of a small creature exposed to the hazards of the larger world as it makes its journey towards what will become its alternative, and securer, home. The feelings associated with the journey and the sense of 'home' which is its starting and end point are never conjured for us explicitly. Rather they emerge from the detailed perception of the terrain over which the mouse moves, of the rhythm of exertion and rest, and of successive dangers successfully overcome. The entry into sleep under the tulip tree is a moment of pure magic, all the more affecting for being so natural. That writing in this genre should have provided access to the expression of such 'poetic' emotion for this boy – who, incidentally, found great difficulty in writing and dictated the story, which he subsequently illustrated – may indicate that there is some

---

A MOUSE AND IT'S JOURNEY

One day there was a mouse called Bruno and he lived in a human house. He was very fed up with living there so he decided to go and live outside. He had never been outside so he did not know what he would see there.

He started to pack his bags straight away and then he left the house. He went through the bushes, over the streams and under the bridge until he came across a cat. He tried to outrun the cat but it got hold of Bruno. Just at that moment a dog howled from far away and the cat dropped him and ran away.

He walked a couple of miles more then it was nightfall, he slept under a tulip tree.

The day after that when he woke up he noticed a signpost which said 'The Spinney.' He was just crossing the road to investigate when a car came along and went right over him, but luckily the wheels missed him and he wasn't hurt. When he crossed the road he came to a flower bed and he walked up a path until he came to a gate. Then he squeezed through the bars of the gate and he found himself on a green, and at the side of the green there was a ditch and beyond that ditch there was a forest. He went through the ditch and into the forest and he found a log with a hole in it. He squeezed through the hole and he decided he was going to live there. He lived there happily for ever after.

The End

Figure 3.2 A Mouse and its Journey

potential for shifting the boundaries of boys' writing too. In most instances this would seem to be more entrenched than the girls' in particular gendered modes, however.

Why this should be is by no means clear. Is there something in the genre ingrained in boys by this age – the episodic adventure mode – that is more resistant to mutation than the forms predominantly used by girls? Or does boys' fear of feminization pervade their narrative performance at a period when girls remain freer to explore masculine aspects of social identity, at least in an imaginative sphere? It is likely, in any event, that the material offered to these children would have elicited quite different responses if introduced in a different way; and there is evidence, at least in the last story cited, that the beast fable form can provide access to the expression of feelings other than those of competition and aggression for at least some boys. But what is perhaps most exciting about this work is the degree to which the seemingly universal form of the beast fable, in some of its older retellings, would seem to have facilitated a group of stories from girls that exhibit shrewd and determined resistance to gender categorization. 'Out of old books comes new knowledge,' as Chaucer himself puts it in his *Parliament of Fowls*.[6] The old stories here arguably provided a base enabling girls to focus on some of the problems encountered in modern existence in fresh and revealing ways that perhaps approximate to a particular kind of new knowledge for our own time.

Notes and References

1. For example: 'The traditional fairy tale relies upon concluding devices such as a "happy-ever-after" marriage or a tragic death for a forsaken lover, and adopts clear and uncompromising stereotypes for heroines. Danger lurks for maidens without men or families: women are clearly not meant to be able to exist alone. Animal stories vary far more in plot, but one of the striking features of animal stories is the way in which they are often almost exclusively masculine. When female characters are used in animal stories, the role is often a stereotyped one. A mother/nurturer is needed? A girl is lost?' (Gilbert, P. (1988) Stoning the romance: girls as resistant readers and writers. *Curriculum Perspectives* 8 (2), 16.)

2. Hastings, S. (1988) *A Selection from the Canterbury Tales*. London: Walker Books.

3. White, J. (1990) On literacy and gender. In R. Carter (ed.) *Knowledge about Language and the Curriculum: the LINC Reader*, p. 188. London: Hodder and Stoughton.

4. It is perhaps significant that editions of the animal fables of neither of these women are currently readily available. The most recent edition of text and face-to-face translation of Marie's *Fables* has not achieved wide distribution and is currently reprinting (*Marie de France: Fables*, translated by Harriet Spiegel. Toronto: University of Toronto Press, 1987). Aphra Behn's pithy four-line versions of some hundred of Aesop's *Fables* are currently only available in the excellent, but expensive, first volume of her complete works (Todd, J. (ed.) (1992) *The Works of Aphra Behn*, Vol. 1, *Poetry*. London: Pickering).

5. National Writing Project (1990) *What Are Writers Made Of? Issues of Gender and Writing*, pp. 20–8. Kingston upon Thames: NWP/Nelson.

6. For out of olde feldes, as men seyth,
Cometh al this newe corn from yer to yere,
And out of olde bokes, in good feyth,
Cometh al this newe science that men lere.

Geoffrey Chaucer, *The Parliament of Fowls* 11.22–25.

Part Two
Developing Discrimination

Current concerns about children's standards of reading have tended to narrow teachers' perspectives. The debate has focused mainly on methods of teaching reading, particularly in the early years of schooling, and has concentrated largely on children's reading of published fiction. Although well worked out methodologies for developing reading are clearly essential elements in any adequate reading curriculum, and fiction remains a central experience for any reader, the overemphasis on these two aspects of reading has tended to neglect some important areas of children's developing literacy. Reading has become a matter of public concern and, inevitably, has become entangled in emotional rhetoric. This is because literacy matters. However, one unhelpful aspect of the public debate about reading is that rather than deal with the fundamental matter of just what 'becoming a reader' means, commentators have focused on the narrow ground of materials and methods. Because of this, the debate tends to take place around polarized descriptive terms. A glib opposition is often made, for example, between a 'real books' and a 'phonic' approach. What is considered of value and what is intended as abuse depends on the stance of the commentator. As ever in educational debate, however, the whole matter is more complex than can be signalled by emotive jargon, as the chapters in this part of the book demonstrate.

The absurdity of this kind of oppositional approach is clear to any who have worked in classrooms with children learning to be readers. Most importantly, trivializing the debate by the exchange of equally imprecise buzz words has not helped children who are learning to be readers. The inflation of a small – albeit important – aspect of reading not only has distracted attention from existing good practice, but has shifted the focus away from some fundamentally important issues about effective literacy. A succession of reports by what was formerly Her Majesty's Inspectorate, and is now OFSTED, stress the importance of extending the range of children whose reading is already competent and of encouraging a wider range of reading strategies. At the same time, they highlight the needs of less fluent and confident readers:

reading received less systematic attention as the children grew older. ... By Year 6 three quarters of the children assessed were reading widely on their own but the majority were not being challenged to develop advanced reading skills ... some children were making less progress than they should, and a very small but significant number were virtually non-readers.[1]

This certainly does not reflect widespread non-literacy, as some of the more inflammatory public commentators would like the public to believe. What it *does* emphasize – and this is what teachers take seriously – is that just being able to read the words on the page does not make for full and active literacy. The most recent report takes the question 'what contributes to effective literacy?' further by considering the range of texts children are introduced to at Key Stage 2: 'The quality of learning was highest where good teaching was allied to the pupils' access to a broad range of reading material.'[2]

In considering what contributes to successful literacy, then, there needs to be a rather wider view than one which simply concentrates on methods of 'decoding' print. Children need to adopt a range of approaches to become effective readers. They need experience of a range of kinds of text and teaching which supports and extends their knowledge of texts and the strategies they use to make sense of them. What is critical is an awareness of the complexities of the process by which children come to be readers. Myra Barrs and Anne Thomas stress that:

The ability to read is not located in any one individual aspect of reading, such as sense of book language, or knowledge of print, but in the whole activity, where these different aspects are orchestrated. And, as in any skilled process, practice is essential to the achievement of this balance and orchestration.[3]

It is important to bear in mind just what 'being a reader' can mean. Liz Waterland says that for children to become fully motivated readers they need some 'vital knowledge':

What is that vital knowledge? Why, of course, it's the certainty that books and reading are worthwhile, personal pleasures. *This* is the secret that all real readers, those who read for choice, know, and it is this that small children must understand if they are to succeed in becoming readers rather than just being able to read.[4]

This distinction is critical. A booklet produced by the North London Language Consortium is a reminder of the complex and dynamic process of 'becoming a reader'. As this extract makes clear, this involves awareness of phonic clues and reading for meaning from books which carry for children that 'vital knowledge' about the world of literacy:

The child is actively involved in the process of making and taking meaning from the text. Children can only read (in any real sense) what they can understand. So, from the very beginning the emphasis is on meaning, not simply on the precise identification of letters or words. Books written by authors sympathetic to this interpretation of the reading process encourage children through the use of familiar and sometimes repeated language structures to read in a holistic way for meaning. Thus children are using all available cues. The emphasis is not only on grapho-phonic cues but also on semantic, syntactic and bibliographic cues. Children learn through familiarity with texts like *Each Peach Pear Plum, Rosie's Walk, The Very Hungry Caterpillar* and *Mr Gumpy*, to name but a few, that books are entertaining and multifaceted. These books allow children to bring their existing knowledge to bear in making sense of the text; they encourage prediction and they invite collaboration. Favourite books are revisited time and time again because they hold layers of meaning and can be discovered afresh with each successive reading as the child's interpretation of the text matches with increasing accuracy the actual words printed on the page.[5]

This revisits the points that Holly Anderson makes in Part One about using quality texts (p. 55) but makes it very clear that reading involves using strategies which, although arising from children's existing literacy knowledge, need to be carefully developed by the provision of material which holds significant meaning for the reader. A further point, important in relation to the chapters in this part of the book, is that children who know they are readers can choose to re-read books for pleasure, returning to favourites when they feel like it. They can use books for their own purposes, will readily talk to others about books and look forward to what they can read next.

Becoming a Better Reader

The fulcrum of any debate about the best way to help children become readers is the tricky question about assessing progress in reading. How does a teacher know when children are getting better at it? It is a central concern, not just for teachers but for young readers themselves. If the comments by HMI are to be satisfactorily addressed, then the importance of being able to describe children's progress in reading cannot be overestimated. If children are to be supported and challenged as developing readers, every teacher, not just those involved with the early years, will need to find a manageable and useful way of observing and noting children's progress in reading. The first two chapters in 'Developing Discrimination' consider just what this means for young readers about to go to secondary school as well as those in the earliest years of schooling.

Mike Millroy's starting point was the regular – and often unquestioned – practice of 'hearing the children read'. His involvement with the Research and Development Group of the Essex Reading Project gave him the impetus to find out what his pupils thought about the practice. Their views sparked off a process of reflection which opened up new opportunities for the class to acknowledge themselves as thoughtful and critical readers, while providing him with opportunities for observation and assessment of progress. Janet Towlson, working with much younger children, began with a familiar question: 'Why are so many children failed or reluctant readers sometimes within a year of starting school?'[6] In attempting to answer this, and prevent her own class falling into this category, she began working with challenging picture books. Her findings strongly indicate how powerful these texts can be in developing discrimination and critical awareness. In both accounts, however, the 'hidden factor' is the teacher intervention needed to energize the classroom potential. Similarly, both teachers indicate just how essential it is to see reading as interlinked with writing.

If children are to be helped to read published material in a way which satisfies them, they need to develop strategies for 'interrogating print'. It has become almost an essential part of any teacher's armoury of quotable quotes that 'children learn to read by reading'.[7] But what is becoming increasingly clear is that this does not mean just surrounding children with inviting books and going through the motions of hearing children read. Close, careful scrutiny of texts – both their own and other people's – is what makes the difference between active, hungry readers and writers and those who are not engaged with their own literacy in any dynamic way. As Jacquie Nunn puts it, if young people are to 'develop preferences and pursue enthusiasms', school can provide a 'critical community' where readers may reflect together on texts.[8]

'Learning to read by reading' involves careful provision of texts and opportunities for developing readers to extend their existing repertoires as well as the chance to re-read familiar and favourite texts. Besides this, it means providing young readers with language which will enable them to articulate their developing critical awareness, and so to take their awareness of texts and text construction further. The technical term used to describe language which allows further analysis of language or text is 'metalanguage'. In the words of Simons and Murphy, this is 'the ability to focus on language itself as an object'[9] and to use appropriate vocabulary to comment on and analyse texts. It is significant that they are referring here to the ways in which talking about literacy helps develop successful reading. The oral texts which children draw on to rehearse what the words on the page ought to sound like are essential precursors to literacy.

Margaret Meek points out that professional storytellers and children when they are learning language 'do the voices' and that this is an important ingredient for literacy:

I believe that children learn to read when they discover that some of the voices they can learn to do are those of storytellers. Then they discover what reading is good for, that learning to read is worth the effort. For most of them, those who are drawn to the factual as well as the fictive, reading means stories.[10]

Through the cadences of heard texts children grasp the shadowy possibilities of written texts and they make the crucial link – the moment of literacy – in understanding how to transmute the words on the page into meaning. When they then have a chance to pay close attention to those texts, to measure them against the other 'voices' they know about, including their own, then they are on the way to becoming readers by reading with their ears as well as their eyes.

If we learn to read by reading with our ears as well as our eyes, the same argument can be used about developing writing. There is a strong case for 'learning to read by writing', to paraphrase Frank Smith, just as the first part of this book proposed the value of 'learning to write by reading'. The written texts which young readers learn to produce themselves by drawing on their knowledge of heard texts become an important element in the range of reading which children should be confident in tackling. The experiences of reading, writing, speaking and listening are therefore vitally interwoven to make literacy possible. Awareness of parts of this intermingling process and discussions of written and read texts adds the dimension of explicit awareness which activates that literacy and begins to establish independence in young writers. As the OFSTED Report makes clear, one effective practice in relation to writing is 'systematic and rigorous appraisal of written work' which addresses 'not only the surface features of spelling, layout, etc., but also structural and syntactic features and quality of content and organisation'.[11] A useful way to challenge young readers to extend their repertoire of critical response to text is just this 'systematic and rigorous' approach in encouraging children to reflect on their own writing.

Writers Reading Their Own Writing

Writers need a range of strategies to help them become attentive and critical readers and evaluators of their own writing. Evaluation implies a process of establishing the value of any piece of writing; it is a positive process which grows out of children's enthusiastic and considered reading of published material. Asking developing readers to comment on what they enjoy (or otherwise) about the reading they encounter provides a basis for future choice and discrimination. Equally, such critical experience should lead to increasing confidence in developing writers who can begin to see how to make improvements in their own texts. Again, however, this does not happen by osmosis. Just asking children to comment on what they have read will not automatically lead to the development of discernment. The key factor is the teacher's contribution in setting up effective contexts for critical awareness.

Part of creating the 'critical community' which Jacquie Nunn recommends is establishing a sense of shared responsibility for improving reading and writing. Just as young readers are encouraged to make their views explicit as well as taking notice of teachers' views, it becomes equally important to establish a view that it is not just the role of the teacher to read and comment on writing. Again, however, reading and writing are complemented by talk. In the gradual process of taking over responsibility for their own writing, developing writers need to learn that discussion and planning are part of the process of getting their writing to do the job they want it to do. Even very young children can do this. When teachers talk to children about writing – whether the children's own or something the class is reading together – they are providing them with a model for evaluation and giving them experience of the kind of vocabulary they might use to identify strengths and weaknesses in any piece.

Certainly, helping developing writers to evaluate their own work means careful provision of opportunities to try things out and to discuss what is happening. Since the aim is to develop readership of writing, it means taking into account the range of reading experiences as well as providing opportunities to write. If writers are to become attentive and critical readers, then they need to understand something about the relationship between reading and writing. Rachel Sparks and Ian Eyres, in the last two chapters in this part of the book, describe how they helped children to develop techniques and strategies to help them get to that point. As both of them point out, helping learners to evaluate their own work is a complex process. Rachel Sparks found that her investigation allowed her to establish more effective ways of providing models, examples and teacher demonstrations of planning, drafting, editing, proofreading and ways of responding. In addition to these strategies, Ian Eyres found that in trying to help bilingual reader-writers he needed to provide frameworks to help the children ask each other questions about particular pieces of writing. Beyond this, both classes demonstrated the need to establish a confident sense of writing as something which could form part of a dialogue with the one significant adult that they work with every day. If young writers see teacher response as merely 'correcting' then they are likely to be inhibited in developing a more wide-ranging and helpful view. Both these studies of children taking more responsibility for improving their own writing give insights into the process by which young writers can be helped to recognize that they can be readers of their own writing and give value to it. Both the successes of the approaches and the unexpected responses of the children shed light on just what 'being a reader' can imply, for the readers themselves and the teachers whose job it is to help them develop discrimination, critical fluency and the beginnings of active literacy.

References

1. Department of Education and Science (1990) *The Teaching and Learning of Reading in Primary Schools: a Report by HMI*. London: DES.

2. OFSTED (1993) *English Key Stages 1, 2, 3 and 4 Fourth Year, 1992–93: the Implementation of the Curricular Requirements of the Education Reform Act*, p. 11. London: HMSO.

3. Barrs, M. and Thomas, A. (eds) (1991) *The Reading Book*, p. 8. London: Centre for Language in Primary Education.

4. Waterland, L. (1992) Ranging freely. In M. Styles, E. Bearne and V. Watson (eds) *After Alice: Exploring Children's Literature*, p. 161. London: Cassell.

5. North London Language Consortium (1991) *Questions of Reading* (pamphlet produced to accompany the NLLC's reading exhibition).

6. Waterland, L. (1988) *Read With Me*, p. 1. Stroud: The Thimble Press.

7. Smith, F. (1982) *Reading*, p. 9. Cambridge: Cambridge University Press.

8. Nunn, J. (1993) Moving on: becoming a mature reader. In P. Pinsent (ed.) *The Power of the Page: Children's Books and Their Readers*. London: David Fulton Publishers.

9. Simons, H. D. and Murphy, S. (1986) Spoken language strategies and reading acquisition. In J. Cook-Gumperz *et al.* (eds.) *The Social Construction of Literacy*. Cambridge: Cambridge University Press.

10. Meek, M. (1992) Children reading – now. In M. Styles, E. Bearne and V. Watson (eds) *After Alice: Exploring Children's Literature*, p. 175. London: Cassell.

11. OFSTED (1993) *English Key Stages 1, 2, 3 and 4 Fourth Year, 1992–93;: the Implementation of the Curricular Requirements of the Education Reform Act*, p. 9. London: HMSO.

Chapter 4

'I Also Read to Jinxy My Kitten'
Children Writing Reading Journals

Mike Millroy

One of the strongest points which Mike Millroy's chapter makes about reading is that it is really about talk. This account outlines the introduction of reading journals with a Year 6 class in a nine-class junior school in a suburban area of Essex. His work was given particular focus by the opportunity to work with the Essex Reading Project headed by Pat Baldry and Liz Slater. One of his starting points was a dissatisfaction about his approach to reading in the classroom. He felt strongly that opportunities to talk with young readers are often cramped by the daily demands made on teachers. In providing spaces for dialogue through offering the class a chance to write about reading, Mike Millroy found out even more about how talk and reading are closely bound together. This emphasis on talk, which led to writing, began from a desire to provide both time to have conversations with children about reading and time for them to enjoy 'constructive silences'. Using reading diaries to replicate the two sides of any communication, both speaking and listening, enabled a richer set of conversations than might be possible in any school day. As Naomi wrote: 'now that we are writing to Mr Millroy I can talk to him and tell him how I feel about reading'. Other factors became evident, too. The children's attitudes to reading and their perceptions of themselves as readers, both essential but often neglected aspects of 'being a reader', gave important insights into the process of reading. Nadine's sense that reading to the teacher got in the way of her relationship with the characters in the books she read is both fascinating and salutary. Finally, two other areas of talk emerge. One is the networked talk between enthusiastic readers – the recommendations, preferences and enthusiasms mentioned by Jacquie Nunn. The other is the important talk about other concerns, unre-

lated to reading, which a carefully planned approach to writing dialogues between teacher and pupil can provide.

We were only two weeks into a new school year, and, although fired up and full of enthusiasm, the children and I had had very little time to establish relationships with each other. The first session of the Essex Research and Development Group, with input from Anne Thomas of the Centre for Language in Primary Education (CLPE), provided the initial stimulus for introducing the idea of reading journals to the class; the momentum and energy to keep it going was provided by the raw enthusiasm and thought-provoking openness of the children's contributions.

I went to the Research and Development course with many questions that begged answers. Among these were: questions of assessment and reporting; reluctant readers (in particular, 'switched-off boys'); and time, one of my major concerns – time to do all that is expected of the classroom teacher in the teaching of reading. I had already begun to doubt the value of the traditional approach to hearing children read after the research by Vera Southgate *et al.* questioned its effectiveness. Southgate describes 'the ineffectiveness of short sessions with individual children'.[1] The findings of her research show that 'the average time solely devoted to any one child at one session was 30 seconds. No effective teaching or help can be given in such a short time.' She advocates less frequent, but longer, contacts with children in which teacher and children are involved in quality discussion about the child as a reader and the material the child has read.

During questions to Anne Thomas of the CLPE after her session with the group, she remarked that few children enjoy reading to the teacher and made the point that they should read when they have something they wish to share. I was also inspired by her description of the way in which reading journals had been used. She spoke about them being a conversation between teacher and child, getting the child to reflect on what they are reading and on their own development, but also extending and challenging readers. I saw in them the potential for trying to find out what made the children tick, what they enjoyed or did not enjoy about reading, a way of getting to know them and their reading habits, and a way of monitoring what they read and guiding and encouraging them.

Reading to the Teacher

On returning to school I posed the question asked by Anne Thomas, 'Do you like reading to the teacher?', to my class of Year 6 children. In a show of hands, not one child indicated that they liked reading to the teacher. I was very surprised by this; on reflection it may have been because the question was asked in an open setting and individuals may have felt pressure from their peers not to support the practice. But I was even more surprised by the responses they gave to the question 'Why?'

I read better to myself. (Edward Shaw)

When I read to the teacher I read slower and make more mistakes. (Gilly Black)

When I read to myself I feel like I'm there. When I read to the teacher it feels like they're there instead of me. (Kathy Chef)

When you read to the teacher the teacher says words for you; I can take my own time on mistakes when I read to myself. (Alison Sawyer)

The children expressed a variety of concerns, ranging from frustration at being slowed down, to nervousness and even fear of making mistakes; one child remarked that when she read aloud she 'couldn't build up the pictures in her head as well'. I decided that this was an opportune moment to introduce the reading diary, as it became known. I quickly gave out a set of exercise books and asked the children to write down their thoughts about whether or not they like reading to the teacher, and why. Analysis of the children's written responses to this question is quite revealing. Four children were less negative about reading to the teacher, one of whom made the comment:

I don't mind who I read to because I like reading. (Jason Greenwood)

and three who made similar comments:

I prefer to read to the teacher because if I get a word wrong they can help me.

Even though they did not necessarily say they disliked reading to the teacher, twenty-four children stated a preference for reading to themselves. One of the more common reasons was that of being nervous. Six children actually stated that they get nervous, particularly about 'getting a word wrong'. Others were 'embarrassed' or even 'frightened'.

When I read to the teacher and get a word wrong I get frightened in case I get into trouble. (Jane Kaye)

I like reading to myself because I don't get muddled up. I don't like reading to teachers because I'm scared you get a word wrong. (Nisa Dell)

What possible experiences must Jane and Nisa have had to make them feel this anxious about reading?

A number of children made some reference to 'making mistakes' in their initial response to the question 'Why?'

I like reading to myself because I don't make mistakes. (Lawrence Slater)

Sometimes I can't say things to a teacher but I can read it in my mind. When I read in my mind it's a lot more interesting and I make a lot less mistakes. (Susan Crowley)

How often do adults read 'unrehearsed' to an audience? If ever I am called upon to present something to parents, governors or my colleagues, I always try to prepare myself for the ordeal by familiarizing myself with the text. Maybe we ought to carry this idea through into our practice and allow children to do the same. What do we gain from children making mistakes purely because they are nervous? If on reading something 'blind' they make mistakes, we make judgements about their ability; but there is the chance that they were merely nervous about reading to someone else. If they can, or cannot, sort out any difficulties with the text after preparing the reading, surely this is telling us even more.

The children also expressed concern about the quality of the experience of reading aloud to the teacher. Martin Zoula summed it up well when he suggested that he can seemingly be performing well when reading to the teacher but in fact he is not reading at all in the true sense of the word:

and sometimes when you're really into a book and you're called up to read, you're so nervous that you sometimes read well but you're sometimes not actually even listening to what you are saying because you're too busy thinking 'I wonder if the teacher is impressed with how good your reading is.'

Martin was also concerned about, or nervous of, the fact that he was continually being assessed:

If I read to a teacher, I tend to get nervous and make mistakes which is a problem, because if you're on a certain colour on a library book and you want to get to a higher colour the teacher might not let you if you make too many mistakes.

This highlights one of the other pressures that children are placed under merely due to the way in which some schools organize their book stock.

Putting aside the idea of being nervous, children commented on many issues that affected their 'performance', such as:

- having more time to 'work things out' without the teacher interfering

- reading more quickly

- stopping to wait for the teacher to talk to others

- having time to picture what is happening

- being there with the character

- getting into the book.

Several children indicated that the speed at which they read, and in particular the way in which the teacher 'interfered', affected the quality of the experience.

Dear MM,
I read more quicker to myself than [to] a teacher . . . when I have a mistake I can take more time working the answer out and I keep it in my memory.

from Helen G.

I like reading to myself because if I make a mistake I would like to break it up instead of a teacher telling me. . . . When I was in Mrs X's class if I did not know the word she would tell me. But I like to break it up. (Kirsty Wales)

I like reading to myself because when you make a mistake you can work it out yourself where's a teacher says it for you. (Alison Sawyer)

I prefer reading to myself because I can read faster and you don't have to stop and wait while they [the teachers] shout to the children because there's too much noise. (Natasha Wells)

These comments highlight the need for teachers to be more sensitive to the need for 'silences' when listening to children, to be aware of both the function and reason for them and act accordingly. How can teachers allow children these 'constructive silences' and not be pressured by the fact that we have 'got six more readers to get through by lunchtime'? It is a matter of letting the children work at their own pace and seek help when they want it. It is a matter of supporting children with their reading and not being there apparently as an agent of assessment, a judge, the oracle. The time spent together should be an enjoyable, shared experience and this puts demands on the teacher to provide the atmosphere and classroom organization to create the minimum of disturbances to the child's involvement with the text. I devoted more of my time to creating a better reading environment than listening to the children read, making it clear that I would be available to hear them read if they wished. I addressed both the physical environment and the children's attitude towards books and reading. Initially I involved the class in redesigning the book corner, organizing book collections and making 'book boxes'. I tried to create a more relaxed and positive attitude to books and reading. I found that after I had involved the children in these ways and heavily promoted books and reading in general, they were more eager for me to share books with them.

The children in my class made powerful statements, not only about the issue of 'listening to children read', but also about 'listening to children talk about reading'.

also I can stop to get a picture in my head of what they are doing but when I'm with a teacher you can not stop you have to carry on … (Esther Whittington)

I prefer to read to myself because when I read to the teacher it gets boring and I can't get into the book but when I read to myself I can get into the book easily. (Keith Davies)

When I read to myself it feels like I am with the character, but when I read to my teacher it feels like she or he is there with the character. (Nadine Burns)

Here the children are describing their interaction with the text, building up images and creating pictures, involving themselves by being 'there with the character'. They are telling us important things about what happens when they read.

How the Diaries Developed

From the outset, when I first asked the children to respond to my question, I said, 'Just write, write what you think!' It was important that the ideas they had were the focus of their attention rather than the handwriting or spelling. The books I had chosen for them to write in had plain pages so that there were no constraints on how large or small they wrote, where they started, or where they finished. I did not stipulate which colour ink they should use or whether to underline with a ruler. During that first session I just encouraged them to write.

After they had become used to the idea I did speak to the class about some issues I felt were important and together we set a few ground rules:

• It was their book, for them to write their thoughts in.

• Spelling and handwriting 'were not important'.

- They should write as openly and honestly as they could.

- I would reply as often as possible.

- The dialogue was between the child and myself, and would be shown to others only with the permission of the child.

My main concerns were to establish openness and trust between the children and myself, where each child has control over what they write. It was important that I responded to what they wrote in an open and honest way, while grasping the opportunities to encourage, guide and nurture them as readers. The reading diaries had become the focus of a lot of our work on reading. In addition to the children's book reviews, comments and self-assessment, we did various class or group tasks and activities, such as designing the book corner, comparison of books by the same author and evaluation of books read to the class. Children began to respond to all manner of things through their reading diaries. For some it became a chatty dialogue about things like pets, the school journey and friendships, while others wanted to talk about maths, design and technology and other aspects of the curriculum. For me they became both a valuable record of the children's reading habits and attitudes and a means of promoting reading in general.

I attempted to introduce new and varied materials to the children in a number of ways, some on a personal level and others with a group or the whole class. I offered the class a list of different types of books in an attempt to encourage them to read more widely. This not only served as a prompt or reminder of the variety of material available, but also provided a record of the breadth of reading children had been involved in, as and when they ticked another one off that they had read. Some children used these more than others and made a conscious effort to choose something else from the list, while others were more selective or independent in their choices.

Another way I found to encourage young readers to choose more widely was by suggesting that they speak to classmates about particular authors, especially if they were becoming 'experts' on those writers.

At the moment I am reading a book called One Hundred and One Dalmatians . . . Gilly B gave it to me. (Helen Gough)

Dear Kirsty,
Have a chat with Natasha and Nisa about Dick King Smith. You might like to try some of them.
MM.

Dear MM,
I am going to go down to the library to get some Dick King Smith books with Natasha and Nisa.
Kirsty W.

Other children comprise a great influence and resource that is worth tapping as much as possible; after all, between them they have read far more children's books than I have and are more in tune with what others might like. But by far the most frequent method of promoting books through the diaries was by way of my making suggestions during the course of our correspondence.

Dear MM,
I'm reading 'Taller Than Before' by Bernard Ashley I've only just started it I got it from the school library.
K W

Dear K,
I have some favourite Bernard Ashley books. I particularly like 'Linda's Lie' and 'Dinner Ladies Don't Count'. They each have a moral at the end of the story.
MM.

A Tool for Assessment

Reading diaries can be used to elicit a wide range of valuable information about the habits and attitudes of the children as readers, and changes in these can be more readily monitored. The written reflections mean that we can draw information from throughout the reading diaries to build up a more complete picture of children as readers: their range of reading experience, responses to particular texts and the different strategies they use. At the same time it is an ideal vehicle for self-assessment.

Throughout the reading diaries it was possible to find descriptions of the variety of reading experiences. There were those initiated by myself, such as reading to younger children and sharing books with friends, and those they experienced out of school, ranging from library visits and membership of book clubs, to reading to the pet cats:

me and Nadine have been reading this book called 'Ramona and her Dad'. I find it really good.

At the moment me and H. are reading 'The Twits' but we've only just started it.

... me and my friend Jane read to the infants, to Yellow class, they are really good at reading. I am joined to a book club my dad gets me books every month.

p.s. I also read to Jinxy my kitten he seems to like Roald Dahl best.

Dear MM,
I like reading to my cat Misty. Helen said that she reads to her cat so when Misty came by the fire I read to my cat. He's the only cat that listens to the story Blacky just looks at me and goes away. Georgy just purrs and rolls on her tummy and Mopsy tries to get in the book by pushing her head against it. My dad says Misty's brain-dead. He can't be that brain-dead. Have you got any pets?

Alison S.

Using the framework set up by the diaries there are many questions the children's writing could lead to – even finding detailed evidence of reading range or interest through questionnaires. The way in which children respond to the text can inform us about their understanding of what has been read and about their preferences:

Just started to read Dracula ... it's starting to get a bit scary. Listen to this, 'the count smiled and his lips ran back over his gums, the long, sharp canine teeth showed out strangely'. (Nadine Burns)

It is evident here that Nadine is revelling in the suspense created by the text in her book. She not only talks about her feelings, about it being 'scary', but is trying to involve others in it by promoting it, trying to get them hooked.

The Church Mouse
Author – Graham Oakley
I read The Church Mouse and I love the pictures. I like the first page because it's a wonderful picture. ... I think its sunny day because it's not a dull picture ... it's only got a bit of writing on it and I love the pictures because it tells you the story. ... I didn't think you needed the writing. ... I would pick the book up and look at it because I think it's a nice cover. (Alison Sawyer)

In this extract Alison is responding not to the written text but to visual clues in the pictures. Her response 'I love the pictures because it tells you the story. ... I didn't think you needed the writing' indicates her appreciation of the wider view of what reading is. An extract can not only show an understanding of the text but also demonstrate empathy with the characters in the book:

Lately I have been reading Anne Frank's diary I have got half way through it now. Sometimes I think of how awful it must have been in the back of the office.

It may be rather more difficult to assess the strategies children use in their reading through their diaries, but a few did give some indication. Alison showed clearly an ability to construct the meaning through the pictures to 'tell' the story in 'The Church Mouse', and similarly Nadine said that:

picture stories help me understand the book ...

Alison also stated:

I work it out myself by splitting a word in two.

However, the diaries did provide much evidence about the children's attitude to reading and their perceptions of themselves as readers, both of which I feel affect performance. Changes in these attitudes and perceptions were evident in several cases and were easily monitored and acted upon.

As a follow-up to my initial questions to the children I asked them to draw a picture of how they felt as readers. I repeated this about three and a half months later, but also asked the children to write about how they felt. If there was any change in their perceptions I asked if they could put it down to anything in particular. As expected, there was a variety of responses:

I feel that I enjoy my reading more now than I did about a year ago because now that we are writing to Mr Millroy I can talk to him and tell him how I feel about reading and he can give me an idea of what books I would like. (Naomi Hobbs)

At a time when Esther had personal problems and was going through an anxious period she wrote:

I do feel a bit more relaxed but sometimes I'm worried because something's on my mind.

followed a few days later by:

Before I felt happy about reading but now I feel unhappy about reading because I can't sit down and get into a book, I read a couple of pages and then I put the book away and I forget about it. I do read if I'm told to but if I'm not told to I don't. (Esther)

Armed with this knowledge it would be evident that her performance and attitude have been affected by her emotional problems and the teacher could take appropriate action.

In the latter stages of the year it was also evident that some children changed their attitude towards reading to the teacher. After using the diaries for some time the three children who were initially reticent about reading to the teacher commented:

I haven't been reading to you lately, I want to read to you more often I want to tell you about 'Honey I Blew Up the Kids'. (Nisa Dell)

I shall bring my book into you and can I read it to you? (Jane Kaye)

and later she writes

I do think I'm a better reader now, I enjoy books better than I use to, I also concentrate more. I wish I could read to you more. (Jane Kaye)

I love reading to Mr M. and my mum. (Kirsty Wales)

I feel pretty confident about reading now, before I came into this class I used to get bored with reading I used to say to myself when are we going to stop reading but now I want to read for longer than we do. . . . I really enjoy reading now, I like all kinds of books like funny, adventures and lots more. (Helen Gough)

The assessment of personal reading preferences and reading diet can be made from a book list kept in the back of the diary. By encouraging children to write a 'Hit List' of books they want to read, the teacher helps them to plan their future reading and can encourage a varied diet.

Much more can be assessed through the use of reading diaries. For example, I have made no mention of the assessment of writing. The diaries are full of prime examples of 'raw', purposeful writing, which could be used for the assessment of secretarial skills, the child's sense of audience or purpose, and numerous other facets of written language.

Conclusions

In response to the children's initial comments about reading to the teacher, one of the strategies I felt I had to adopt is that of 'waiting until they want to share something with me' as suggested by Anne Thomas. I had to work on their self-esteem and my relationship with them. I had hoped to do this partly through the reading diaries, in particular through my responses to their comments and questions. By making them feel at ease with what I felt reading was all about, I hoped they would be more willing to share their books, ideas and views with me. The diaries gave the children a sense of audience which made the writing 'real' and worthwhile.

This account is not an argument in favour of reading journals, but one in favour of an honest, open dialogue with the children in our care. Teachers are finding it more and more difficult to give time during the hectic working day.

So, as needs dictate, we must curl up at 10 o'clock at night with our thirty-odd young readers 'on our laps' who are waiting patiently for our attention, not tugging at our sleeves or vying with classmates.

As the diaries developed it became increasingly obvious that the children did not want to be restricted to writing about reading: there was a multitude of other issues begging to be addressed. There were requests for a maths journal and numerous personal and social problems to be discussed:

I can't wait to go (on the school journey). It's just that I want to share a chalet with S. and G. I also want to share a chalet with K. but you see that's the problem S. and G. don't want to share a chalet with K.

But there was an even more serious side to the 'spin-offs'. This was highlighted by the case of one child who has hearing difficulties and rarely spoke to anyone except a close friend. She works well and is quite capable but it took a great deal to get her to open up in any way about her work or school in general. She was, however, happy to write reams in her diary about the books she had read. Occasionally she got upset about things and it was difficult to find out what was troubling her. On one of these occasions, towards the end of the school day, she was inconsolable and I could not work out what the problem was. I did not have her friend to help me, so, thinking about her reading diary, I suggested that, if there was anything troubling her that I could help with, she could write me a note and give it to me the following day.

The following morning she arrived, earlier than usual, envelope in hand. The content of the letter quite clearly expressed the difficulties she had in relating to others in her class, and her anxieties about the fact that, as her friend was not going on the school activity week, she had no one to share a chalet with. The problem of the school trip was resolved very quickly and easily; the other was a little more difficult, but we worked on it. She found it a lot easier after that occasion to send me little notes when she needed to say something she could not express verbally.

A natural progression would be to that of a 'work journal' or a 'chat book', in which children can have that much sought-after time alone with the teacher. But, powerful and rewarding though they may be, the diaries should not be seen as a substitute for talking about books – or anything at all! What I discovered was a valuable way to create some 'constructive silence', so that the readers in my class could reflect on reading. What became very clear was the children's need for conversations with me and with each other – written or spoken – as they tried to become more confident and discriminating readers.

References

1. Southgate, V., Arnold, H. and Johnson, S. (1981) *Extending Beginning Reading*. London: Heinemann.

2. For clarity the journal extracts in this account have been transcribed in standard form.

Chapter 5

Up and Up
Young Critical Readers

Janet Towlson

This account of Years 1 and 2 children in a suburban Essex school becoming literary critics bears out the importance of having greater expectations about children, reading and writing. There is no doubt that the young readers whose voices are heard here are on the 'up and up'. It is also no surprise to those who know the book that Shirley Hughes' classic wordless text should have been an important motivator for engaged and sophisticated discussions and writing about reading. The different picture books which Janet Towlson used provided constructive spaces equal to the constructive silences of the previous chapter. Carefully chosen, their complexity and challenge allowed the children to soar above the restrictions of the kinds of reading material often offered to developing readers. But there is even more to it than that. Throughout this account, hidden only just below the surface, is an essential component of the debate about how best to help children become active and interrogatory readers – the role of the teacher. Much of the polarized debate mentioned in 'Developing Discrimination' turns on just what the teacher is supposed to do to teach children to read. If children are to become fully literate, it is not just a matter of providing challenging and satisfying texts. What makes the difference is a planned, purposeful and reflective classroom approach. This extends both to the 'mental environment' of the teacher's attitude to the process of becoming a reader and to the provision of a stimulating physical environment for reading. The account which follows shows just how powerful that combination can be.

I try as far as possible to create opportunities within my classroom for all children to show me what they can do and I understand that they can improve, grow and progress only if they are given the chance to take risks, experiment, make choices and continually refine their skills. I do believe that children can be critical thinkers and my aim is to try to 'construct environments in which critical thinking can take place'.[1]

I want to encourage children to be problem-solvers, decision-makers and independent. They are encouraged to take risks, make mistakes and learn from their mistakes in a safe and secure environment which values all of their contributions. The children are also actively encouraged to make choices and know that their decisions will be honoured. I try to create an environment where children do not run the 'risk of punishment, failure or embarrassment' and to ensure as far as possible that they certainly and confidently want to 'join the literacy club'.[2]

Since our new reading policy was implemented, parents and relatives have been invited into the classroom from 8.45 a.m. to choose or read books with their children or chat to the teacher. This also happens during the last twenty minutes of the day. It has been a time when I can model read and discuss books with the children for parents to see. This for me has been a significant time of learning. As Hilary Minns says:

Teachers and parents must set up a two way flow of information with teachers sharing their more developed expertise with parents, and parents sharing with teachers their knowledge about the kinds of literacies they offer to children, including ways of sharing books. This action would help to give parents confidence by making them conscious of their own hidden skills. At present many parents expect professionals to construct their role for them within the school setting.[3]

Children are powerful and active language users and their language extends far beyond the classroom; it is learning based in social and cultural contexts. Within the classroom the children are treated seriously as readers, writers and speakers. However, I did just wonder how wide-ranging their knowledge about literacy was.

Children as Literary Critics

During the year I was made aware of how very competent some of the children were as writers. They could make and write cards, letters, shopping lists, posters and labels, they had the ability to create beginnings and endings to known texts, and they could write stories that displayed all sorts of intertextual links. I still felt, however, that there was an area which I had not explored with the children and their reading picture books. I wondered on what levels the children were reading these multilayered texts; what did the multilayered readers in my class know? I really had little idea about their range of knowledge when reading picture books and what they really thought of them. I wondered whether they could cope with literacy criticism beyond comments such as 'I like that book' or 'I didn't like that book, it was boring'.

When I read books with the children I do try to keep in mind the two extreme ways of reading picture books: one where you explain every detail on every page, and the other where you offer no clues or explanations at all. I expect that however hard I try to take a middle-of-the-road path, perhaps I 'intervene too much and do not allow literature to do its own work'.[4] One of my concerns about setting out to observe the children working with picture books was the time factor involved. I had allowed only two to three weeks to try to glean as much information as possible about children's insights. I was also aware of the fact that a wide range of 'real' books was a relatively new phenomenon in the classroom. Therefore, some of the texts the children were about to work with were not going to be too familiar to them.

It was also difficult for me to select a group of children to focus on. I thought at first I would look at an 'able' group, but 'able in what way?' I asked myself. Certainly what I had in mind did not require reading or writing fluency skills in the traditional sense. Maybe I was looking for highly articulate children, but the work did not require those skills. Eventually I chose eight children with a variety of skills which I felt could be used in a collaborative way. For the first text I decided to use *Changes* by Anthony Browne.

Although this book was not in evidence in the classroom before this activity, some of the children may have seen it at home or in the library. The children were asked to read the book, using the words and the pictures, and they were to tape themselves. They chose to work in twos and went off to the library with a classroom helper and a tape recorder. I deliberately asked the children to tape their readings and discussion and write about them. I did this for several reasons. I am aware that certain children are far more voluble than others and perhaps some children would be unable to articulate what they felt or perhaps they would feel a little inhibited about airing their views in a not so familiar situation. I also felt that if I or the classroom helper had written down what we thought we had heard it might have been incomplete and very different from the actual thing; it is easy to make wrong assumptions about what children mean. I thought that some children would feel far more confident writing their responses, but again there would be children who preferred to use the tape recorder. The taping and the writing occurred on different days, the bulk of the taping having been done before the writing. Giving the children the opportunity to articulate orally and write their responses meant that they would have at least two opportunities to read *Changes*. In fact this would be the absolute minimum number of readings. The children re-reading the book would perhaps reveal to me whether they could read or unravel any other layers of the text.

When the children embarked on this project some had only just celebrated their sixth birthdays. What follows has been nothing less than a revelation to me. I had thought it might be enlightening to do as Margaret Meek suggests:

let children talk to you about what they see in the pictures. They look more closely than their skipping and scanning elders – what texts teach is a process of discovery for readers, not of instructions for teachers.[5]

The following 'snapshots' of three pairs of readers show how this project exceeded everything I ever hoped would emerge from it.

Reading Picture and Text

Bella and Angie read *Changes* together, reading alternate pages of the text. Although a transcript of their tape would be too lengthy to include, it is certainly worth 'listening in' to some of the comments they made as they read. As they turn from page 7 to page 8, there is a lot of oohing, aahing and gasping:

Bella: Crocodile is changing – no, the settee is changing into a crocodile.

Angie: I think the chair's going to turn into a gorilla ... and I don't know what that is ... mmmm ... I think that's going to be a bit more of the crocodile – yes.

By this time, both of them are expecting more and more strange objects to appear on the page; they are always ready to risk a guess and enjoy predicting what may happen. It all becomes a game, sometimes quite competitive, to determine who can see the most and say it first.

Bella: I think the crocodile is going away ... there's a bird – it's the slipper. The cat is hunting the bird.

Angie: Oh, the tail's going to turn into a snake, or this, or this ...

Bella: The chair's turning into a gorilla and I think that this is the fingers – and, look – there's a snake and a crocodile.

Anyone who knows Anthony Browne's picture books will know that these two are not just enjoying getting inside the story, but are also reading very carefully and accurately a complex and difficult pictorial text. They use all the strategies of developed readers when they pick up cues and clues from the text, predict the narrative flow and how difficult with a text like this!) and, most impressively, as they show when they get to page 12, refer back to earlier incidents:

Bella: Look, I was right – they *did* turn into fingers and the chair *has* turned into a gorilla. The crocodile tail has turned into a banana! (much laughter from both girls). The baby has turned into a pig in the photo.

Angie: The baby bird looks as though it's just about to be eaten by the blackbird.

This was, to me, a fascinating observation, drawn from the image on the television screen in the picture which changes throughout the narrative. They start with a bird in flight; later there is a nest with eggs, and at this point there is a large cuckoo nestling being fed by a parent blackbird. I certainly would not have expected either of them to know about usurping cuckoos and babies. I was further intrigued when Bella said, 'I think the baby bird is feeding its mother when the mother should be feeding the baby.' She has clearly associated size with age, since the cuckoo is so much larger than its 'parent'. What is important, though, is the way in which such a small detail of text, which underpins the written text, becomes a matter of discussion and speculation, bringing in all sorts of other knowledge to inform the girls' reading – yet another strategy associated with a developed reader.

All the tapes from each pair gave equally fascinating insights: some worked more 'as one', saying things together; all of them read with extraordinary attention to detail, bringing their existing knowledge to the text. I was encouraged by this, since if children could offer this knowledge when they were not particularly familiar with the text, what would they be telling when they had re-read the book a number of times, over a period of time? As Judith Graham points out, multiple reading develops 'an ability to link picture and text and text and picture'.[6] During the next few days the one and only copy of *Changes* was available in the classroom for all children to read. All eight children sat down together, collaborating, exchanging and sharing ideas, and then each of them wrote individually about the book.

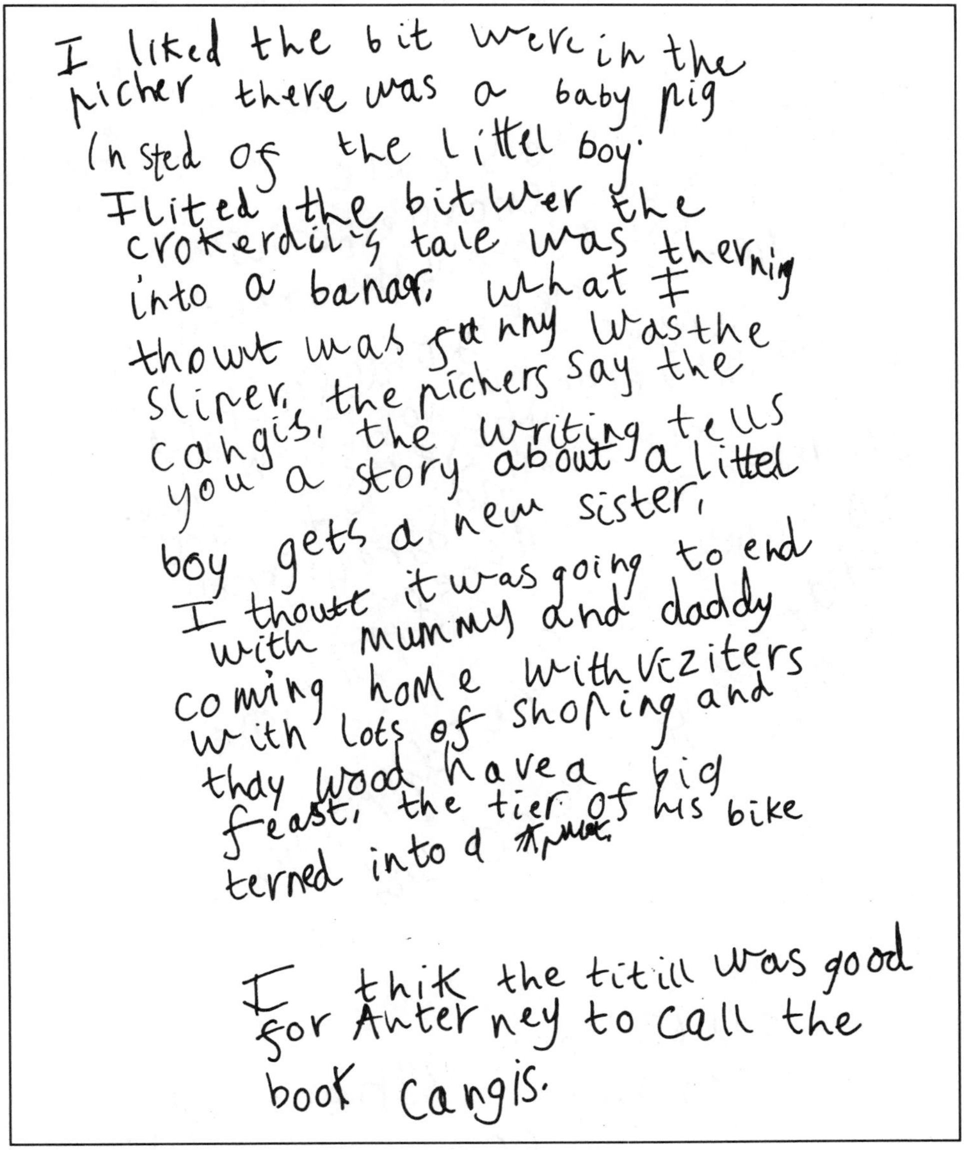

I liked the bit were in the picher there was a baby pig Insted of the littel boy. I Lited the bit wer the crokerdil's tale was therning into a banar, what I thowt was funny was the sliper, the pichers say the cangis, the writing tells you a story about a littel boy gets a new sister, I thoutt it was going to end with mummy and daddy coming home with veziters with lots of shoping and thay wood have a big feast, the tier of his bike terned into a ∗∗∗∗∗ ∗∗∗∗ his bike

I thik the titill was good for Anterney to call the book cangis.

Figure 5.1 *Changes*: Angie's comments

In the written work (Figures 5.1 and 5.2) Angie and Bella show that after re-reading the book they add to the perceptions they discussed on the tape, although they both refer to parts they had enjoyed during the reading:

Angie writes: I liked the bit where in the picture there was a baby pig instead of the little boy. I liked the bit where the crocodile's tail was turning into a banana. What I thought was funny was the slipper. The pictures say the changes. The writing tells you a story about a little boy gets a new sister. I thought it was going to end with Mummy

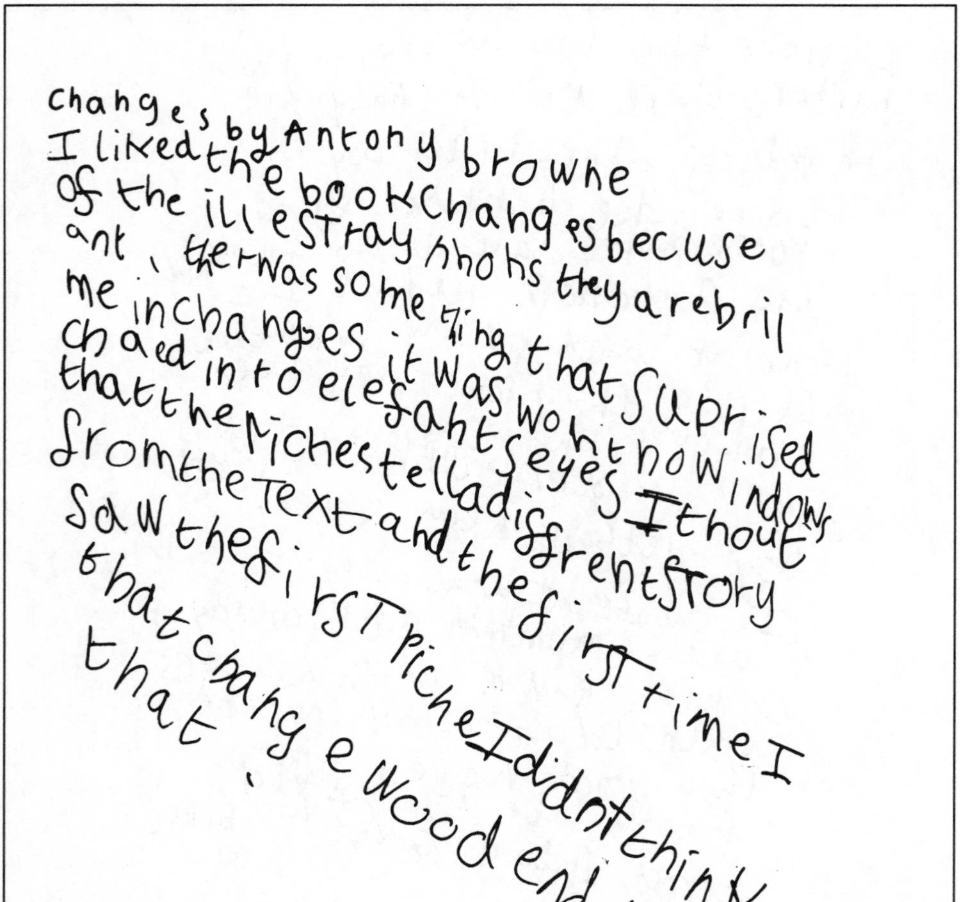

changes by Antony browne
I liked the book changes becuse
of the illestray hhohs they are brill
ant. herwas some 7ing that suprised
me in changes. it was wohtnow indows
chaed into elefahts eyes I thout
that the Pichestelladissrentstory
from the Text and the first time I
saw thefirst Piche I didnt think
that change wood end like
that.

but I know why he called it
changes becuse the thing change

Figure 5.2 *Changes*: Bella's comments

and Daddy coming home with visitors, with lots of shopping and they would have a big feast. The tyre of his bike turned into an apple.

I think the title was good for Anthony to call the book *Changes*.

Bella writes: I liked the book *Changes* because of the illustrations, they are brilliant. There was something that surprised me in *Changes*; it was when the windows changed into elephant's eyes. I thought that the pictures tell a different story from the text and the first time I saw the first picture I didn't think that *Changes* would end like that, but I know why he called it *Changes* because the things changed.

Another reader, Victoria, had made similar observations about the pictures and text telling different stories, but perhaps most stunning is her concluding comment: 'I think all the little changes make up into one big change; that was the baby.' Victoria's perceptive comment displays her ability to read beyond the literal. I felt elated and excited when I read what the children had written.

Entering the Conspiracy

We then moved on to do an author study of Anthony Browne and I collected as many of his books as I could lay my hands on. Meanwhile I was also informing parents about what I was doing and I asked them if they would consider noting what their children said about books they were reading. I sent home the Anthony Browne books, reminding parents to keep a watchful eye on the illustrations. If the children wanted to write or draw about these texts I would certainly welcome looking at them in school.

Piggybook, *A Walk in the Park*, *I Like Books*, *The Tunnel*, *Gorilla* and *Willy the Wimp* were just a few of Anthony Browne's books that we began to focus on. Anthony Browne had become probably the best-loved author in my class; children are drawn to his surreal pictures. Some children also began to realize that he is sometimes making a comment on a controversial issue or is putting over a moral message. They come to expect the secrets and hidden jokes in his illustrations and become adept at seeking them out. They are attracted by the outrageousness of his books. Barbara Jordan says:

Authors engage and sustain readers' emotional regard in worlds rich in metaphor, subversion, jokes, innovations of many kinds and questions. Readers of all ages encounter the nature and variety of written discourse and enter the network which links readers, writers and illustrators in the conspiracy of knowing that much more has been said and recognised than appears in the surface features of this language.[7]

Through their writing and taping, these children demonstrate that this is precisely what is happening.

To read any of Anthony Browne's books is to confront the unexpected, which probably is one of the main attractions of his work. Margaret Meek says, 'Storytelling can be surprising, and move away from what we consider the norm.'[8] What the children have said about Anthony Browne's work has proved to me that they are certainly capable of moving away from what I considered the norm, being far more critically discerning than I ever anticipated.

Reading Wordless Text

Victoria and Kim were introduced to Shirley Hughes' *Up and Up*. This is a sepia wordless text in strip cartoon form and they were not particularly familiar with it. I had specifically taken the text into school that week with the intention of seeing how they would read a wordless text. During the course of the day Victoria and Kim familiarized themselves with the book and later in the week they wrote what they thought about *Up and Up*. Their story was beautifully fluent; the content and the expression with which it was read made it very evident that Victoria and Kim certainly had an audience in mind when they tape-recorded their reading:

Victoria and Kim together: We've been talking about this book called *Up and Up* by Shirley Hughes.

Kim: One day there was a little girl who wanted to fly. She tried one day but a stone got in her way and she tripped over.

Victoria: Then she had an idea she drawed a wing on a piece of paper and then she cut it out and then she drawed another wing and cut that one out. She put one strap on it and then another on it and then she put two more on the other. She got a step ladder out of the garage. Then she jumped off it and started to fly. Oh it's no use and she bumped down. Then she had another idea. She got out the balloon box and blew up all the balloons, she tied them around herself. Unfortunately there was a tree in the way and they all bursted on the trees.

Kim: Then she came down. She was in a sulk. And then she heard the door knocking and it was the postman with a great parcel. She started to open it, it was a big egg with a ribbon on it. She started to open it and then she fell in. She started to nibble and nibble and nibble.

Victoria: and she went 'Oh no, it's gone now but never mind I still had a lovely time, didn't I?' [spoken in both sad and mischievous tones]. She walked up the ceiling and walks along a bit and then she walked down the walls. 'Oh no!' said her mum, 'What on earth is happening?'

Kim: Then her father came home. She whizzed around and made little patterns in the sky. Then she flew out the door her mum and dad chased her down the street, over the people's heads at the bus stop and knocked all their hats off. They started to chase her as well.

Victoria: Then Miss told the children to go downstairs and see if they could catch the little girls. They ran downstairs and they couldn't.

(Evidently Victoria has turned over two pages. Kim goes back a page without interrupting the flow and still makes perfect sense in story form. Their story still hangs together very well.)

Kim: Then she flew up into the tree and a man had an idea. He climbed up the tree and she had an idea too she flew off but they tried to catch her but they couldn't. She went over the fruit stall and she knocked a few bananas down and then everybody came and they knocked all of it down.

Victoria: and then they ran away chasing her. She flew over the gates into the school. She made funny faces on the window even when Miss wasn't looking and when Miss was looking. All the children said 'Hello, what are you doing there?'

Kim: Then she went round and round and made little patterns in the sky and others as well all around the sky. One day a man came out and saw a balloon in the garden.

Victoria: He jumped on it and then he started the fire engine [I think she means he was inflating the balloon with hot gas], and it went up and up.

Kim: Then she flew away. She saw it coming nearer and nearer. He tried to grab her but couldn't. So she flew and flew as fast as she could.

Victoria: She flew onto the house top and then the person began to pull her off but he couldn't and then he grabbed hold of her and began to pull her as the balloon rose up. She came off with the telephone aerial bit.

Kim: Then she had an idea, she slapped it on the balloon and punched it in the balloon. The balloon began to sizzle up. It came down and down and down and luckily she was on the top. She crawled out and all her friends came to meet her then she said to the man 'sorry' and her parents came.

Victoria: Then her parents took her home and all the people had a chat about her flying. Then she thought about it. 'I had fun flying.' Then she went home and into her house and her mum and dad said, 'come on eat your egg and cheer up'.

The end.

After I had heard their taped story, I had a chat with them about it:

JT: So she had an egg for her tea. And do you actually see her eating the egg for tea?

Victoria and Kim: No.

JT: You don't actually see her eating it?

Victoria: No, you don't actually see her eating it.

JT: You see her looking at it, what do you think she's thinking?

Kim (in funny voice): Will I be able to fly with this egg?

Their visual literacies are sophisticated. The story flows, it is exciting and their sense of audience is sharp and real. It is well organized and hangs together well; it is clear and coherent. Their knowledge of ironic humour is impressive; their use of standard forms of grammar is sound and there is evidence of risk-taking. Together, Victoria and Kim have devised a very strong, exciting and sophisticated storyline. When at the end of this transcript Kim says 'Will I be able to fly with this egg?' she seems to have made the assumption that the chocolate egg delivered to the little girl has given her the magical power to fly. I think that the children's ability to 'bring a personal understanding of the inner world of fantasy to these pictures'[5] has been essential to their being able to read the pictures. When Victoria realizes she has turned two pages instead of one there is no panic; no one would guess from listening to the tape that this in fact has happened. She reads the text and calmly turns the page back to where she should have been and Kim continues reading the pictures.

Kim's writing probably highlights her admiration for this little girl and all her naughty antics. Perhaps the power of the imagination transports her into wondering what it would be like accomplishing similar feats:

I like the illustrations because they are good and the book is all pictures. It's about a little girl who wanted to fly.

This is particularly interesting because in a wordless text there are no clues about the characters' feelings, but Kim has (quite accurately, I think) been able to impute emotion to the central character, solely from her reading of

Shirley Hughes' evocative pictorial text. Victoria gives specific examples of her enjoyment of the narrative – precursors of selecting quotations, as is common in the practice of literary criticism? She confidently writes as an accomplished reader who can identify with the situation of the central character and who is able to discriminate the elements of a text which are satisfying:

I like the illustrations because there's so much to look at in the pictures. I like it when she makes funny faces on the windows. I don't like it when she trips over a big stone and I like the first picture because there's lots of things to look at and I like the way they wrote it. What surprises me is when she starts to fly. I like it because there's no writing.

Victoria's final comment, 'I like it because there's no writing', suggests that she feels totally uninhibited when reading this book in exactly the way she chooses to. There are no restrictions.

Both Victoria and Kim have shown how very young children can read wordless texts in a very competent way. As Barbara Jordan says: 'How to read *Up and Up* is culturally and specifically learned and we shouldn't overlook its significance, or texts like it, for the reading experience of children of any age.'[7]

The Promise in the Text

Maria and Caroline were asked to read *The Frog Prince* by Jan Ormerod. The three of us, Maria, Caroline and I, discussed the book in great detail. Jan Ormerod's pictures are intricate and the borders on each page promote a great deal of interesting talk. In one of the pictures there is a black mark almost like a thumbprint which extends out of the border and on to the edge of the page. I asked the two girls what they thought could have made this mark. Christine said, 'It could be where the ball has fallen into the pond and where it is', and Maria suggests, 'It could be where the ball's been taken out of the pond and came up making it all muddy and left a smudge.' The borders held great fascination for them:

It looks as though the flowers are dancing, it looks as though one flower is a maid and another flower is a dinner plate. . . . I think that's a man and that's a lady. That could be smoke coming out of the plate because it is very hot.

They spent a lot of time paying close attention to the borders. Maria says, 'The border is lizards – looks like the music signs', where she is referring to the lizards' feet, and:

the flowers look like dancers; it could be the prince. The flowers are dancing a bit like people playing with a guitar, or the double bass or the mandolin.

When I asked Maria and Caroline, 'Do you think if you look at *The Frog Prince* again you would see things there that you didn't see first, second or even third time around, different things in the pictures?', Caroline replied, 'It's a bit like when I got on my climbing frame I got to know more and more things – how to do it the more I had goes on it.' I am convinced Caroline and Maria will re-read and re-read *The Frog Prince* and more and more will be revealed and unravelled to them from childhood through to adulthood. Maria's opening line when she writes about *The Frog Prince* sums it all up in a very sophisticated and succinct way: 'I think the text is telling you to keep a promise.'

With all the children's taped responses and writing I am left in no doubt about their total involvement with the text. Through their collaboration they exhibit concern and anticipation; they laugh; they help one another; and above all they enjoy what they are doing. They have a firm grasp of the narrative formula, the texts. Their understanding of incident, sequence and cause and effect has been demonstrated very ably in what they say and write about the texts. All the children have shown a strong reflective interest in aspects such as the action, characters, illustrations and other features that are prevalent in the text they have been exploring.

During this very short space of time when I took a very close look at how these children read picture books I was continually amazed at their knowledge of how texts work. Embarking on this enterprise I was rather sceptical about the children's ability to take on literary criticism. This fascinating study of a small group of children's achievements has convinced me not just that all children should read picture books but that all children should be given the opportunity to develop confidence in analysis and critical comment on texts.

I feel that every child should be helped and shown how to make explicit what they know implicitly about picture books. The way in which the children read these picture books has revealed to me a range of reading behaviours, reading strategies and reading performance as parts of reading competence that I know would never have been revealed to me through using a reading scheme. Certain children in the group I worked with might well have been termed non-readers or slow starters if the only literature they had been offered had been scheme books.

Some children were not fluent readers in the traditional sense but they certainly displayed a whole range of reading strategies shared by developed readers when reading *Up and Up* and *The Frog Prince*. I am also convinced that none of the children would ever have wanted to re-read scheme books, whereas they constantly re-read picture books, learning something different with each reading.

These children have been exposed to a wide range of literature and they also experienced a system of independent writing. They have proved that they are sophisticatedly adept at unravelling the layers in multilayered texts, spot numerous things we miss and often present different views. When given the opportunity, they hold exciting and complex discussions which are reflected in their written work. They show me that they have definite ideas about certain books and can also inform me of the range of their knowledge about literature. The children are active language users when they come to school and through the activities I have outlined they can inform me very well about what they already know. I am now committed to finding a variety of ways in which I can ensure and develop the children's reflective analytical vocabulary, continuing to involve parents in the process.

This has been an area where children can make their voices heard, and by their doing so we are made aware of the extent of their knowledge through capturing their insights. Through making choices and taking risks these children are empowered. The triangle of learning is now in place, and parents, teachers and pupils are working together in a mutually supportive and trusting way. Gordon Wells states: 'Risk taking is necessary in any enterprise that aims to move beyond the status quo and this is particularly true of learning in school.'[9] To achieve this I feel that being a teacher must allow the power to shift to the children. They are, after all, already active language users. If you take the risk, in turn the children will show you just what they know.

References

1. Smith, F. (1984) *Essays into Literacy*, p. 10. London: Heinemann.
2. Smith, F. (1984) *Essays into Literacy*, p. 12. London: Heinemann.
3. Minns, H. (1990) *Read It to Me Now!*, p. 114. London: Virago Educational.

4. Meek, M. (1991) *On Being Literate*, p. 157. London: The Bodley Head.

5. Meek, M. (1988) *How Texts Teach What Readers Learn*, p. 3. Stroud: Thimble Press.

6. Graham, J. (1991) *Pictures on the Page*. Sheffield: NATE.

7. Jordan, B. (1992) Good for any age – picture books and the experienced reader. In M. Styles, E. Bearne and V. Watson (eds) *After Alice: Exploring Children's Literature*, p. 117. London: Cassell.

8. Meek, M. (1988) *How Texts Teach What Readers Learn*, p. 12. Stroud: Thimble Press.

9. Wells, G. (1987) *The Meaning Makers: Children Learning Language and Using Language to Learn*. London: Hodder and Stoughton.

Chapter 6

The Marks on the Page
Children as Editors

Rachel Sparks Linfield

The previous chapter urged risk-taking in order to discover just what children can do. This is exactly what Rachel Sparks Linfield did. In a piece of research stemming from her own urge to help her class of 8 and 9-year olds improve their writing, she opened up to the class what is often a hidden area of the teacher's role. In doing this, she offered a model for future possibilities for her pupils. When teachers receive children's writing they may respond to it in a variety of ways. Even before it is handed over, the teacher may have been involved in some kind of response to the text as it is being put together. One of the most regular – and very often unquestioned – areas of responding to children's writing is the kind of 'marking' which is familiar to everyone who has ever written in a classroom. For some it is a mysterious process, where it may not seem in the least bit obvious just what the teacher wants in selecting apparently arbitrary points to be corrected. For others, where there has been some discussion of the criteria which a teacher is operating, it becomes a more balanced process, where the teacher is acting, perhaps, as a more experienced proofreader. All teachers who mark work, whatever the perceptions held by the pupils, want to help children get better at writing. The tricky bit is to find out just what kinds of marks on the page will do that. In taking the risk and investigating the effects of her own marking, Rachel Sparks Linfield not only found ways of developing her practice, but discovered also the power of teacher modelling for editing and the important part which explicit discussion plays in helping children to become more attentive and critical readers of their own texts.

The investigation involved the Year 4 class I was teaching in a primary school in a university town. I had been working at the school for seven years.

Although the children tended to be able and articulate, this was not always reflected in the quality or presentation of their written work. Since the kinds of response made to children's writing seem to be critical in helping them to make progress, during the summer term I decided to look closely at the way I marked writing.[1] I wanted to consider how useful my marking was for my class: whether their understanding of my comments and markings was the same as I had intended, and what value they gave to my comments and symbols. Marking children's work should always help them to learn and encourage them to learn further, as well as enable teachers to assess their pupils' progress. I decided to investigate marking from my pupils' points of view since I felt that my marking did not seem to be yielding the results I wanted. To make the investigation manageable, I decided to restrict my researches to the children's personal imaginative writing.

There was no marking policy for teachers at the school, although there were guidelines for the presentation of work by the juniors. No systems of numerical or letter grades or house points operated. Teachers all had their own schemes based on symbols such as ticks and underlining words, comments like 'good', and fuller comments, especially in the area of personal writing. Marking was qualitative rather than quantitative. It assumed that the phrases and symbols used by teachers carried a meaning which pupils shared. Each new year children had to take on their teacher's method of marking and possibly a different set of meanings. As a result I wanted to see just what the children understood about my personal marking system.

When marking children's work I prefer, where possible, to read it over with them so that problems may be discussed and feedback is instant. Understanding of written marking is crucial if the child is to benefit. Inevitably, however, much of the children's sustained personal writing is viewed without the child present, because of the practical factors of time and quantity. For personal writing my marking takes place at a variety of levels. Sometimes children draft and I provide many of the technical corrections before they redraft – a form of sub-editing. In this case the main criterion for assessment would be the content. At other times I would provide response throughout the writing process; children draft, talk to me and continue redrafting until they and I are satisfied. Here my marking of the final piece would extend to technical details and presentation. A third type of marking is where children write immediately 'in best' and again it covers content, technical details and presentation. The amount of technical detail and presentation commented on varies according to the nature of the task and the child's present position in terms of writing development.

My investigation was carried out in four stages:

1. I analysed the symbols and comments I used to mark children's personal writing.

2. I asked children in a questionnaire to explain the symbols I used.

3. A child's piece of personal writing was marked by children.

4. Interviews with seven children were carried out to discover their views on marking.

Before I began it was important for me to establish what the children understood by the word 'marking'. As part of a general discussion about school I asked my class to define certain words, one of which was 'marking'. Three of their definitions were:

You can mark in different ways – ticks, crosses, question marks, squiggles, words. I suppose it depends on what you're correcting.

Marking is what teachers do to work so they know how well we're doing and what we still need to know.

It's what you do when you take in our books. I wouldn't mind marking with an answer book but it must be hard to do stories.

The children realized that 'marking' went beyond ticks and crosses, encompassing all the words and symbols teachers used in their books, and could take a variety of forms depending upon the subject matter. They understood that marking personal writing could be more problematic than perhaps a sum which was either correct or not. Through this discussion, I found that my class and I held shared views on the purposes and general methods of marking. My investigation, therefore, needed to check my pupils' understanding and use of my actual marking.

Analysing My Marking

I began by listing all the symbols and comments which I had written in the margins of Class Four's books to accompany personal writing during the year, and considered what I intended them to mean. I then went on to look at three pieces of work and noted all the comments I had written at the end of each one. I coded them for key words such as 'enjoy', comments on the content, and questions and instructions for presentation or punctuation. I wanted to see what I tended to focus on most and whether my comments gave children the chance to develop. The 'enjoy' remarks show that I particularly like something. Whilst they perhaps encourage children, they do not give specific advice. Similarly, the content ones simply indicate that I have read and appreciated the personal writing.

Within personal writing I always comment on the creative content. Where a negative comment is necessary, I try to balance this with something positive. I might indicate a paragraph which is particularly successful; depending upon the child, I might correct up to three spelling errors, punctuation or a handwriting feature. I would also mention areas of presentation – not using a ruler or not dating work. Occasionally I would use the 'see me' type of comment. 'See me' would indicate poor work. 'Come to me and talk' or 'Please see me' would indicate a problem I wished to discuss or something I wished to explain to extend the child. 'See me now!' generally means that a child has failed to act upon a 'See me' or has completely disregarded vital instructions!

Hence, whilst sessions spent on personal writing may have a creative aim, my marking often includes presentation, punctuation and spelling. Figure 6.1 indicates the range.

All work is marked in blue or black pen so that my marking is not too intrusive. When children have spent time and effort in writing I do not want to spoil the outward appearance. Neither do I wish to use a colour such as red to emphasize mistakes. As children write in pencil or blue ink, marking in a similar colour tends to be viewed as advice. Though readable, it does not stand out and thus the child's work is still important to the child and to other readers.

My initial analysis (Table 6.1) showed that the majority of markings within the margin concerned errors of spelling. Generally, I felt, my margin marking was negative. Of words misspelt, only one child repeated the error, and only five children ever made the same mistake twice. Within the comments I investigated, the majority reflected the creative element of the story rather than presentation; for example:

A good ending. Also 'well done' for using speech marks. Please check through for capital letters and then see me.

I enjoyed your second chapter. Please though remember that we do not join from b, p, s, y or g. [for handwriting]

FIGURE 1

SYMBOLS AND WORDS I USE IN THE MARGIN ALONGSIDE PERSONAL WRITING

	EXAMPLE	MEANING
with	He ran home whit the box.	"with" spelt incorrectly. Write it in the margin, in your word book and learn to spell it.
x10 with	He was whit me.	"with" misspelt again. Write it ten times in the margin.
Date?		Work not dated. Date it.
Ruler	Black Beauty	Title/date not underlined. Underline.
Ruler?	Black Beauty	Ruler not used. Repeat with a ruler.
wr	with	Use top line please. Top line not used. Next time use top lines. Letter not in Jarman style. Future "w"s should be straight. [Could be for any letter or incorrect letter or incorrect joining.]

Additional margin marks and meanings:

	EXAMPLE	MEANING
Good ✓		Indicates a good part – description, beginning or end.
Missa line	Crossing the Creek in 1890 we were	Next time leave a line between the title and story start.
	Angela and and I	Word not required.
A	angela and I	Angela needs a capital.
?	He went also School to tree.	What does this mean? Check it and change/ add words.
	capital letters and punctuation are used where necessary.	
	One upon a time there lived a	Start at the margin next time.

Figure 6.1 Symbols and words I use in the margin alongside personal writing

Table 6.1 Frequency of marking symbols used within Class Four's personal writing

	Spelling	Presentation	Style
Alan	4	1	1
Neil	13	2	3
Mark	10	2	0
Chris	0	2	0
Cathy	2	1	0
John	6	1	0
Paul	1	3	0
Mary	3	2	0
David	5	1	1
Ruth	1	3	0
Bob	3	1	0
Joe	6	3	0
Jonathan	0	1	0
Edmund	5	1	3
Jane	0	5	1
Nicola	1	3	1
Elizabeth	9	2	1
Ian	1	2	0
Nick	10	1	0
Stephen	0	1	0
Rachel	3	1	2
Lucy	7	0	0
Becky	3	0	1
Matthew	2	0	0
Stanley	2	0	0
Giles	3	0	0
Lisa	5	0	0
Charles	6	0	2

Was it magic that got you out?

An action-packed story which I really enjoyed.

I thoroughly enjoyed your story. I wonder what your father would do if this really happened. Also how did you become your real size?

I'm glad you had a happy ending.

Table 6.2 Analysis of comments made on 72 stories

Question	3
Instruction	14
See me	3
Good start	2
Good end	6
Good describing	2
Well done	8
Like	4
Enjoy	8
General comment on complete story	41

Table 6.2 shows the balance between types of comments on a number of pieces written over the year. These were mainly positive. For example, 3 out of 72 comments were 'See me'. Thus my marking seemed to reflect my aim to balance positive and negative statements. I was, however, surprised by the number of remarks I made concerning presentation. Few remarks related to the structure of the stories, although ten indicated 'good parts'. Given that few mistakes were repeated, but that a large proportion of margin marking was negative, I was keen to discover how my class viewed the way I marked.

Children Explain My Marking

To find out what my class understood of the way I marked, I used a questionnaire depicting all the symbols and markings I made on their personal writing. I included examples of marking showing a margin and work as if it were in their books and asked the children to tell me what the marking meant. Although one or two children showed some confusion, the completed questionnaires indicated that most of the children understood most of the markings I used within their personal writing (Figure 6.2).

The mark to indicate a good part of personal writing was not understood by two children and left unexplained by three. Of the two who misunderstood, one stated, 'Good shouldn't have a capital letter', yet in his own work he had had this marking on three occasions. A second simply stated 'Start a

| w | <u>with</u> | The next time i would try and do a w straight. Though i do do my w's curly |

| Good | | Its a good bit of writing. |

	See me	see miss sphars
	See me now!	see miss sparks that second
	Please see me	miss sparks starting to get a bit angey
	See me	go and tat talk to you because you don't understand
	See me now!	you have seen see me you didn't come so your in a bit of trouble.
	Please see me	you woneed) to have some-thing explained.

Figure 6.2 Children's explanations of my marking.

new line.' One problem in interpreting 'Good' may have been that on the questionnaire nothing was written after 'Good' whereas examples were given after the margin for all other marks. Out of 15 children who had never received the mark, however, 12 were able to interpret it. Children's under-

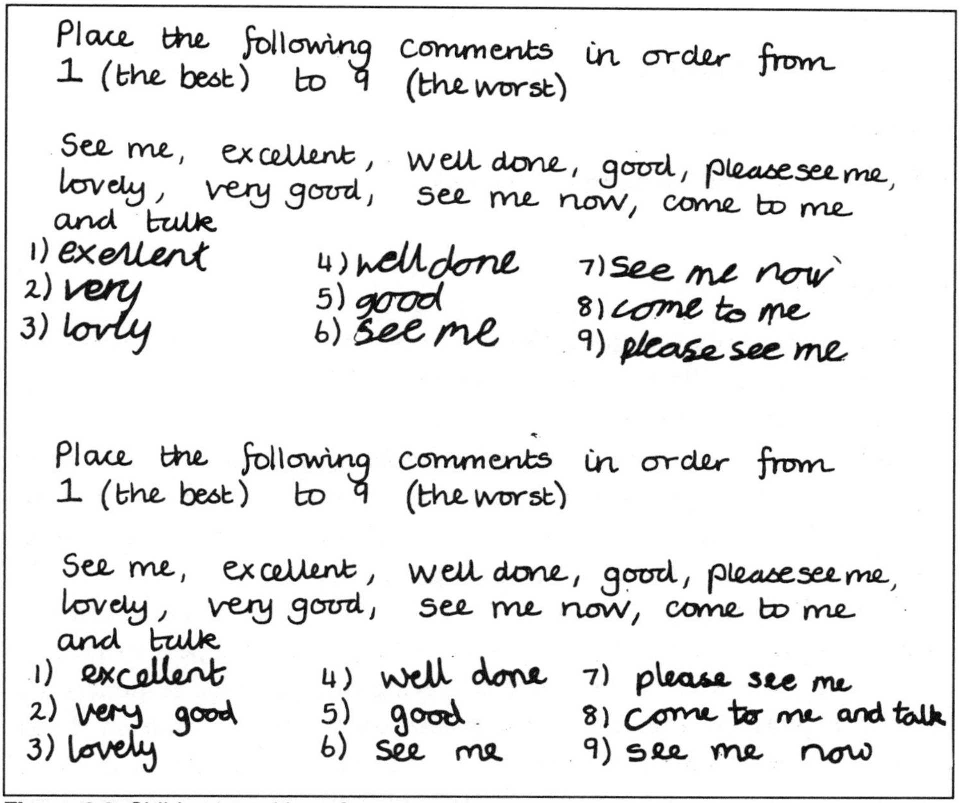

Place the following comments in order from
1 (the best) to 9 (the worst)

See me, excellent, well done, good, please see me,
lovely, very good, see me now, come to me
and talk

1) exellent   4) welldone   7) see me now
2) very   5) good   8) come to me
3) lovly   6) see me   9) please see me

Place the following comments in order from
1 (the best) to 9 (the worst)

See me, excellent, well done, good, pleasesee me,
lovely, very good, see me now, come to me
and talk

1) excellent   4) well done   7) please see me
2) very good   5) good   8) come to me and talk
3) lovely   6) see me   9) see me now

Figure 6.3 Children's ranking of my remarks.

standing of 'See me', 'See me now' and 'Please see me' was varied. When
writing 'See me now!', 'See me' and 'Please see me', I would rank them in that
order both in terms of urgency to come to me and in the seriousness of error.
Although children's definitions of these words indicated that 'See me now!'
was more urgent than the other two, seven children saw no difference
between 'See me' and 'Please see me'. One child felt 'Please see me' would be
given for 'something nice'. Of all the children's comments only three were
written negatively: 'You're in a bit of trouble', 'They aren't good' and 'Miss
Sparks is starting to get a bit angry.' The rest merely meant the child had to see
me. I was surprised by the lack of concern shown for these comments. This
lack was later shown in the interviews.

I had also asked the children to rank some of my comments (see Figure 6.3).
In ranking the nine comments from best (1) to worst (9) I would do it as
follows:

1. Excellent

2. Very good and Well done

4. Lovely and Good

6. Please see me and Come to me and talk

8. See me

9. See me now!

I would also use the words for different things: I might say an illustration was 'Lovely', whereas a display of effort would get 'Well done'. Personal writing would never be marked with a single word such as 'Good'; I would say precisely what I thought was good. When ranking the comments, 'Excellent' was clearly the best, gaining twenty-six firsts, although 'Very good', 'Lovely', 'Well done' and 'Come to me and talk' were bracketed first once. Fifteen children felt 'See me now' to be the least good phrase.

One child's handling of the task alerted me to a problem associated with such a ranking exercise. At first, his list of rankings did not appear to have any logic. I felt this may have been due to having to order nine responses and an unwillingness to alter the questionnaire once it was completed. Later, however, when I asked him to read his list to me, I realized that the vocal expression and intonation which he gave to the words influenced his thinking. As a result, although I found my class had a general understanding of my written comments, based on their experience of working with me for almost a year, I decided that I needed to investigate even further when I later interviewed some of them.

Children Mark Personal Writing

Before the interviews, however, I wanted to see how well the children could operate a system of marking themselves. I hoped that by seeing their marked work I would be able to check the information I had gleaned from the questionnaire. I copied out a piece of writing by an 8-year-old former pupil which contained a variety of technical errors. I asked the class to imagine that they were teachers and to mark the piece. They could do what they liked and use anything to mark it with. I told them that the piece had been written by a Year 5 writer who had done his best. I agreed to show them my marking after they had looked at the piece – 'My Cat Rodney' (Figure 6.4).

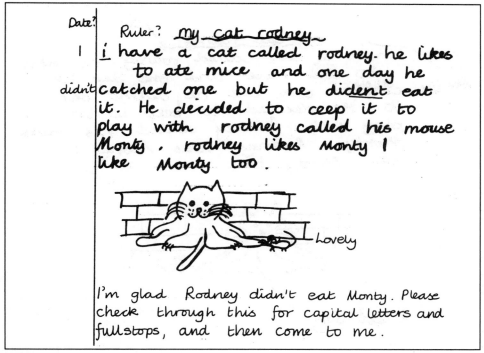

Date?

Ruler? my cat rodney

1 | i have a cat called rodney. he likes to ate mice and one day he

didn't | catched one but he dident eat it. He decided to ceep it to play with rodney called his mouse Monty . rodney likes Monty I like Monty too.

Lovely

I'm glad Rodney didn't eat Monty . Please check through this for capital letters and fullstops, and then come to me.

Figure 6.4 My marking of 'My Cat Rodney'.

The examples in Figures 6.5 and 6.6 show how some of the children responded to the work. Other comments were:

This is a good story but im shuere you could have tried harder I aspecialy licked th picture!!

and

I think rodney is a kind cat   good

To analyse the children's marking I compared their attempts with the way I had marked the piece. First of all, I noted the colour they used to mark with. Only one used red (crayon); ten used blue pen and seventeen used pencil.

Table 6.3 shows the range of types of feature the children marked. There was emphasis on presentation: the highest numbers noted that a ruler had not been used and that the date was absent. When marking spellings, I had focused on the two words I felt it would be most useful for the writer to know – namely 'didn't' and 'I'. Far fewer children marked these two words compared with the numbers who noticed 'catched' and 'ate'. Although there were five spelling errors, eleven children marked only one. I later checked whether the class could, in fact, spell all five which were mistakes in the piece,

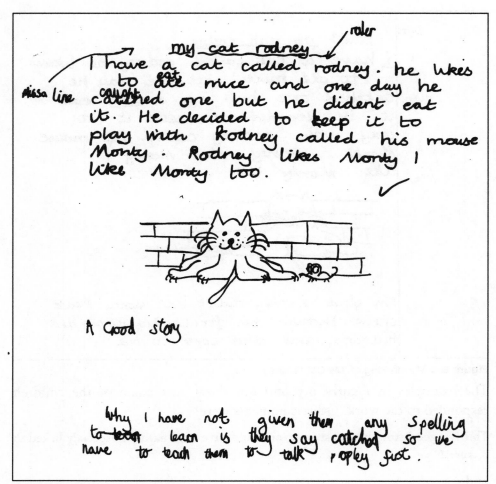

Figure 6.5 Children's marking of 'My Cat Rodney'.

to make sure that their lack of marking of these was not simply because they were not aware of them as errors. All of them could spell all five, with the exception of just three children who misspelt 'keep'. It appeared, then, that the children did not feel that all mistakes should be corrected.

All of the children gave a comment at the end of the story. Of these only three were totally negative. In all other cases where negative comments were given, something positive was also said (Table 6.4).

Overall, the children showed a good grasp of the way I marked personal writing. Many of the comments made could have been mine. However, although these results indicated understanding of the symbols I use, I could not determine whether the children genuinely found them helpful, and so used them, or whether when asked to mark 'My Cat Rodney' they had simply tried

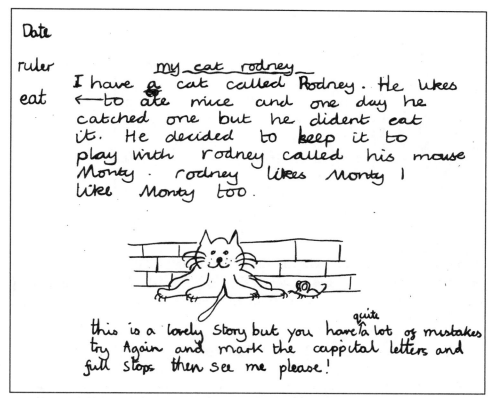

Figure 6.6 Children's marking of 'My Cat Rodney' (cont'd).

Table 6.3 The frequency of markings in the margin

Marking	Frequency
Ruler	23
Miss a line	2
Date	17
diden't	3
ate	16
catched	11
ceep	7
i	2
mice [word not misspelt]	1
friend [word not actually in story]	1

Table 6.4   The range of comments made

Comment referring to	Frequency
Capital letters	21
Lovely picture	7
Story content	11
Story mistakes	7
Please come and see me	1
Good	12
See me	5
Check your story and then see me	3

to imagine they were me! Clearly the children had used my comments as a model for the possible ways in which they might mark. With this in mind, I decided to interview some of the children about their views of my marking.

Children Talk to Me

I interviewed three girls and three boys, all with varying levels of confidence in personal writing. I used a schedule of questions but did not stick rigidly to the wording or order. I was guided by the children's responses to one question in deciding how I asked the next.

Before the tape recorder was switched on, I asked each child whether they were willing to help me discover more about marking by answering questions about their own writing and the cat story. I also asked they if they minded being taped, and then used the following as a guide:

1. Why do you think I mark work?

2. When your personal writing book is returned to you after it has been marked, what do you do with it?

3. What do you think work should be marked in? (implement/colour)

4. Look back through your personal writing book.
   (a) which piece pleases you the most? Why?
   (b) which piece pleases you the least? Why?

5. Is there anything you don't like to see in your personal writing book when it's returned? Why?

6. How would you feel if you saw 'See me'?

7. What, if any, is the difference between 'See me' and 'Come to me and talk'?

8. Do ticks matter in personal writing?

9. What would you say you have learned this year by doing personal writing?

10. Look at the cat story. Can you explain why you marked it like that? How would you have felt if I had marked your work like that?

Of course their answers may have been influenced by my being both the teacher and the interviewer. But, generally, children within the school tended to be fairly eloquent, and used to stating what they believed as opposed to what they felt was expected. It can be hard, though, for children to disagree with their teachers and hence some of their remarks may have been made to please me, although as the interviews took place at the end of the school year I feel that the problem of teacher bias, if present, was small.

On being asked why I marked work, children saw marking as being to correct work and to improve it. Edmund felt it was 'to encourage us and to make sure we don't make the mistakes again'.

By asking what children did with their books once they had been marked, I wanted to ascertain their interest in what I had done. With the exception of Mary all looked through their books. In mentioning ticks I wanted to see how aware children were of my marking. (Rarely would I tick a story; only where I made no comment.) Children were unconcerned and Jonathan felt that ticks were for mathematics. Three children thought they might have had ticks but overall they considered comments more important.

For marking work, children decided that blue or black was appropriate. Edmund said these would 'stand out', whilst the rest chose these colours because they were not obvious and did not spoil work. Jonathan stated 'Not red. Red is sort of blood colour. Blue is sort of nice. It's like good.'

Asking what pleased them the most, in their own writing, I was interested to see whether children would be influenced by the way I had marked their books. Jonathan picked his favourite comment, which did not go with his favourite story. The others chose the stories they preferred, regardless of my marking. Joe's reason for his favourite personal writing was 'I just found myself doing a piece of work I was satisfied with. It had quite a lot of corrections but I didn't really mind that.'

I also saw that all children were aware of their books' contents, being able quickly to find the pieces and comments they wished to show me. For two children, length influenced the choices of what pleased them the least. Of his least favourite piece Joe commented, 'It's a short one and I like doing longer things. I like doing stories. I once did six hundred words at home and I still haven't finished it.'

No one seemed to mind their work being corrected. Elizabeth and Joe disliked seeing too much, but realized why correction is necessary. My corrections and the occasional 'See me' did not disturb most of them; only Joe appeared to mind. Of the interviewees, only Rachel and Edmund had never received a 'See me' for personal writing. Differences in 'Please see me' and 'Come to me and talk' were not perceived to be very great. Answers to the question 'What have you learned this year by doing personal writing?' focused on presentation. Children mentioned joined-up writing, speech marks and a variety of letters. Edmund felt he had learned a number of things:

I've learnt partly about different stories, and how you can properly write. . . . I always got used to putting a capital 'J' or if it wasn't a capital I used not to cross it at the top whereas you go under the line and dot it. I didn't quite get used to that. That's helped me – em. One thing I do like is your comments. I mean sometimes I have a little laugh about them. Some of them are quite funny I've found.

The children were less explicit about the creative content, reinforcing the fact that the majority of my marking was for reasons of presentation, spelling and punctuation.

Conclusions

At the start of my investigation into the understanding and feelings children show for the markings I put on their written work, my expectations were coloured both by my own understanding of my marking and by my own past experiences of my work being marked as a pupil and as a student. Thus I found some surprises. In terms of understanding I realized that whilst most of my symbols were understood, it was not until I spoke with children that all of them could be correctly interpreted. Some children shared my meanings whilst others did not. On reflection I realize that I had never explained what my comments meant. With regard to the emotional impact of marking, phrases which as a pupil would have caused me concern did not concern my class. I discovered that they viewed marking with a mature, even objective, attitude.

Looking back at the investigation as a whole I found that the time I spent interviewing the children was very rewarding. It made me realize that although I frequently talk about work with pupils it would be helpful in the future to take more time to discuss marked work with children.

When the children marked the piece 'My Cat Rodney', I discovered just how capable they could be at editing. They could correct spellings and punctuation, and make evaluations of the creative content of the personal writing. I realized, however, that their willingness to correct the piece was not evident when redrafting their own normal work. As a result, after my investigation was finished I encouraged children to read peers' work and make helpful suggestions. Although I have no written data I believe that the children became more critical of their own work. They realized that errors of spelling and punctuation could alter the meaning of what they wanted to say and that different styles of writing could be used to put a message across.

I continued this practice of discussing work with neighbours with my next Year 4 class. As children made suggestions about ways in which peers could improve their writing, they became more aware of improvements possible in their own. Discussions with me also became more fruitful as children came, not to seek approval, but to ask for advice over particular problems they had noted for themselves. In this way we became more equal partners in the process of writing.

Note

1. I have used the term 'marking' throughout, to make clear the distinction between the varied kinds of responses I make to the children's work – often spoken – and my written marks on their writing, which is the area I was keen to investigate.

Chapter 7

Looking for the Pattern
Bilingual Readers Writing

Ian Eyres

This chapter describes how literacy can become even more critical when the learners have access to more than one language. Eventually, of course, this will become a major strength in their understanding of language, but while bilingual children are getting to grips with two (at least) languages, teachers need to develop carefully structured ways to help them move towards confident literacy. Ian Eyres gives an account of work with a class of developing bilingual children at Gladstone School, an inner city primary school in Peterborough. As members of Cambridgeshire's peripatetic ESL support team, Ian Eyres and a colleague were invited to work in the school because the headteacher was concerned about the reading performance of some of the older children. Within a relatively short period they were concentrating their efforts in one of the two Year 6 classes. All but two of the children were of Pakistani heritage, speaking the same variety of Punjabi, although proficiency in spoken English varied widely across the class. Tina March, the class teacher, and Ian began by concentrating on the children's writing as a means of developing reading, being aware of the important links between reading, writing and, indeed, the children's oral language and finding that their reading did not seem to release the meanings of texts for them. Through the work outlined in this chapter, Ian comments: 'I learned a great deal about how bilingual children operate with texts and encountered many opportunities to test my belief that there are essential common patterns to be observed in all kinds of language learning.' Not only this, but he and Tina March found that the children used their language resources to help them become more discriminating in the ways they tackle texts.

As a starting point in our work with the class, we decided to conduct miscue analyses with a large sample of the children to find out just what their strengths were as readers. Although, as I soon discovered, reading ability varied widely within each class, there was one feature which seemed to be common to virtually all of the bilingual children. While all of them showed at least some mastery of the phonic and syntactic cueing systems of reading, their grasp of the meaning of a text appeared much less sure. This imbalance manifested itself in a number of ways. Less confident readers often employed the (widely used) technique of establishing what a word says by 'sounding out' the initial letter and then offering a guess without any reference to the semantic context. At the other end of the scale, some of the children showed themselves to be capable of reading aloud with great fluency and appropriately expressive intonation. With even the best of these it was obvious from their answers to questions about the text that there was much that they had not understood. Many would search for an answer by scanning the text for a sentence containing what they decided was the key word in the questions. Just as often, though, simple questions were answered by silence. These children seemed to be able to use their existing knowledge about language, derived from their experience of both Meierpuri Punjabi and English, and in particular to be able to use knowledge about formal linguistic structures as a short cut to reading aloud. I say reading aloud because in no other sense could many of the children be said to be reading.

The neglect of meaning in the process of reading disturbed me for two reasons. Obviously there is no point in 'reading' without understanding. It is literally a meaningless exercise. In addition to this, however, children who turn their backs on meaning are abandoning an essential tool for learning to read. Competent readers use the meaning of a text to help them to predict what comes next, to check what they have already read and to self-correct. Being able to make use of all available semantic information substantially reduces the range of possibilities offered by words and phrases as they are encountered and correspondingly reduces the burdens imposed on other cueing systems. Using meaning makes reading a lot easier. And if this is true for competent readers, how much more must it be true for those less confident learners, for whom the uncertainty they experience as they progress through a page is so much greater. And if it is helping these beginner readers read, then it is helping them learn to read. As well as providing an essential strategy for readers as they progress through a text, the re-creation of meaning provides a reason for embarking on the task in the first place. If a child comes away from a text without either having learned something new or having been in some way intellectually stimulated or entertained, why should they believe that reading is a worthwhile activity? And why then should we anticipate that they will engage in that activity except at those times when a teacher or some other adult requires them to perform the trick of reading aloud? If children, as I believe they do, learn to read by reading, it seems likely that a lot of vital practising is not going to get done.

'Reading' which rests heavily on the use of syntactic cues and word recognition requires the reader to bring relatively little to the text – simply the knowledge of a set of syntactic patterns and the ability to recognize (and then maybe only in the 'seen it before' sense) a number of words. Compared with reading proper, or 'reading for meaning', where the reader needs to bring a wide range of personal knowledge to bear in order to interpret the print fully, it is a rather passive activity. My overwhelming impression in this case was of children who were not in control of their reading. Rather, their reading was controlling them.

So much for the problem. What strategies could help the children work towards a solution? Tina and I decided to work on three fronts. First, we organized the class for regular group reading sessions. Second, I worked on developing materials for topic work of a kind which would necessitate reading for meaning. Third, I initiated a workshop approach to writing. It is this strategy which I would like to examine in some detail in this chapter.

There were a number of interrelated reasons why I felt that it would be useful to address through writing what was, on the face of it, a reading problem.

Putting Meaning First

First of all, my approach to teaching writing (an approach which owes much to the work of Donald Graves[1]) is one which stresses the primacy of meaning. Children choose their own subjects and are encouraged to fix their ideas on the page quickly, refining and elaborating them later, and giving attention to surface features such as spelling and punctuation only in the final stages of a draft. Children continue their drafts from day to day, working towards the eventual presentation of their work in the form of books which are displayed in the classroom and available for other class members to read. The children refer to this as publication. The writing process is supported by individual conferences based on questioning procedures which are, again, designed to bring children to say what they mean. It is specifically intended to leave the writers 'in control'.[1] This way of working leaves all the decisions in the hands of the writer – not just choice of subject but also the length of a piece, when to edit, what vocabulary and structures to employ, which pieces to publish and so on. All authority remains in the hands of the author. I wanted to use this approach, which I had used successfully before, so we set out to write and publish books.

A distinctive bar to many bilingual children's access to a text to be read is the disjunction between the experiences (both linguistic and general) of the author and those of the reader. If the reader is not herself able to bring to the text all those elements which are implicit in it, then no matter how well she is able to decode the words, that text remains impenetrable. By asking children to tell their own stories (in the widest possible sense of the word) we can give them the opportunity to develop their own meanings and to produce texts which they (and children whose experiences are similar) are able to engage with fully. So often as teachers we ask children, in their writing, to tell us what *we* mean. At the best of times this is difficult for many children to do and difficult to defend on any communicative grounds. So far as communication is concerned, the difference of experience obtaining between writer and teacher/reader is a positive gift. The teacher needs to ask questions, the writer needs to explain. When we ask children to talk or write about their own experiences we are able to help them develop the medium of their expression through matters of which they have the firmest of grasps, simply by asking them what *they* mean.

Supporting Children at the Early Stages of Literacy: Linking Reading and Writing

A small number of children in the class appeared to be at the very earliest stages of literacy. My experience of working with young emergent writers told me that the development of reading and that of writing are intimately related and that skills learned in one mode may be practised and consolidated in the other. Phonic correspondences, for example, which are perhaps most commonly associated with the development of reading, may best be learned through the opportunity to experiment and play with letters offered by writing. In addition, these beginner writers especially were in need of reading material which would, in its subject matter, be accessible and interesting without presenting them with too many structural difficulties. I hoped in this case that a substantial number of the books published would help to meet this need and I expected that most would prove popular with many of the class.

The link between the reading and writing processes does not end once a child has 'taken off' as a reader-writer. My own classes had shown me that writers who are experienced in taking the many decisions an author has to take become more critical and insightful readers. I felt that the experience of being an author would help children overcome what I saw as their passive relationship with 'reading' texts. Another aspect of this link concerns the use of reading as an element of the writing process itself. Experienced writers are constantly reading greater or lesser chunks of their own texts to help them maintain direction and cohesion.[2] This variety of reading is a very active one, entailing both searching and questioning. It involves on the one hand moving swiftly back and forth between different sections, and, on the other, slow, detailed examinations of particular stretches. It is a far cry from the helpless slide from top to bottom characteristic of so many of these bilingual children's encounters with the printed page. I felt that if, through becoming aware of their readership and through the effect of my questioning, the children could be brought to re-read their work (something which, when I began to work with them, they were emphatically unwilling to do) then this experience of being active readers would benefit their approach to any text.

Getting Started

My usual practice in getting writers' workshops off the ground is to ask the children each to list four topics which they feel they could write about. Then I ask them to choose one of the four and to start writing about it. This usually gets most of the class started on the first day, with perhaps two or three unwilling to commit themselves to paper just yet. These more reluctant writers are usually willing to start after another day or two, when they have seen what their classmates have produced and how their teacher and other children respond to their work. With this class, however, I did not feel that this approach would work. My intuition was that many of the children would lack the confidence to write without asking for my support (one of my strictest workshop rules is 'don't come and see me, I'll come and see you') and therefore disrupt the essential calm atmosphere. Even if this did not happen, I feared that the number of reluctant starters would simply influence the rest of the class. A productive and inclusive first session is essential to set the right tone for the future.

I knew that most of the children would be happiest if they were given clear and precise instructions as to what to write (maybe a set format, a suggested subject and a list of 'useful' words) but I could not see how such a start could ever lead to the point where the writers were making all their own decisions. I decided therefore to begin by offering a task which, although it made specific demands, left the children free to respond (or not) in whatever way they chose. I explained to the group that I had begun to write a story and that I needed their help to finish it. I then read them the beginning of a piece about a 10-year-old animal lover who has been promised a trip to a safari park if he manages regularly to get to school on time. My draft ended at the point where he has to decide whether to free a trapped bird and risk being late or to leave it and get to school on time. When I had finished reading it I asked the class to help me with their suggestions, perhaps by writing the ending as they thought it should be or by writing me a note with their ideas, or in any other way they chose. I hoped this would be an effective way to start because the story and its main character would be ones the children could identify with and because they were left with a dilemma to resolve. I also hoped that they would feel able to follow the two models I had offered them. The first was the text itself – I hoped that its form and style would appeal to them as something to try to emulate. The second was the model of myself as a writer – I wanted the children to see that writing an absorbing (I hoped!) story was an activity which an ordinary person of their acquaintance could indulge in and that they could be writers too.

In the event, all the children showed an interest in the story. A few wrote very little in the first session, but about half the class wrote notes on possible outcomes and the remainder completed the story for me. After the lesson I took all the texts which were capable of standing alone as narratives (about ten of them), typed them out, edited spelling and other conventions and spiral-bound them into individual books.

At the beginning of the next session I showed the books to the whole class and read some of them out as preparation for a discussion in which we looked at different possible endings. This was moving an important step on from the first session because now the models I was showing were provided by the children themselves and by their own books. I was also introducing a purpose for their writing – publication – and this in turn introduced the concept of audience to them. Someone was going to read what they wrote. I invited (genuinely) those who had not already done so to write an ending for the story and gave the authors of the completed books paper on which to draw a cover and write a short piece 'about the author'. This left a few children undecided as to what to do, and I drew the attention to the sheet of paper which I had included in everybody's folder and which was headed 'Ideas for writing'. I told the class that if they did not want to work on my story they could think up some ideas of their own and list them here. No one was therefore under pressure to start out writing on their own and this meant that the number of children needing support from me, as they began to plan their own pieces, was relatively small. Within a few sessions most members of the class were busy on their own texts. A few were still working on the bird story, some were writing accounts of personal experiences, and most of the rest were writing versions of folk or fairy stories. The writers' workshop had become established.

Talking about Writing: Their Language or Mine?

Much of my teaching during these sessions is done during writers' conferences – one-to-one meetings in which authors talk about their writing. I find that if they are asked the right questions, children can be led to say quite clearly and explicitly what it is that they want to express in their writing. By the right questions I mean questions offered in a genuine spirit of enquiry – when the child really believes that the teacher wants to know what it is that they have to tell. The questions need, therefore, to be very open indeed, and I have to resist the temptation to look for answers going in any particular direction – a direction which may lead to territory which is familiar to me but (more or less) alien to the child. This, of course, is a greater danger in the case where the child and teacher do not share a common culture. Often conferences are of use in helping a child to develop and elaborate something that has already been written but at other times they may provide the support necessary to enable them to get a piece started. I found that with this class I was spending more time than I would usually expect to on the latter. In the early days this was in large part due to the fact that many children insisted on 'finishing' a piece at the end of each session, leaving themselves with a blank sheet at the start of the next. It took a good while before some were prepared to accept that what they wanted to say was more important than the (now self-imposed) imperative to finish a piece of work in a single session. This attitude reminded me of the behaviour I had observed when children were reading from books. In each case the task was 'get to the bottom of the page' and meaning is sacrificed to the perceived (formal) demands of the task. I soon learned that the best way to help a child arrive at a subject for writing was to try to get them to forget about the writing at first and just have a chat. A question I used very commonly was 'What did you do at the weekend?' Whatever the answer, a few follow-up questions would soon bring us to the point at which I could say, 'Do you think you've got something you could write about there?' Usually the answer would be 'yes'.

One of the purposes of the writers' conference is to give children an opportunity to rehearse orally the words which they may subsequently write. One technique which I use frequently therefore consists of giving children their own words back – echoing what they have said in order to affirm its value and to confirm it in the writer's memory. In principle, and usually in practice, I think it is essential that the words a child gets back should be exactly those originally offered. I am not the author and it is not for me (however implicitly) to suggest editorial changes during the composition of a first draft. All good rules have their exceptions, however. It is not completely truthful to say that I just repeat what children say. I could not possibly repeat everything they say. They say too much for that, and, besides, one of the functions of the conference is to help them to give order to their thoughts. The bits I choose to repeat are the bits which I think can be best put together to make a coherent text. This pattern of dialogue, of course, mirrors normal conversational patterns where a listener is keen to understand a developing narrative (a pattern frequently used between adults and young children learning to speak) and is, I hope, perceived by the writer as natural conversational support, rather than as an intrusion. However, since I select for repetition only certain of the sentences and phrases a child offers I am implicitly proposing a structure for their developing text. I choose to say that I am *proposing* a structure rather than *imposing* one because the writer is perfectly at liberty to ignore my implicit suggestions. My suspicion is that the closer my selection fits the writer's original intentions and understanding of the subject, the more likely they are to make use of it. If what I choose to highlight fails to strike a chord it will be ignored. (Some information is more equal than other!)

Where there is conflict between giving children their exact words back and talking sense then, naturally, sense prevails. If, for example, a child says 'I played football' I would naturally reply 'You played football.' Repeating the sentence in the first person would not fit in with my usual conversational behaviour. What then if they say (still referring to a past event) 'I play football' or 'I runned with the ball'? I want to value their language. I do not want to reject forms they habitually use[3] and impose the forms of standard English, so maybe I should say 'You runned with the ball.' But what if the child concerned recognizes that I am using an unfamiliar form? There is certainly a risk that I will appear patronizing and, as I have said, I try to keep the language patterns of conferences as close as possible to those of ordinary conversation – and ordinarily I do not say 'runned'. On top of that I have to remember that one of the functions of the writer's conference is to help the writer shape their own language into the forms of written language. Even for the child who grows up speaking standard English all the time, part of the process of learning to write is the learning of forms of language which they would not use in speech.

I decided that the best course was to stick to my own customary classroom variety of English for three reasons. First, I felt it important to offer these children a consistent model of standard English. I felt this to be particularly important in the context of these children's writing because the school environment offers relatively few examples of this variety (apart from books, broadcasts, etc., only the teaching staff are consistent users of standard English) and as writers the children will eventually need to be in command of standard forms. Second, I felt that most children in the class would be happiest to hear this form from me. The more sophisticated users of English would have become accustomed to the way I speak and accept that different people speak in different ways, while others may well not have noticed the difference, or not considered it important. I see this as another example of children accepting the kinds of information which are in some way close to their existing state of knowledge whilst being much less receptive to less familiar forms. Third, I see the retention of my own usual mode of speech as in keeping with the integrity of the workshop approach to writing, which is about using *real* language in real contexts.

Setting a Written Standard?

The dilemma somehow feels more acute on those occasions when I am scribing what children say. If they are instructing me to write 'runned', can I in that case write 'ran'? Children who would not notice the difference in an oral exchange might well be aware of a change when it is written down. My way out of this one is to ask the speaker. I treat the difference as personal rather than one of status and say something like, '*I* usually say "ran". Do you want me to put "ran" or "runned"?' Some children are quite adamant that it should be 'runned'. There would be absolutely no point in arguing with this point of view. The likelihood of a child at this stage of English language development learning the standard form from being told it is negligible. Quibbling over it can only give them the message that I do not like their writing and do not want to hear what they have to say. Such learning will not advance their performance as writers.

On the other hand, there are children who will say, 'Oh, yes, "*ran*"', with a tone of recognition which shows they are not simply being obedient to what they assume to be a teacher's thinly disguised instruction. These children will probably already be employing a relatively high number of standard forms in their writing and for these the opportunity to reflect on the choices of form available to them should enable them to enlarge their standard English repertoire further.[4]

Although I have argued for the need for children's written language to develop towards standard forms, I cannot overemphasize my belief that this will only be achieved in an environment where children have the opportunity to write frequently, purposefully and for a known audience, where plentiful models of the standard forms are offered and where children see the need and actually *want* to use standard forms in appropriate contexts. Any insistence on the production of standard forms for their own sake can only detract from the real purpose of the writing (or speech for that matter) and undermine the writer's willingness to take risks, often to the point where they choose to write less and sometimes to the point where they choose to write nothing at all, a state of affairs unlikely to lead to greater proficiency in the use of standard written forms.

Most of the difficulties I had with conferences arose from the fact that I simply did not have time to hold enough of them. Even if I managed to see ten children in a session, that meant that the average child could expect only two visits in three weeks. In addition to this, the facts that four or five children needed direct support every day and that (at first at least) an unusual number of children needed help in getting started on a new piece meant that it was a mathematical certainty that some children would get very few conference opportunities. This in turn meant that many children did not really get the chance to develop conference techniques which would enable them to make the most of the conferences which they did take part in and it also meant that the majority of all conferences took place with children who were having problems. One of the most valuable teaching opportunities occurs when working with a child who is on the verge of grasping some new aspect of the writing process; often the indicator of this is that they are starting to demonstrate that they can get it right some of the time. Often I would make a note to visit a child who was just beginning to use dialogue effectively, or to demarcate sentences or to find ways of bringing a narrative to a conclusion, only to find all my time during the next session taken up by children with difficulties, the opportunity to affirm these positive developments thus being lost. Another negative effect of this is that it encourages children to see their own development as writers in terms of dealing with problems, with the teacher in the role of problem-solver. I wanted to move on to the much healthier situation in which children feel confident to experiment with the forms of language and willing to seek ways of solving their own problems, seeing the teacher as a fellow writer.

One obvious way out of the problem of low conference-contact rate would be to give children the chance to respond to each other's work in paired conferences. I have already said, however, that shortness of time had prevented most children from developing their own conference habits and my feeling was that most of the class were not yet ready to take on a task which requires a good deal of tact and sensitivity. It did not, however, seem unreasonable to expect children to work together on original drafts, so when one pair of boys asked if they could collaborate on a story, I not only allowed them to, but made sure the rest of the class knew about it too. The practice became very popular and at any given time for the rest of the period I was with the class probably about half were writing collaboratively. The advantages were obvious. Children were highly motivated. They enjoyed inventing stories together. It was very rare for children working together to claim to be stuck for ideas. The texts of children who had previously insisted on finishing within one session, however brief their offering, became impressively (and sometimes excessively!) lengthy, and there was a great deal of talking going on. At first I believed that this talk was in English. It seemed to me obvious that bilingual children writing in English and negotiating about which English words and phrases to use would automatically carry out these negotiations in English. I was therefore very pleased to have found a way of getting these Punjabi speakers to conduct purposeful discussions in English. I was, however, wrong. Further eavesdropping and some tape-recording suggested that probably the majority of this discussion was conducted in the children's mother tongue. I did not consider this finding disappointing, however, since it clearly demonstrates the value of allowing children to use their mother tongue even in a situation where it seems only common sense to see English as the most suitable medium. There is no doubt that the quality of their writing in English was improved by these discussions. Of course an awful lot of what the children were planning and learning was independent of any particular language. When looking at details of plot and action, the order in which details are revealed, the inclusion of elements of surprise and humour, when to use dialogue and when to use narrative, how to arrange a text as paragraphs and chapters and no doubt countless other elements of a piece it really does not matter in what language one works. An awful lot of what the National Curriculum calls 'English' can clearly be developed without speaking English at all. These children are developing *language* (a word which would make a better title for the National Curriculum for English) and so, although it may appear paradoxical, to discourage their use of their mother tongue would hinder their development of skills which are essential to the development of English.[5]

Writing Together

As well as the conventional form of collaborative writing, involving two (or more) children working closely together as they compose, another form of collaboration, *parallel writing*, developed spontaneously within the class. This involved groups of two to four children working on the same story-line without necessarily using the same words. While the conventional collaborators were composing their pieces together line by line, parallel writers produced texts which consisted of a sequence of similar episodes expressed in sets of words which differed from each other to a greater or lesser extent. The collaborators were talking constantly, while parallel writers wrote silently for fairly long periods, before meeting again to discuss and plan their next episode. Collaborators' work had the 'who can tell what might happen next?' quality of make-believe play, while the parallel writers' work appeared rather more planned and measured. Interestingly, a great proportion of the parallel texts produced in the class were retellings of familiar stories, maybe because the familiarity of the plot made it easier for the writers to agree on the shape of sizeable stretches of plot, maybe because it meant a lesser burden on the memory or maybe because the security of a preordained narrative leaves writers freer to concentrate on other aspects of composition. Interestingly, this kind of writing was more common among the girls in the class, while the boys, when working collaboratively, seemed to prefer to remain immersed in the action of their stories the whole time, often producing narratives very reminiscent of make-believe play.

I have tried to convey the impression of a busy classroom in which children were writing with energy, with pleasure and with a real sense of purpose. Bachani's story (Figure 7.1) shows the kind of vigour and fluency young writers are capable of when they are in command of their subject and not inhibited by a compulsion to get everything right first time. The pace of this piece and the tension created by the reader's not knowing exactly how badly injured the parents are far outweigh any possible difficulties of comprehension which might be caused by non-standard forms of language.

I did, however, feel that there was one respect in which the children's writing urgently needed development. At this point the children were working purposefully and energetically on first drafts and although they were willing to accept editorial correction of them, they were not at all interested in changing them in any other way. Many of the children's drafts showed great promise but lacked detail and elaboration and were often difficult to understand fully because of gaps and inconsistencies. Most of the pieces were much briefer than I would have expected from children of that age. I needed to find a way of getting children to revisit their work which would let them improve it without losing the freshness and originality which make up the author's unique voice.

I usually approach the question of redrafting through individual conferences. By showing an interest in what the author has to say and a desire to have as clear a grasp of the facts of a piece as possible, I find that I can usually bring children fairly quickly to the point where they choose to make small additions to, deletions from or transpositions in their work. Behaviour learned in conferences soon begins to manifest itself in children's solo writing. For example, the frequency of crossing out increases while the use of rubbers declines as authors cease to be ashamed of what they once perceived as errors

MY DADS car wasexcident 25/1/93
One day when my dad wasbuying
some fruits when he was going home
One man came speed with
his car and smashed mydads
car, my dad wasabit of injured and
my mum was injured. Then my
dad came home he didnt tell
any one in the house. In the
school one of mine my friend
told me that your car is
is been exccident. I was fr
frigten when I went home
I told my grandmother that
what had happen. She could
not believeme so when my
dad come from his work my
dad told them what had
happed. than my dad told

nothing to worry about none
is injured. then he told the
car will be soon here.

Figure 7.1 Bachani's story.

and now begin to see as part of the process of getting things right. Children who have reached this stage in their writing development have learned to use writing to help them reach new understandings. They are still learning to write, and – for as long as they continue to write – always will be, but they are now also writing to learn.

The Rights of an Author?

The children of Class 6M were not always interested in my concerned questions. In the middle of a draft they would generally be willing to discuss what they were writing about, but would repeatedly refuse to take any hints about making changes, and even when frustration reduced the subtlety of my suggestions they simply refused to amend anything they had written. If we were discussing a completed draft the situation was even worse. So far as they were concerned, a finished draft was the end of the story. On the one hand they were proud of (or at least content with) the achievement represented by a substantial body of text, while on the other they gave the impression that any questioning was to be interpreted as (hurtful) criticism. How then was I to bring these children to an attitude of confident self-criticism without offering a model of criticism which, however benignly intended, they viewed as destructive and disheartening? It was with alarm that I realized that all these thoughts were leading to the conclusion that although I had started out with the intention, through their writing, of improving the children's reading, they were not in fact even willing to read what they had written themselves.

Essential to a developmental approach to writing is the creation of a classroom culture which promotes and offers models of language and literacy throughout the school year. From the outset I had conducted individual conferences in which children's intentions were questioned and explored; I had read children's pieces to the class and invited comments and questions; I had written pieces together with small groups and with the whole class; I had written pieces of my own and invited children to question, comment and help me to improve and sometimes complete them; in short I had tried to do everything I could to encourage a view of writing as a craft which involves repeatedly revisiting what has already been written in order to arrive at what the author really means. The children had undoubtedly learned a lot about writing – they had learned about choosing interesting subjects, about using their own experience and about continuing with a theme to its conclusion. On the way their use of the conventions of English had developed too, but over this particular aspect of writing they were just not taking the hint.

If children were unwilling to reflect on their work in collaboration with me in conferences, would it be better to try to develop reflection through collaboration with other children? It was clear to me in conferences that one of the obstacles to success was my position of power within the classroom. Any remark on my part which could be construed as dissatisfaction with a text was perceived as a threat – or at least as disapproval – and I did not seem able to influence the development of a text by any means short of usurping the author's own authority.[6] Criticisms offered by one's peers, on the other hand, are far easier to rebut and the ensuing debate is often what is needed to arrive at a text which is consistent both with itself and with its author's intentions. As I have already noted, however, owing to time constraints these children were not very experienced conference participants and because of this I did not feel that putting children into pairs to receive and respond to each other's work would be likely to succeed. I decided to make the task more accessible by removing the element of threat and by making it more concrete.

I selected two of the class's recently completed drafts and typed each out as a block in the centre of a sheet of paper, leaving wide spaces all around. During the next writing session I gave four pairs of children copies of one of these, asking them to use the space to write any questions they felt would help them understand the text, and to use a line to link these to particular words. I encouraged them to invent as many questions as they could, even if many seemed to be trivial. This turned out not to be so easy as it might sound and most of the pairs managed to formulate only a few questions (Figure 7.2).

The important thing in my view, however, was that they were asking questions at all; that, thanks to the collaborative nature of the activity, they were talking about different parts of the text; that they were, as they read, using the scanning techniques of the writer rather than the beginning-to-end approach of the reader of narrative; and that they were willing do work on a text which they perceived to be complete. When the children felt they had asked as many questions as they could, I asked them to invent their own answers, consistent with the original text. Finally, I asked some of the faster workers, using scissors and glue, to assemble a new text combining the original with their written answers. Figure 7.3 shows one pair's beginning to this final version. They have managed to add an explanation for the mother's absence, 'out shopping', some less useful detail, 'I was washing 10 dishes and 5 cups', and a significant plot element, 'I heard my sister say I am going to

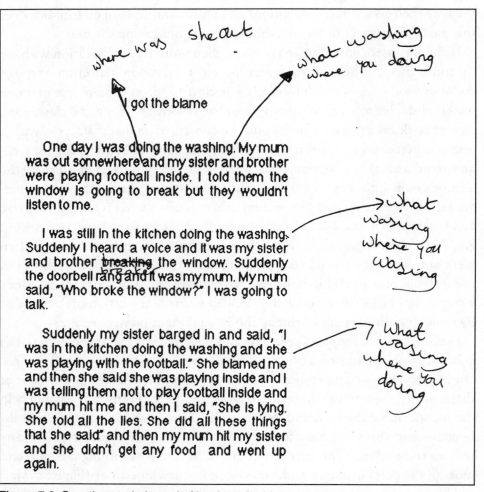

Figure 7.2 Questions to help re-drafting *I got the blame*.

break the window'. There is also some evidence, in the form of words squeezed in and of erasures, that there has been some redrafting in the process of its composition. Heartening as this is, a look at the notes made by the two girls suggests what might have been possible had they had more time.

In addition to the shopping and the crockery, Ruhina offers:

My brother and sister were playing with a hard ball and they were playing roughly.

My sister kicked the ball very hard and it nearly hit my brother but he ducked down and it hit the window and the window broke.

I did not tell my mum that I was washing the dishes because I wanted it to be a surprise.

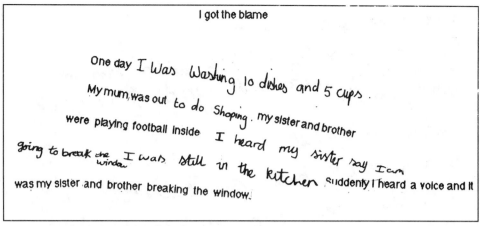

I got the blame

One day I was washing 10 dishes and 5 cups. My mum, was out to do shoping. my sister and brother were playing football inside I heard my sister say I am going to break the window I was still in the kitchen suddenly I heard a voice and it was my sister and brother breaking the window.

Figure 7.3 Making a new story: *I got the blame*.

My sister said that I broke the window, but just then my brother said that my sister broke the window.

These points seem to indicate an attempt to take the story over, making it more interesting by adding details and developing a plot (which in fact still contains an inconsistency to be ironed out – was it an accident or was it planned?) and making the stylistic change from use of brief sentences to the adoption of more elaborate ones.

Jameela's notes (Figure 7.4) offer a further interesting element. At first sight, it appears that Jameela's mastery of English is not as good as her partner's. However, after a closer look, it seemed to me that the non-standard forms of language are due not to any lack of competence but to the fact that she is writing in note form – a conclusion supported by her use of abbreviations in the final sentence (bro[ther], sis[ter], Ash[faheen] and fb [football]). In fact the whole page reads like a (not quite complete) plan for a story – from a child almost certainly in the habit of developing stories line by line, as she writes them.

Small as each of these developments may appear, they are significant in so far as they indicate a shift of attitude away from one which views texts as objects to be created word by word, line by line, completed and forgotten. Instead these writers are beginning to see texts as objects on which they can reflect, objects which can be viewed even before their creation in the guise of ideas and plans and which, in their more fully developed forms, can be questioned and improved upon. If they are beginning to understand these things then writing is becoming a craft for these young authors. Children's performance in the context of exercises such as this does not of course

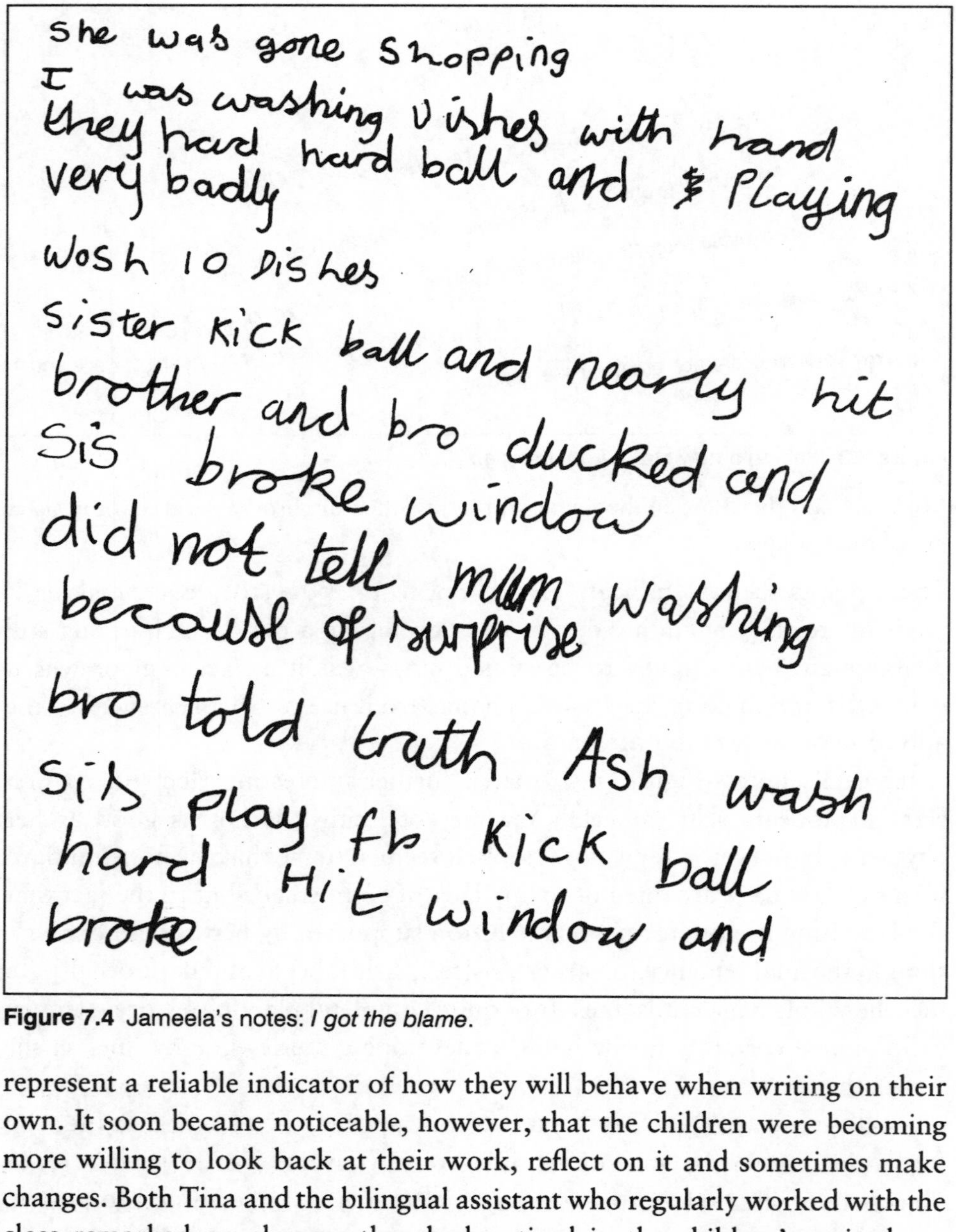

she was gone shopping
I was washing dishes with hand
they had hard ball and $ playing
very badly

wosh 10 Dishes

sister kick ball and nearly hit
brother and bro ducked and
sis broke window
did not tell mum washing
because of surprise

bro told truth Ash wash
sis play fb kick ball
hard Hit window and
broke

Figure 7.4 Jameela's notes: *I got the blame*.

represent a reliable indicator of how they will behave when writing on their own. It soon became noticeable, however, that the children were becoming more willing to look back at their work, reflect on it and sometimes make changes. Both Tina and the bilingual assistant who regularly worked with the class remarked on changes they had noticed in the children's attitude to writing outside the workshop sessions.

By now I felt that enough of the class were convinced of the primacy of the content of their writing and felt able to place greater emphasis on the process of editing. I felt that many of the children were capable of bringing the pieces they were offering for publication to a higher standard of finish but again it

Questions to the author

author *Tahira*

title *The frog prince*

date *2/3/93*

Questions

Why didn't the princess see the frog?
Why did the frog go away for about
two or three months?
Why did the frog say to the princess,
Can I marry you?

Because the Frog was behinds her.
Because the Frog went away to think about
the princess.
The Frog said to the princess can I marry
you.? because he liked her very much.

Figure 7.5 Editor's questions and author's answers: *The Frog Prince*.

seemed that the children were apprehensive about criticism of their own work. For this reason I began this phase of work by allowing the class to edit one of my texts, which I had written on the board. This exercise allowed many to demonstrate a comprehensive knowledge of useful forms of punctuation and other conventions, so the following week I set up the 'editors' table'. Each week one group of four children was relieved of the responsibility of their own writing and asked to sit at the editor's table. On this were copies of texts submitted for publication, typed out (double spaced) exactly as they had been written, editions of various dictionaries, pencils and rough paper. The editors were asked to work in pairs and they mostly worked quickly and efficiently, with the only instances of reluctance arising where children would have preferred to spend more time on their own work.

The Pumking ~~thet~~ *that* grow bigger .

One day there lived a girl called ~~s~~hamila. ~~s~~he planted some seed at here mums garden.   And then she went to bed.   *In* ~~At~~ the morning ~~s~~hamila ~~wok~~ *woke* up and went out to see the seed's that she growed.   *The* ~~and~~ it was small she took them out but exspeter for one.   She ~~had~~ fogot and went to bed. *In* ~~At~~ the moning ~~s~~hamila woke up and went out she saw a big pumking.   She *pulled* ~~pulling~~ it but she couldn't.   She called her mum and she helped her to pull but they couldn't do it. *So* ~~so~~ ~~s~~hamila called her dad they pulled and pulled but they couldn't pull it out they called the dog. *T*he dog pulled and pulled but it couldn't take it out. *T*hen they called a little ant. *T*he ant pulled and suddenly the pumking fell over. , Shamila fell over, her mum, her *dad* ~~mum~~ fell over, her *dog* ~~dad~~ and *the ant* ~~her dad~~ fell over, ~~her little sister and the dog and the dog fell over the ant and~~ *It* was dead every one said you help~~p~~ed as a lot and he is dead *know* ~~now~~ and they bried him, ~~the~~ *They* eat the pumking.

the end

Ashfaheen

Figure 7.6 Amendments to a typescript: *The Pumking That Grow Bigger.*

In some cases omissions and unconventional use of punctuation, spelling, word order and so on meant that a text could not be understood without reference to the author. Because I wanted the editors to do the editing, rather than simply throw the job back at the authors, I put on the editors' table a pile of question sheets. These were simply blank sheets, headed 'Questions to the author', on which the editors were asked to note any problems they had in understanding a piece. The author could then answer all the questions together, in writing, and the editor would be able to make the final changes necessary. The kinds of questions the editors came up with did not really fit into this pattern, however. For example, Figure 7.5 shows a (typical) set of

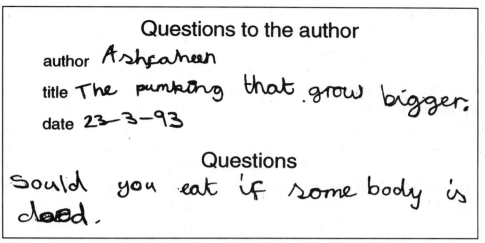

Figure 7.7 An editor's very personal response: *The Pumking That Grow Bigger.*

questions and answers arising from Tahira's version of *The Frog Prince*. These questions do not seek clarification but ask the author to explain and extend the text. Not only has Tahira answered them on the sheet, but she also went on to incorporate this new information in her story. Of all the question sheets completed by the editors, not one included a question of the type I was anticipating (What do you mean by ... ? Who said that? How could that happen?). Moreover, it was clear from the amendments being made to the typescripts (see Figure 7.6) that the children were able to give attention to surface features whilst at the same time engaging with the texts at the level of meaning. Occasionally a reader would get carried away by involvement with a story and allow a personal view to intrude, as in the response to a version of *The Enormous Turnip* shown in Figure 7.7.

Back to Reading: Making Messages Explicit

I began to feel that at last the children were beginning, in their writing, not simply to work at the level of meaning, but to see meaning as the most important level at which to operate. And if that was true of the texts they were writing, then surely they would automatically see that it was also true of the texts they chose to read. This, however, proved not to be the case.

Even at this point, towards the end of the spring term, many of the children, including, again, some of the most fluent (in terms of both English language and literacy), were still willing to perform the trick of reading a text aloud while, as questioning revealed very plainly, having little understanding of its meaning. Since this had been the starting point of the project it is possible to say that we had made no progress at all. I think this would be less than fair, however. Some of the less confident children had made considerable progress in both reading and writing. Early gains in confidence were reflected in a developing competence. Some became keen writers when they had been very reluctant indeed. Across the class the children had become much more skilled as readers of their own writing and of each other's writing. Why then was there still this problem with commercially published texts? I should like to offer two strands of explanation, one related to the particular reading activity and one arising from the way in which we taught.

In reading aloud, the children were able to demonstrate competence in a range of reading skills and knowledge. They could decode words using knowledge of letter/sound correspondences; they recognized a large number of words, even if they did not know what all of them meant; they had a grasp of grammatical structures so good that they were able to assign correct intonation to strings of words they did not fully understand. All this must give them a good deal of satisfaction. Their difficulties of comprehension arose when the text contained unfamiliar vocabulary items, cultural references and the use of metaphor. These last two are of particular relevance to more fluent readers, who tend, because of the level of their decoding skills, to choose texts which are longer and more sophisticated but which are, at the same time, much more likely to contain expressions which are figurative and less direct. This group of children, at least, will have benefited from the classroom publishing programme if only because it meant that in the classroom there were at least *some* fully accessible texts which met their need for more complex stories about subjects which interested them.

The second strand concerns the link between reading and writing. Although the decision to try to develop children's reading through their writing appeared to be a way of exploiting this link, we had failed to alert the children to its existence. As a class teacher I always found numerous opportunities to make (often spontaneous) connections between on the one hand the children's own personal reading, and the stories and poems I read aloud to them, and on the other their own writing and the writing process in general. Because of the way in which we had divided our activities it was much more difficult for Tina and me to make this connection. In fact, far from showing children the intimate relationship between reading and writing, we had in fact seemed to demonstrate that they were two separate fields of activity.

If we had been able to continue the project we would certainly have had to find ways of establishing the reading–writing connection more firmly in the conscious minds of the children. As it was, it does seem that the work we did substantially influenced the way in which the children wrote, and in particular affected the ways in which they read as they wrote.

Although the full impact of the project may not be seen until later, the opportunity to work with these children – to watch their use of two languages, to witness the power of what they had to say – convinced me even more of the importance of observing the patterns of language use. These children drew on their considerable language resources to make sense of all the new ideas presented to them. By watching this happen, and trying to respond to their own language repertoires, I am convinced that we made the right decisions, and – we hope – laid the foundations for the task of extending their new reading skills in ways which would enable them to tackle less familiar texts.

Notes and References

1. Graves, D. (1983) *Writing: Teachers and Children at Work*. Portsmouth, New Hampshire: Heinemann Educational Books.

2. It is worth pointing out here that writers who are inconsistent in their use of verb tenses are usually manifesting a failure to exercise such reading strategies. They are unlikely, therefore, to benefit from an explanation of the tense system, which they probably mastered some time previously – in one of their available languages.

3. In a homogeneous linguistic community such as Gladstone School, few non-standard forms can be written off as 'mere errors'. The fact that most children in the class will say 'that's mine's', for example, cannot be dismissed; it is a part of everyday dialect.

4. Even in cases where children's writing appears to be very 'non-standard', careful analysis can often reveal the use of more standard rules and items than non-standard ones.

5. In fact, the picture is probably more complex than this as I observed discussions held in both English and Punjabi, with each language being used to a greater or lesser extent by particular individuals, in particular contexts, and for particular purposes.

6. It has been suggested to me that in certain cultures, traditional respect for the written word may also be a factor inhibiting children's willingness to change or 'deface' a text in the course of redrafting.

Part Three
Text and Intertext

Critical literacy is a central thread in this book. All the classroom work described here reverberates with the sense that getting to grips with literacy is critically important and that developing a critical approach to literacy is equally important. This is because literacy is to do with power – but not just the power of the individual in relation to some view of literacy held 'out there', important though this is. It is not just the case, either, that those who are literate have more power over those who are not but that those who have power to *define what counts as literacy* hold the greatest power. Literacy, then, can be exclusive as well as inclusive. Frank Smith points to the importance of 'joining the literacy club'[1] and indeed this *is* important for every child, but who writes the rules for the club? And what if they change? Margaret Meek, ever a 'shifter' of educational perspectives, challenges any complacency about stating that 'literacy is a matter of human rights' without taking such platitudes further.[2] She continues: 'have we also asked ourselves about the ways in which reading and writing can be used against people? Differences in literacy are not only the results of social differences. Literacy also helps to perpetuate them.'[2] This is because texts, the ways they are made and the ways they are given value or status, are part of wider cultural practices. As the quotation from Ursula Le Guin in the introduction warns, book-held knowledge inevitably becomes someone's property, needing gate-keeping to make sure that only those who have the right, or permission of the holders of knowledge, can gain access to what is seen as valuable (p. 4). When children move from the home into the school they pass through the gateway of a 'literacy interface' where the literacy practices of home may not meet those of school on equal terms. There is nothing 'natural' in taking on literacy in any culture, as Marilyn Cochran-Smith points out:

Children ... are not born knowing how to connect their knowledge and experience in 'literate' ways to printed and pictorial texts. Rather, they must learn strategies for understanding texts just as they must learn the ways of eating and talking that are appropriate to their cultures or social groups.[3]

This bears out the work done by Shirley Brice Heath, detailing her research into 'ways of taking' texts in different communities.[4] What is clear is that when considering literacy and schooling, nothing should be taken for granted. Much of the work in this part of the book emphasizes that teachers' openness to the experience of texts which children bring to school will allow developing reader-writers to get a stronger grip on the versions of literacy which matter in any particular society.

Mary Waterson's work with Leila is a powerful example of just how important this can be. Coming from a home where literacy is not taken for granted, Leila nevertheless drew on her considerable knowledge of spoken texts to lead her into literacy. Most importantly, as Shirley Brice Heath found, those spoken texts which provide the possibilities for future literacy were often narratives. They may have started from everyday anecdotes, repeated and shaped in the home in pleasurable retellings: 'do you remember when ...?' or 'it's like that time ... ' – the kinds of polished home narratives common across cultures. Equally, they may have grown from more formal storytelling sessions by older members of Leila's extended family. What was certainly true was Leila's capacity to be a spellbinding storymaker.

After lengthy and detailed research into the linguistic structures of children's storying, Carol Fox believes that this kind of storymaking can 'reverse the usual power relations' in children's lives:

This includes areas of experience which are often suppressed in their interactions with adults, in the interests of politeness and learning 'appropriate' forms of address for various addressees and appropriate registers for conducting what are largely the discourses of the adult language and of adults.[5]

She points out that this may well stretch the resources of any language learner. However, that kind of effortful success suggests the robust way that literacy needs to be understood. Harold Rosen quotes Bakhtin's reminder that 'language is not a neutral medium that passes freely and easily into the private property of the speaker's intentions ... expropriating it, forcing it to submit to one's own intentions is a difficult and complicated process'.[6] This makes children's reworking of narratives all the more impressive when they are known to have been wrought by effort and intention. However, even these powerful narratives are set within cultural contexts, moulded by historical shaping. In an earlier consideration of the power of narrative, Harold Rosen points out that 'The composer of a story is not a free agent':

however universal our human bent for narratising experience, we encounter our own society's modes for doing this. There is no one way of telling stories; we learn the story grammars of our society, our culture. Since there are irreconcilable divisions in our society of sex, class, ethnicity, we should expect very diverse but not mutually exclusive ways of telling stories.[7]

Angela Ridley certainly discovered this when she began her investigation into young reader-writers' perceptions of gender images. Their experience, depicted through narrative, revealed the many kinds of texts they drew on. Their knowledge of film, television, advertisements, magazines and conversations at home, as well as books provided in school, contributed to their perceptions of gender. However, to Angela's surprise, they were aware of this intertextual weaving and knew that different texts carried different meanings according to social and educational expectations. In other words, at a very early stage in their schooled literacy experience, they were aware of how the cultures of home and school can contribute to the meaning a reader or writer encounters in any given text. Through some apparent contradictions between what the children said about gender images and what they wrote, Angela Ridley discovered something important about what these children, and no doubt many others, know about cultural reflections in texts. This parallels what Gemma Moss, emphasizing the social construction of texts, points out – that conflicting readings or remakings of texts are to be expected, suggesting a need to reappraise texts:

Positively valuing girls' activity and raising questions about boys' provide new and much more useful approaches to questions about reading (and writing). For it also suggests a different way of thinking about the relationship between pupils and texts, both the texts they read and the texts they produce . . . what matters about texts is not the content alone, but the way that content can be mobilised and used by readers.[8]

Further, she urges different views of 'reading' according to the kinds of texts under scrutiny and according to the different groups of readers. In a study of 10-year-old boys and their reading, Hilary Minns recognizes the diversity of literacy experience and its gendered implications:

It is worth speculating about the areas of literacy encountered by the boys which are likely to be gender-related: certainly computer texts, farming magazines, adventure comics and books, fighting fantasy books, and the sports pages in newspapers come to mind. If I had chosen to work with three girls, would their reading practices have been different?[9]

Angela Ridley's chapter suggests some of the possible differences as well as bringing into sharper focus the ways in which school operates as an institution to perpetuate socially constructed texts and their 'accepted' readings. It raises, too, the ways in which young readers – of all kinds of texts, including the broadcasting media – make valuable connections between their different visual and verbal experiences of reading. Angela Ridley's discoveries about the kinds of texts which the 9-year-olds in her study drew on to explain their views about representations of men and women in narratives of different kinds, their use of film, television, magazine and other forms of literacy, offer a much broader view of the significant texts which make up literacy experience. This raises the notion of 'literacies' rather than just one form of literacy, replicating the diversity mentioned by Harold Rosen and Gemma Moss.

Nick Jones, working on the Language in the National Curriculum Project, assumes this view of 'literacies' when he refers to 'the associative networks of textual memory from which our sense of a culture is woven'.[10] He goes on to point out that although readers of print and television across the world 'share the same stories, the same slogans, the same photographs', they need not 'share the meanings they make of them'.[10] In pointing to the versions of texts which readers carry with them, he adds a further – and necessary – complexity to the matter of just what literacy might mean. Not only should school approaches to reading and writing take into account the cultural shadings of any texts which children read or make, but they must also allow for the culturally developed readings which children bring with them in their lived histories as members of particular families and communities. Meanings are made in specific contexts through the meeting of readers and texts. Readers and writers of texts have particular points of view. Coming from their own directions they may, on meeting, begin a conversation which will be sustained for a while or returned to, like the meetings of established acquaintances; they may be in dispute with each other or even pass each other by. Teachers have a special responsibility to make some of the introductions; this is what classroom literacy is all about. It places texts and the intertextual meanings that readers may bring to them into a specific environment – the context of a cultural institution for education which is itself a continually shifting construct. Readers, texts and institutions change and so should ways of helping children get hold of the kinds of literacies which are given high prestige.

Valuable Texts

The National Curriculum takes little account of the shifts concerning cultural literacies outlined above. In assessing reading, writing, speaking and listening, there is a clear and unequivocal requirement for children to be able to deal with a canon of texts which are seen to be of most value. This is not the place to rehearse the implications of such a view.[11] Teachers in schools of all kinds have had to get on with it. This is a tall order, especially if the young people involved lack confidence or experience in their practice of school forms of reading and writing. Peter Fifield's account of working on *Romeo and Juliet* with a class in a special school in north London provides an insight into the intertextual weaving of oral, media and 'canonized' texts which released potential in a group for whom the achievement of full literacy in school terms remains elusive. The literacies of everyday news coverage as well as the spoken texts of home and the playground provided a basis which allowed entry into text territory which is often carefully protected as the domain of only the most literate in school traditions. Michael Rosen refers to this historical process of deciding which texts are considered more or less valuable in a culture as a 'conversation between academics'. Over the years it has been used as an authority to determine the 'greatness' of any piece of text and so influence decisions about which texts are worthy of detailed school study.[12]

This returns to the earlier point about who defines what counts as useful or valuable literacy. Peter Fifield's class broke through the barrier separating children who have literacy difficulties from satisfying texts. This class demonstrated what so many classroom teachers know – that an exciting narrative which has meaning for a group of readers will stimulate them into greater efforts to make those meanings their own. Imaginative approaches which draw on other familiar texts are often the entry point to previously forbidden-by-difficulty terrain. Further to this, acknowledgement of the conceptual maturity of young people whose literacy has been hampered leads to possibilities for future learning. The television and film experience which Peter Fifield's class drew on is a reservoir of 'spontaneous concepts'.[13] Vygotsky suggests that children come to school with everyday concepts 'saturated with experience', whereas school introduces 'scientific concepts' – the systematized knowledge of the school curriculum which is learned through conscious attention. Everyday and school-learned concepts are related through 'complex inner ties': 'The formal discipline of scientific concepts gradually transforms the structure of the child's spontaneous concepts and helps organize them into a system.'[14] This 'system' includes developing generalizations of experience as a basis for comparison with other or later experience. This, then, leads to further conceptual development. There was ample evidence from these otherwise inexperienced reader-writers that the chance to tackle a complex Shakespearian text can lead to significant extension of knowledge – about narrative construction, about the process of reading and writing and about fictional and real characters. And the development of understanding need not just be on the part of the pupils!

The teacher, then, becomes the provider and reflector of a range of literacy experiences which can use children's active intertextual interpretations to gain value from new readings. What is important, though, is not so much the provision of these experiences, nor even allowing texts to enter the gaps of school experience, but the commitment to young learners' attainment. This is where the critical element of literacy cuts most sharply. If certain texts are considered to have greater value than others and if these are used to test the capabilities of developing reader-writers, then it is essential to find ways of getting the texts and the readers together in a context of challenge and support. To lose these opportunities has serious consequences for those who might already be vulnerable to the power of the definers of valuable literacy. As Peter Fifield argues, if certain texts are used as the basis for assessing achievement, then access to them is a critical matter, especially, perhaps, for those groups of children for whom literacy is hard won.

Reaching Out

The final chapter in this part of the book weaves all the threads of intertextuality together. Sarah Theaker's work with nursery rhymes summarizes the range of aspects of powerful literacy reflected by the other contributors to this book: that texts are socially and culturally constructed; that linguistic experience out of the classroom feeds the development of literacy; that forms of text are historically shaped as features of a particular culture; that oral texts inform readings and making of other texts; that developing readers should learn to tackle a range of texts with confidence drawn from experience of different ways of reading. Starting with an urge to 'make time for rhyme', Sarah Theaker's study extended into discoveries about the oral culture and literary tradition of the school community. The researches her class began ended by stretching far beyond the classroom into the playground, into the homes and community, into the nearby infant school and back over centuries of the oral transmission of cultural symbols. The texts ranged from the spoken, sung and rhythmic to encyclopaedias and reference books, well-loved anthologies and new ones, picture books and television. The discoveries led beyond the curriculum boundaries of English to geography, history, science, ecology, maths, etc.

However, by using nursery rhymes which are so deeply embedded in historical and cultural experience – and very much children's own subversive and private territory – Sarah Theaker did not fall into the trap of cultural colonization. Cathy Pompe warns against this all-too-easy pitfall:

And so another attempt to find sensitive and empowering ways of tackling the contemporary cultural environment of which children have so much latent knowledge *could* turn into something that is driving children's real feelings and opinions further underground and out of reach.[15]

Sarah Theaker set out with the intention of respecting the privacy of children's own cultural texts while offering opportunities for them to bring these into the classroom if they wished. Certainly, though, she gave scope for the exciting personal texts to mingle with the taking on of more school-based kinds of reading and writing. This awareness of the importance of spaces for learning meant that the children involved were able to reach out over those spaces and grasp new meanings for themselves. In Marian Whitehead's words, Sarah Theaker ensured that school literacy practices could be 'acquired in ways which further empower children and leave them free to exercise their literacy in life-enhancing ways'.[16]

In rounding off this collection of descriptions of classroom practice, the final voice we hear is Natalie's – subversive, pragmatic and unafraid, using the known and practised forms of parodied verse to express a serious political issue. It is difficult to tell how serious it is for her, but what is clear is that her capacity to juggle the texts of her own cultural experience makes her a sturdy representative of the voices of all the children in this book who have rewarded their teachers' greater expectations for their developing literacy in so many diverse ways.

Notes and References

1. Smith, F. (1984) *Essays into Literacy*, p. 12. London: Heinemann Educational.

2. Meek, M. (1992) Literacy: redescribing reading. In K. Kimberley, M. Meek and J. Miller (eds) *New Readings: Contributions to an Understanding of Literacy*, pp. 224–6. London: A&C Black.

3. Cochran-Smith, M. (1986) Reading to children: a model for understanding texts. In B. Scheiffelin *et al.* (eds) *The Acquisition of Literacy*. Cambridge: Cambridge University Press.

4. Brice Heath, S. (1983) *Ways with Words*. Cambridge: Cambridge University Press.

5. Fox, C. (1992) 'You sing so merry those tunes.' Oral storytelling as a window on young children's language learning. In K. Kimberley, M. Meek and J. Miller (eds) *New Readings: Contributions to an Understanding of Literacy*, p. 14. London: A&C Black.

6. Rosen, H. (1992) The politics of writing. In K. Kimberley, M. Meek and J. Miller (eds) *New Readings: Contributions to an Understanding of Literacy*, p. 128. London: A&C Black.

7. Rosen, H. (1984) *Stories and Meanings*. Sheffield: National Association for the Teaching of English Papers in Education.

8. Moss, G. (1992) Rewriting reading. In K. Kimberley, M. Meek and J. Miller (eds) *New Readings: Contributions to an Understanding of Literacy*, p. 187. London: A&C Black.

9. Minns, H. (1993) Three ten-year-old boys and their reading. In M. Barrs and S. Pidgeon (eds) *Reading the Difference: Gender and Reading in the Primary School*, p. 71. London: Centre for Language in Primary Education.

10. Jones, N. (1990) Reader, writer, text. In R. Carter (ed.) *Knowledge about Language and the Curriculum: the LINC Reader*, p. 165. London: Hodder and Stoughton.

11. For an invigorating argument about 'the canon', see Styles, M. (1994) *The Prose and the Passion*, pp. 36–54. London: Cassell.

12. Rosen, M. (1992) Poetry in all its voices. In M. Styles, E. Bearne and V. Watson (eds) *After Alice: Explorations into Children's Literature*, pp. 155–9. London: Cassell.

13. Vygotsky, L. (1962) *Thought and Language* (translated by E. Hanfmann and G. Vakar), p. 109. Cambridge, Mass. Massachusetts Institute of Technology.

14. Vygotsky, L. (1962) *Thought and Language* (translated by E. Hanfmann and G. Vakar), p. 117. Cambridge, Mass.: Massachusetts Institute of Technology.

15. Pompe, C. (1992) When the aliens wanted water. In M. Styles, E. Bearne and V. Watson (eds) *After Alice: Explorations into Children's Literature*. London: Cassell.

16. Whitehead, M. (1993) Born again phonics and the nursery rhyme revival. *English in Education* 27 (3), 49.

Chapter 8

'Why Are We Doing This?'
One Child Coming to Literacy

Mary Waterson

This case study gives a detailed insight into the coming to literacy of a powerful storymaker from a home with a strong oral culture. The evidence was collected by audio tape, the tape recorder being left running whenever possible. Leila herself, or the other children Mary Waterson worked with, made the decisions about whether to let it run or not. As it turned out, the tape recorder became such a significant part of the group's joint experiences that its presence was for the most part ignored. Mary collected and dated the children's written work as back-up to the tape-recorded evidence. Throughout the longer study of which this is a part, Leila emerged as an engaging storyteller. When she had been in school for about a year, she held two children, slightly younger than herself, riveted by her told story – she was 'making out', in her own words. By the time she was at the top end of junior school she kept two classes listening for 30 minutes!

What comes across most strongly from extracts from Leila's journey into literacy is her assertive hold on meaning as a way of learning to deal with the symbolic language of reading and writing. Her home stories were told to her – not read. She acted as a role model for her peers, influencing the perform-ance of the children who worked alongside her. All of the evidence in Mary Waterson's account of Leila's early moves towards literacy confutes anyone who suggests that stories from books are the sole route to literacy. Leila shows that the cadences and structures of her home oral culture produce their own 'literary' style, one which feeds strongly into Leila's introduction to schooled literacy.

Children vary considerably in the strategies they evolve for themselves when approaching literacy – strategies which are inevitably influenced by their own views of life and their teachers'. The interaction of those views with their own home environment and that of the school and local community are drawn on as they develop their own philosophy of learning. In the account which follows, I hope to provide some evidence of one child's strategies and also of the tremendous power of memory, persistence and concentration developed by Leila, who at 6 years 3 months had very little experience of school.

The language competence demonstrated by this child and others like her, given their experience of school – often brief, fragmentary or still to come – points to such competence being potentially inherent in all new-to-schoolers, a competence which may not show up in the classroom, its strengths being neither realized nor capitalized on. Why had Leila had so few days in school before she was six-and-a-quarter? It was because she is a Traveller. And while following Leila's 'effortful success',[1] let us be mindful that Traveller children are often the subjects of negative stereotyping, being described as children with low powers of concentration.

My coming to know Leila really began at her second infants' school, where I would be supporting children with their reading. There were six children new to the school on the day Leila and I started. Luckily her class teacher suggested my working with all six new entrants: it helped to integrate both Leila and me into her class. As well as initiating the children into activities usual for newcomers, I made time for extra stories: some I chose, some they chose. One of the first I offered was *Where the Wild Things Are* by Maurice Sendak. At the first mention of Max's mother, Leila wanted to know: 'Where is his mum?' and added, 'I think she's got black hair'. When, a few days later, the same children were discussing with me how a writer made a story, it was Leila who knew what the storyteller did: 'He "makes out",' she said. During the same month, listening to *Green Eggs and Ham* by Dr Seuss, when Sam's persuasive campaign had been in operation for some time, she interjected, 'He ought to try it!' *Rosie's Walk* by Pat Hutchins had her musing aloud:

We haven't seen her owner – he might have gone shopping or he might be inside having a cup of tea, or his dinner – or . . . it might be a magic house and he . . . [tailing off].

From the outset, Leila showed a robust readiness to interact with text, wanting to find a story in whatever she met.

In Leila's class the newcomers' first encounter with school reading was learning to recognize their own first names from their personal drawer labels, and from the flashcards provided for tracing and later copying. Next came the matching of ten red flashcards with enlarged captioned illustrations from the reading scheme, on permanent display above the carpet area. The custom was for the children to become proficient in recognizing the red cards, and then transfer to the white ones relating to the same book (and of course to others) before tackling the introductory book from the scheme. Most children took to the system happily and proceeded rung by rung up the book ladder.

Ten days into Leila's first term when she was working at matching the red cards with words on the wall she asked, 'Why are we doing this?' The following day she dictated her version of 'Roses are red' and after writing it twice I cut one copy into mini-flashcards. At that time she did not see how to go about matching the words to those on the original copy. She said then, 'I wish I could read.'

My diary that week contains 'Flashcards yes – but no spin-off for reading.' At the class teacher's suggestion I worked with Leila at her flashcard assignments.

The first day of October, five months from the time she became a regular schoolgoer, I handed her *Mary and the Wild Cat* by Chessex to 'read'. We were by ourselves in the staffroom. She began. 'One day the little girl see some houses', paused for seven seconds, and then said, 'Oh, I don't know how to read it.' But on my saying 'Well, you make your own mind up,' she said 'All right' and began again.

Leila made her own 'reading', led by the illustrations, concluding, 'But she growed up to a fine young girl and she got married to a Chinese fellow. She lived happily ever after.' I read the story to her immediately afterwards. She gave voice 37 times as I read the printed story: the first 3 times she commented on illustrations; there were 7 mms, giggles, or oh/ahs; and the other 27 were comments questioning, predicting, confirming or evaluating.

In her 'reading' Leila thought the fox/cat had taken off Mary's shoes and was going to eat her up. Later, as she listened to the part of the story where they 'curled up together and went to sleep', she said: 'I thought he was going to eat her up.'

'Yes I know you did,' I said, 'looks a bit like it in the picture doesn't it?'

'Mm. There's her shoes.'

'She must have kicked them off do you think?'

'Yeah.'

Much further into the book, when the cat is inveigling Mary into going for yet another walk in the woods, Mary says she would love to but ... Leila interjected, anticipating Mary's reasons for saying no: 'What about her mummy and daddy?'

It was nine months before we picked up *Mary and the Wild Cat* again.

Tackling the Mechanics of Text

When Leila was approaching word-corresponding reading of Book 1 of the scheme the school used, she retained her will to 'find a story' in the book; she 'read' that the characters were 'hiding' and that the boy 'can mend his own bike' – both ideas distinctly more interesting than the print on the pages before her! It was then she first noticed that there were three rabbits pictured on one double-page spread. She had started at this school at the end of the previous April. It was 15 October, after four and a half months of regular schooling, when I found she was actually reading the text of the scheme book. It was two weeks after her first meeting with *Mary and the Wild Cat* and she took on the producers of the reading scheme as authoritatively as she had Chessex over his 'failure' to explain in line with her own interpretation. As she again examined the illustrations on the double spread she read:

I can see three r r rabbits. I can see two rabbits. But they was wrong wasn't they?

I agreed with her because I knew what was coming:

because there was two – there was two there – he shouldn't 'a' written two there.

Again I agreed.

No 'cause 'cause there was two there, one there, and there's three.

I concurred.

Must be a silly person who writ it. Cause they've got two there and anybody'd think Well – really you'd think to yourself – if you want to look at that page – just looking at that – you'd think 'that's two' wouldn't ya.

I mmed in response and she concluded:

Some silly person writ on there.

At the end of the following January, Leila was reading Blue Book 1 and by 5 February Blue 4. This taped reading gives a very different aspect of Leila from that shown by her comments above – a halting, word-by-word, delivery almost all through the book.

Leila's read text	Book text
Mother, Mother	Mother, Mother
We can go in a car	We can go in a car
We can have a ride.	We can have a ride.
Do you want to go/come?	Do you want to come?
w-wid wid come/go to the zoo?	We can go to the [illustration of zoo]
You like the animals.	You like the [illustration of zoo]

These scheme books substitute thumbnail illustrations for one, two or three words on each printed page. Leila improved on the word flow by going against the intention of the material. She self-corrects 'go' to 'come' and 'come' to 'go', semantically interchangeable items, and although she has, mistakenly, predicted that 'with' is likely to follow 'come', this is a prediction based on meaning reinforced by graphophonic information. She is using several cueing systems to tackle this text, but there is none of the verve of her chosen reading.

Memories of Story

Six months later, shortly before term ended, I read *Mary and the Wild Cat* again, this time with Leila and two other children – Jan and Chloe. The three girls all made quiet sounds of amusement at the idea of Mary raising a large family with the cat, and, when he was caught in the cage, Leila said softly, 'Poor cat.' It was nine months since she had heard the story; as I came to the last word of 'he loves the woods as much as she does', Leila threw in:

I know, that's the cat 'cause he had green eyes.

This was a significant moment, because the text has not yet told about the young man's green eyes. Leila's memory had stretched back nine months.

Every story we read evoked questions, predictions and evaluations, revealing a storytaker who both articulated and endeavoured to solve the enigmas that lay within the stories she heard. During the last week of term Leila elected to 'read' *Mary and the Wild Cat* to Jan and another child, unfamiliar with the story. It was exactly three weeks since I had read it with her, Jan and Chloe. Leila began:

Once upon a time, there was Mary. She went to school, she was a good little girl. And one day she decided to have a day off, course she went into these woods and used to eat nuts at springtime.

Leila had not yet ordered the seasons in her memory but the relevant text reads:

She feasted on wild strawberries and nuts in season . . .

She went on:

and that winter she used to hear the birds sing.

I wish there were space to give you all Leila's text. Occasionally, when she substituted one character for another in conversational exchanges, Jan quietly interposed, making Leila conscious of her slip, which she corrected as she continued her reading.

Compare the prosody of the child telling a story with that of the same child reading from a book in a scheme. Even if it is felt useful or, in many schools, perhaps thought essential for children to work through a scheme, even then their reading could be tuned in to sense if more teachers read these early reading books to the children first, before asking the child to read. This practice can build a child's confidence as well as providing important intonational patterns – a difficult thing to achieve with so little text to go on.

If aural experience is important to a child's 'coming to read', so is visual patterning. Leila drew very strongly both on what she had *heard* of stories read and told to her and on the visual elements of pictorial text in the books she enjoyed. She tried strenuously to use these strategies with any book she encountered and, like many other children, drew on aural, visual and contextual cues to help her tackle unfamiliar text. These contributors to the development of reading, as well as Leila's love of story, can be traced also in the development as a writer.

When I'm by myself I can do it.

It was 29 April when Leila started her new school. On 13 May, at her dictation, I wrote about her two ducks: she illustrated this and added her own caption (Figure 8.1). There is no doubt about her visual awareness. Eight weeks later she produced two drawings of Snow White after listening to the story. She dictated what she wanted to be written beneath her first picture after captioning that and her second picture herself.

Figure 8.1 Leila's illustrations for 'Two Ducks'.

In these very early stages Leila was showing what she knew about text layout. At the same time she was vigorously experimenting with her own writing. She produced pages of letter strings during her first year at school and often I read to her what she had written. Gradually, from these strings, sequences emerged. It was 4 May when she wrote:

nok
nekc bwis
lowecehiyinv
howevieR

in that order.

It had seemed a long while before she could write her own first name. After six weeks in school she was still writing the last letter of her name at the beginning, lower case 'a' followed by capital 'L' and lower case 'eil'. She did write her first name before the end of her first term but was still practising her family name the following September, five months after beginning school, although on 16 September Leila said: 'When I'm by myself I can do it.'

We were still practising it at the beginning of October, and on 19 November she was within an ace of writing her family name; it has eight letters. That day, at the first attempt she omitted the third and sixth letters and the rest was there, letter order correct, the 'e' written facing left. At the second attempt it was all there but the third letter had been added after she had written the others so that it hung in the air between the second and fourth letters. The third attempt had all letters in the correct order, the 'l' hanging down and the 'e' about-faced in both cases. A month earlier I had noted in my diary that

Leila was getting correspondence between the word in the 'reading book' and her voiced version, and that she was 'beginning to listen to writing guidance'. Perhaps she had had too much of that? Back in July I had been explaining how letters needed to be written 'just so', so that her teacher could read what she wrote, saying 'she does not know what is in your head like you do'. Because I was often her scribe, Leila's response was, 'You know what it is because you've done it.'

That July, a child whose family was staying alongside Leila's had been very ill with suspected polio. Her illness was still uppermost in Leila's mind when school started again in September. She began her own book; it was about her friend in hospital. The first two pages read:

When I	no-one didn't
was tiny	know me
I was so	and I had
little that	a party and
	I know
	another little
	girl
Page one	Page two

On 15 October, to illustrate her story, she was sticking a cut-out drawing of 'Pluckaduck' (the ill child) on to a background she had drawn of grass and sky, tree and trailer. We had just finished reading *Mr Gumpy's Outing* by John Burningham and had checked the title page to see if John Burningham had been his own illustrator; I started to explain that if anyone else had produced the illustrations, there would have been another name, saying 'there would have been ... ' and Leila completed it for me with: 'some other name'. I had pointed out that she needed good drawings for the book she was making. She said, 'I'll have to put "Mrs Waterson helped me to do it".' I asked if she should add writing to the illustration of Pluckaduck to show who it was. 'Yes,' she said, 'write me name on it.' When I had offered a number of ways of captioning it to show who was depicted, Leila said,

Er, yeah, but what about if I writ me name on it? And then you'll make a cover.

Oh, we've got more to write yet haven't we?

Mm, takes you a long time to write a story.

I agreed.

She worked on her book over a period of two months. She could have called it complete in December but she looked at it one day and then decided to add to it. She wrote another story during that time called 'Three Traveller Girls', a short one, copying her dictated text:

Once upon a time there was three Traveller girls and they ran away from their mother and got married.

And she wrote a letter to her uncle too, to accompany one I had written for her grandmother; she wrote:

Dear . . . [using her uncle's nickname]

We are stopping at the same place where we were before and don't worry about your dog.

Establishing Control

I do not think that Leila had one particular learning strategy when it came to writing. Within the classroom she endeavoured to follow the normal classroom sequence of events that led to becoming an independent writer. She was in school fifteen months before she touched the threshold of independent writing. But parallel with that development went her own experimenting, play-writing, try-writing – Kelly's characterization of a scientist is as one whose 'ultimate aim is to predict and control',[2] and Leila comes into that category. She certainly wanted to predict in relation to the stories written by others and to control the meaning she abstracted from their texts. It seems to me that very gradually she came to predict which letters could follow others, as evidenced through development shown in her letter strings. All the time she was working towards greater control of letter formation. She certainly wished to control the meaning she had within her.

Conclusion

But what can teachers learn from one child's 'coming to literacy'? What questions should we be asking ourselves?

If my evidence from Leila's experience is anything to go by, some of the questions are pretty hard. On several occasions I found myself 'interfering' with her process of thought and so with her progress. With delicate courtesy she never pointed this out to me except obliquely, when she explained that she could write her name better when she was on her own. My other observations of the complex and varied strategies she brought to bear on print – both her own and other people's – suggest very strongly that one question we need to ask is 'what can this child already do with text?' rather than assuming that we have to provide everything. This may be particularly true when we think we are dealing with a child from a home where literacy may be minimal. Deciding when to stand back and when to intervene is a tricky business.

Another question is to do with the quality of text we present to children. It is very clear from Leila's progress that she was prepared to have a good go at any text she met; but how much more vital and involved were her encounters with books which gave her something to bite on. Alongside this question of quality comes the matter of presenting completely unfamiliar texts to children unrehearsed. Just why do we do this?

Vygotsky describes Luria's study carried out in the 1930s of children not then literate.[3] They were told to remember a certain number of phrases that greatly exceeded their expected memory capacity. Some children who produced 'meaningless and undifferentiated squiggles and lines' appeared to make specific reference to the marks when reproducing the phrases: the children seemed to be 'reading' the marks and could repeat phrases, indicating the same marks each time. 'For the first time the marks became mnemotechnic symbols.'[4] Vygotsky and Luria regarded this 'mnemotechnic stage' as the first precursor of future writing. It has equally important implications for the development of reading. Vygotsky was conscious that 'Instead of being founded on the needs of children as they naturally develop and on their own activity, writing is given to them from without, from the teacher's hands.'[5] All this was sixty years ago. Are we still giving too much from our hands?

Certainly, Leila's robust and inventive approach to the demands of schooled literacy suggests that in coming to read and write, it is as well to listen to what children have to say and to be prepared to try to explain 'why we are doing this'.

References

1. Meek, M. (1993) What will literacy be like? Paper given at Homerton College conference, A Critical Time for Literacy, March.

2. Kelly, G.A. (1963) *A Theory of Personality*. New York: Norton.

3. Vygotsky, L. (1978) *Mind in Society; the Development of Higher Psychological Processes* (translation), p. 114. London: Harvard University Press.

4. Vygotsky, L. (1978) *Mind in Society; the Development of Higher Psychological Processes* (translation), p. 115. London: Harvard University Press.

5. Vygotsky, L. (1978) *Mind in Society; the Development of Higher Psychological Processes* (translation), p. 118. London: Harvard University Press.

Chapter 9

'It's Not the Same as the Real World'

Boys, Girls, Books and Gender

Angela Ridley

In this detailed and intriguing study, Angela Ridley discovers just how profoundly children's reading diet in school can influence their writing. However, there were one or two surprises. This part of the book begins by drawing distinctions between children's home and school versions of literacy. The children in the class Angela worked with, and the six individuals whom she studied closely, come from diverse home experiences, some quite troublesome, others more tranquil. Their school is an attractive, welcoming new building in a village-suburb of Cambridge with staff alert to new approaches to literacy. It was to be expected, then, that the children would represent a range of experiences of gender reflections in their home and school 'reading' (including media texts) but the differences went wider than that. Angela began by looking at how the children's writing in a variety of forms might reflect images presented to them about gender. At the same time, as she points out, discussion with the group was 'of fundamental importance'. It was through these opportunities for the 9-year-olds to voice their opinions that she met the unexpected: the children were perfectly aware of the differences between school-based and home reading and writing and its implications; even more clearly, they saw the differences between everyday lived reality and texts of all kinds. In other words, they were perfectly aware of the constructedness of texts. Not only this, but they were able to analyse the gendered images of the popular literacy which they met in their out-of-school experiences. Despite all of this, they continued to write in ways which suggested deeply embedded gender stereotypes. The complexities of this chapter leave many interesting questions to be pursued.

Through working directly with children I wanted to discover how children's reading influences their own writing. My specific interest was gender issues, and the extent to which images portrayed to children in books influenced their own notions of gender.

The investigation involved working with six Year 4 children in a newly built primary school. I had worked for a term with the class before I began this investigation. The particular children were selected simply because I knew they would be willing to share their views and put forward their own ideas. I spent about eight weeks working with the children on this investigation, which certainly clarified some issues, but provided a few surprises!

Over the course of the study the children were involved in a series of written tasks; these included completing questionnaires, making story plans, creating character outlines for stories, and writing stories. The pupils' writing was then used as a means of exploring gender issues. As well as this written work, discussion was also of fundamental importance; through discussion and reflective discussion the children's awareness of gender issues and their particular perspectives and feelings were illuminated. The children knew me, of course, but I tried to project an impartial attitude about gender issues; I did not want to influence the children into adopting particular points of view. I did direct the discussions and raise certain points, but my objectives here were to explore as many avenues as possible.

As the investigation developed, it became apparent that there were significant differences between girls' and boys' writing, with regard to both style and content. I had expected some variance but I was surprised by the extent of the differences.

Girls and Boys Writing: Starting the Investigation

In the first session I gave each of the six children a clean sheet of paper and asked them to write a story of their own choice – a prospect which delighted the girls, but filled the boys with dread. This outcome might be expected according to Joan Swann, who remarked that 'girls tend to enjoy reading and writing activities more than boys'.[1] The girls instantly set to work, conjuring up characters and imaginary worlds, while two of the three boys sat staring at their paper as if waiting for something to appear by magic. Eventually one of them was brave enough to venture the question, 'but what do you want us to write about?' – a simple enough question, but one which was to bear much relevance to, and reveal later, the criteria children consider when writing stories.

When informed that I did not mind what they wrote about, as long as it was of interest to them, the two boys smiled radiantly, their bodies relaxed and they were able to launch into their own narratives. They both chose to write about the world of football, and were careful to make sure that everyone else in the group knew so. It was as if they wanted to masculinize the writing process; they seemed to consider the world of storywriting to be a female realm. Paul kept announcing that he was writing about a football match, as if to say, 'I am a proper boy, I write about *boys'* things.'

Both of their stories were male dominated and full of action. Action was more important than feelings; there was a distinct lack of emotion. This 'male' approach to writing contrasted with the work produced by the girls which, by comparison, was more personal and private, and gave more import to feelings, attitudes and responses. This is illustrated in the following extracts from Paul's and Jill's work. Paul's protagonist is introduced as 'Chris Kiwo-mya ... the man of the match'. He is described in stereotypical masculine terms; he is sporty and a winner, a true hero. Later we are told he is a 'strong lad' and not 'a wingeing moan'. Paul's character portrayal is simplistic and conforms to preconceptions of what 'real' men are supposed to be like. When the boys were asked to elaborate on their characters, the details offered were limited to appearance, e.g. 'Well, he had yellow hair and blue eyes'; feelings were avoided. In contrast to this approach, Jill presents us with a character who has more dimensions to her personality; first we are told that she is a 'nice' lady, and then more details are disclosed with regard to her likes and dislikes. She is much more emotional than the character created by Paul; for example, at the end of Jill's story the heroine is feeling 'over the moon' at the outcome of events, yet we never know how the man in Paul's story feels.

The work that the children produced surprised me. Discussion revealed that the children were very much aware of gender stereotypes and I expected their stories to reflect this. However, there were inconsistencies between what the children felt and what they wrote. Some stereotypical notions were deeply embedded in their work; for instance, in every case the villains were male. When I pointed this out to them the group seemed quite surprised that this had happened; it was as if it had been a subconscious decision.

There was a distinct difference in the writing styles adopted by the girls, compared with that of the boys. This remained so throughout the investigation. The differences were so marked that it is possible to distinguish whether a girl or a boy has written a particular item. The feminine approach was chatty and descriptive, whereas the boys' narratives concentrated on events and action. The girls seemed to give more of themselves to the text. For instance, Jill's character has a similar disposition to her; she is feminine but refuses to wholly accept convention as she embarks on an adventure to solve the problem she is faced with. She is not a helpless, dependent female; she takes the initiative. We are told '*She* decided to go there', and '*She* went back to look for some more clues.' She did not wait for a man to come and help her.

On the whole the boys avoided the inclusion of females in their stories. When asked why, David said 'well I forgot!', while Paul declared, ''cause girls don't like to play football' (this resulted in gasps of horror from the girls!) and Martin remonstrated that his story involved lots of eating and he did not think that girls would want to be seen like that. Andrea's response was probably the most accurate when she proclaimed, 'If a boy had a girl in his story, probably other boys would call him a sissy.'

The girls were quite happy to involve boys. They were less constrained by issues of gender. However, it is interesting to note how the girls often chose to portray the boys unstereotypically. Andrea included a sensitive boy in her story. During the narrative we witness him feeling 'frightened' and 'scared'. He is not a hero, but he is 'lonely'. It is as if Andrea subconsciously realizes that the character she has created would not be well accepted in society because of his femininity.

When questioned on the content of their stories the children all agreed that they had written about something which they would have enjoyed reading about. This fits in with Pam Gilbert's notion that we write what we read.[2] The presence of the children's literature in their writing was very apparent: Martin's story, 'Greedyguts the Gaul', was strongly influenced by his own reading of *Asterix the Gaul*, whereas Susan's work had many of the elements of a fairy tale, and Jill chose to write an animal drama.

My first session with the children was interesting in that it illuminated the fact that boys and girls write in very different ways from one another. But this has been suggested by other researchers, such as Janet White.[3] What intrigued me, as I paid my second visit, was *why* did this happen? What influenced the way they wrote?

A Matter of Gender

The differences I observed were gender based. I decided, therefore, to explore how the children perceived male and female. I gave the children two questionnaires, one about Earth Women and another about Earth Men, and said that the inhabitants of another planet were interested to find out more about Earthlings. I was careful not to indicate to the children what sort of responses I was hoping for from them. The children completed the questionnaires in private, and then the results were shared and discussed. The cumulative answers were revealing. Women were described as pretty, with long hair; their favourite pastimes were shopping, buying clothes and hairbands (!), going out, and hanging around with men, although they spent most of their time working – in supermarkets or schools, or doing domestic tasks. Their main worries were related to their children, their pets, bills or men. Men were described as having short hair and beards, and big hands; their favourite pastimes were estimated to be going to the pub, playing football, and going on holiday; they were said to spend most of their time either down the pub or at work in offices, as salesmen, accountants or football players, and their main worries were caused by women. When asked what the 'visitors from another planet' should bring as a gift for the Earthlings, there was unanimous agreement that women would like flowers and chocolates, whereas the men would be happy with a range of items such as books, a football, or tools.

AR: What do women spend their time doing?
Martin: Mostly shopping.
Susan: They go down town to buy some new clothes.
David: Working.

AR: What sort of jobs do women do?
David: In supermarkets, schools or offices.
Jill: House jobs, cleaners. Everyone thinks women are weak.

AR: Why don't women do all the same jobs as men?
Jill: 'Cos they might get their dresses dirty.
Andrea: The government doesn't help women.
Martin: Women have to look after the house, do the housework.
Jill: They have to get married, and look after the children.

AR: Do you think men should look after children more?
All: Yeah.

AR: Do women have any worries?

Martin: Erm, bills and feeding the cat.
Andrea: Children.
David: They worry about their husbands.

AR: What sort of worries?
Jill: That they'll leave them.
Susan: Because they don't spend much time with their wife and children, they go down the pub.

AR: What do men spend most of their time doing?
Susan: Going down the pub.
Jill: Going boozin'.
Paul: Getting drunk at the pub.
Martin: Playing football and swimming.
David: Watching TV.

AR: Why don't women go down the pub as much?
Susan: 'Cos they have to look after the children at home.
David: 'Cos the men have spent all the money.

AR: Do men have worries?
David: Yeah, bills and women.

AR: What worries do men have about women?
(Long pause)
Martin: Because women irritate men.
Andrea: 'Cos when women are trying to clean the house, the men want to watch something on the television.

The children's notions of masculine and feminine were very strong. Women were placed in domestic settings and portrayed as rather frivolous creatures who could be won over with a box of chocolates and a bunch of flowers. They were also seen as being dependent on men, to whom they were nothing but trouble. In contrast to this, men were portrayed as much more active and outgoing, with many diverse interests.

Having established that children saw men and women as very different from one another, I then endeavoured to discover where these assumptions had originated from. A lengthy discussion ensued. We began by discussing women's appearance:

AR: What do you think every woman wants to look like?
Andrea: Quite tall, long hair.
David: Skinny.
AR: Why do you think they want to look like that?

Jill: Because they want a boyfriend.

This response is reflective of the image presented to girls by the media, particularly through magazines, where looking good in order to get a man is what life is all about. But this sort of literature did not just affect how the girls saw themselves; David commented that if he had a girlfriend and she didn't bother putting make-up on and didn't get dressed up to go out with him, then he would feel that she didn't really care about him.

It became apparent that the children were receiving very strong messages from what they read. Through their reading they absorbed images which were internalized and became an integral part of their own writing.

It emerged clearly that children were reading more than just the written word. Indeed, Margaret Meek perceives that 'There are many different forms of modern literacy.'[4] She points out that television, for instance, is but a metaphorical extension of literacy, a 'secondary literacy'. Literacy is in constant evolution. In modern times children are confronted by 'new technologies of literacy'. Quoting Paolo Freire, she points out that 'they must learn to read the world'.[5]

Reading the World

As the investigation evolved it became apparent that it was of fundamental importance to explore the 'world of reading' in order to appreciate the influence of various forms of reading on the children's own writing. We began by considering comics – a medium in which illustrations and text are juxtaposed, with the result that messages are reinforced. The girls tended to read comics which were about animals; either real ones, such as horses, or cute imaginary creatures, like My Little Pony. The boys, on the other hand, opted for sport journals, or comics such as the *Turtles* or *He Man*, which are action packed and full of heroes and violence. This fits in with observations made by Sarland, who additionally claimed that girls also bought comics which focused on romance, where girls are the passive victims of circumstance.[6] Boys are encouraged to enjoy activity, while the message for girls is to accept passivity.

Comics are very clearly targeted at boys or girls. They are a 'gender package';[7] girls and boys are given very definite roles. It is interesting how the children's own writing is so reflective of the genres they read. The question is, do the comics reflect the gender roles that young children take on for themselves or are children conditioned into adopting these roles because of the images they are subjected to in their comics? Living as we do in a society which encourages conformity, it is perhaps natural that the children would want to create characters in their own writing which fitted in with everything they had met with previously.

However, comics alone cannot account for children's perceptions of gender; children are, as Mary Hilton points out, surrounded from birth by 'a "blowing dust" of iconography, texts and messages'.[8] Media images are powerful, and television is a particularly influential medium. This was illustrated when I asked the children where they got the idea from that women like flowers and chocolates. I felt this was an important point to raise in view of the fact that all the girls confessed that these were not gifts they would hope for:

AR: Where have you got this idea from?
Jill: TV.
Andrea: Romantic films.
Susan: Adverts.

Their answers illuminate the extent to which stereotypical notions are continually being offered to them. The impact of the media is so great that even though the girls do not passively accept the ideology of 'romance' they are seduced by it: 'and the forms of resistance possible are restricted'.[9] As Pam Gilbert regretfully points out, romance makes 'female subordination bearable: it fills a vacuum created by social conditions'.[9]

The children went on to illustrate further their understanding of the media's promotion of stereotypical representations of male and female as the discussion about television developed. They explained to me that most of the leading characters in the programmes they watched were male; Andrea protested, 'the girls get all the boring parts'. David did point out that there was a female leading character in *Maid Marian*, but it is interesting to note that this is a comedy and so the idea of a woman being in charge is treated lightly anyway. Most of the cartoons the children watched involved male characters performing heroic deeds or taking part in violent action and having adventures; genres which are reflected in the boys' own writing.

It was revealed that even the adverts treated girls and boys differently. The group had astutely perceived how the advertisement of products for girls was done through what Andrea described as a 'soppy' approach: fades and dissolves were used, and soft music formed a background to the narration. In contrast to this, adverts for boys were noted to be full of action with 'lots of noise', and the characters were more aggressive. The adverts directed at boys were considered to be generally more exciting and dynamic. It is extraordinary and surprising that children can have such high consciousness of what is going on, yet their writing still reflects gender stereotypes.

The children displayed a sensitive awareness of gender issues. They illustrated that they were conscious of the fact that the advertising media were trying to influence the way in which they perceived things. They also realized that society in general expected them to behave in certain ways. For example, Jill complained that her mother wanted her to wear dresses all the time because she was a girl, when she was more comfortable in jeans. Yet for all their perspicaciousness they failed to consider that the books they read may also be responsible for influencing the way they think.

The Effect of All This Reading

Texts impose lasting impressions on readers, and exert a powerful influence both on the way they live out their own lives and in the production of their own texts. Gemma Moss believes 'Identity, reading and writing are all somehow intimately connected.'[10] Writing is close to reading; indeed, Bruner states that 'the two are part of the same system of signification'.[11] Consequently, children 'reproduce values they have imbibed from their reading, in their writing'.[12]

This was reflected in the next piece of work that the children were involved in. I asked them to produce an extended piece of writing. This time they were given a direction for their writing. The story was to be about life in a particular street; Malvern Road was chosen by the children to be the name of the street. As a focus the children had to construct their story around house number 79, which was unoccupied.

The group were excited at the prospect of being given time to develop a story. They liked the idea of being able to write about life in a particular street; it was a genre they were all familiar with: 'It'll be sort of like "Neighbours", or "Coronation Street".'

This story was intended to be a space in which the children would have an opportunity to explore their own understandings of society. As Margaret Meek points out, literacy is 'useful ... for helping us to understand what we understand'.[13] My hope was that if the children were given a familiar setting to write about they would produce work which, in the light of recent discussions, would contain realistic male and female characters.

Each of the children began by making notes on how the street actually looked, what the characters who lived there were like, and what their relationships were to one another. They were asked to visualize the whole scene. This was to help them clarify in their own minds just what they were dealing with, and the direction in which they wished to take their narratives. It was interesting that it also brought about responses such as 'Can we act this out?' and 'Can we video this and make it like on the TV?' This underlines the fact that a definite relationship exists between television and children's own writing; as children 'read' what they see on television, so they transfer it into their own writing. The influence of television was apparent in the first pieces of work that the children produced and was evident again in their Malvern Road stories: the first story that Paul wrote was reflective of the sports programmes which he enjoys watching on television, with phrases such as 'the man of the match' and the classic 'rounding off' of a sports report with 'Ipswich still haven't lost at Portman Road this season.' In the Malvern Road stories there was a recurring theme of treasure in abandoned houses, a popular motif of children's television programmes. In Martin's story the villain's mask is peeled off at the end to reveal the criminal's true identity; this is a regular feature of the popular cartoon *Scooby Doo*. There was also much coming and going in several of the stories; in Martin's story the 'ding dong' of the doorbell appears three times. This is in keeping with many of the soap operas that the children watch, such as *Neighbours*, where people are in and out of each other's houses all the time.

Some Common Features of the Children's Writing

The stories which the children produced were interesting, but also rather alarming. Although each child chose a different setting, wrote about different events, and portrayed different characters, their stories all had several common features. The children continued to be confined by accepted norms and did not feel able to challenge them.

In every case it was boys who led the action. Jill did start off with a female protagonist, but as soon as the boy entered the narration he became the dominant character. This was detected later by David who pointed out 'Mark has all the ideas, not the girl', to which Jill replied, 'The girl's supposed to have the main part.' Jill's story does begin by focusing on the girl's situation, but the male character soon takes control. He gets the girl to come outside with him, shows her a supposedly haunted house, and tells her, 'I want you to go in there with me.'

It is true that the female character does question his demands – she enquires, 'Why can't you go in yourself?' – but ultimately she accepts and follows his instructions. Later she is seen looking to him for guidance as she enquires 'Shall we go in?'; she waits for direction from him. Jill's writing reflects her resistance to, as well as her internalization of, the cultural images of female stereotypes present in books.

Similarly, in Susan's story it is a boy who takes control. The children, two girls and one boy, arrive at the funfair on Malvern Road, but they are uncertain what to go on first. The male character takes the initiative by declaring, 'Let's play a game', and he goes on to instruct them: 'I'll leave clues on the stalls. See if you can find me.' The girls accede to this. They then follow David around the fair and have 'a real good day'.

The third girl in the group presents a heroic male character who saves everyone; when panic hits Malvern Road he steps forward, saying, 'Stay calm and quiet and you'll be okay.' Then he bravely barges through a crowd and faces danger. It seemed ironic that Andrea chose to have a male hero in her own story, considering that she felt strongly about male bias in other stories she had read. When questioned about her choice of leading character she admitted that she had opted for a male character rather than a female one because 'you can do more with boys' and felt that 'it wouldn't seem right' to portray a girl in such a role. The boys in the group also chose male characters as the leading personalities in their stories, an outcome which was expected on the basis of previous work done. However, the male characters were even more dynamic and active than those produced by the girls. They were the epitome of what is perceived to be male – competitive, active and sporty.

It is said that children's writing provides them with a wonderful medium through which they can explore ideas and feelings. However, it would seem that this does not extend to notions about gender. The boys were unable to explore other possible roles for their male characters; previous impressions were obviously too overbearing. In addition to this, the males remained the violent characters; for instance, in Jill's story we are told how 'Mark grabbed a stick and went to hit the man.' Furthermore, they did not overcome the notion that it is men who are the villains.

The children, it would seem, have very definite ideas about male and female roles within stories. This is reflected further in Martin's work. As a result of discussion about the absence of female characters in his last piece of work, he attempted to involve one in this piece of writing. The best he could do was to involve a 'tomboy' called Georgina. She is not remotely 'feminine'; indeed, she is described as a 'clumsy clot'. The story opens with her chastising Dick for getting in her way, and then the two of them go over to Julian, 'tripping over each other's feet' on the way. She is very much a 'boy', and being such she is able to move the action along as boys do. Georgina is very much the type of female character that is portrayed by one of Martin's own favourite authors, Enid Blyton. Again, the influence of other reading is evident, but I shall discuss this later.

I felt somewhat despondent and dismayed, frustrated even; I knew the children were aware of gender issues, and I had encouraged them to create realistic, unstereotypical characters in their writing. Indeed, in the planning stage of the work the characters they sketched were comparatively well balanced compared with those which finally emerged in their writing.

Time for Some Non-sexist Literature

I decided to present the children directly with some 'non-sexist' literature. The selection of texts I chose included *Princess Smartypants* by Babette Cole, *The Paper Bag Princess* by Robert Munsch and *Benjamin and Tulip* by Rosemary Wells.[14]

Princess Smartypants is an anti-heroine who challenges the stereotypical female role. She is a 'modern'-minded young Ms, who rides around on a motorbike. She does not want to get married, but would rather 'do exactly as she pleased'. Various suitors try to win her over throughout the course of the story but she outwits them all. Even the most successful of them is thwarted in the end as the Princess kisses him and turns him into 'a gigantic warty toad!'.

In *The Paper Bag Princess* we are offered an alternative fairy tale; the princess rescues the prince who has been carried off by a dragon. When she finally outwits the dragon she looks rather worse for wear and the prince complains: 'Elizabeth, you are a mess. You smell like ashes, your hair is all tangled, and you are wearing a dirty old paper bag. Come back when you are dressed like a real princess.' To this the princess replies: 'Roland ... your clothes are really pretty and your hair is very neat. You look like a real prince, but you are a toad.' And 'They didn't get married after all.'

The children found the stories very amusing but regarded them as 'one offs'. They did not take the female characters seriously, although the girls did declare that they made a 'nice change' to the usual 'wimpy princesses in stories'.

There is some doubt about whether literature which is anti-sexist and pro-feminist is more useful than that which raises gender issues. But there can be no doubt that 'Literature that tackles issues of sexism needs careful preparation, handling and a willing investment of time.'[15] I feel that generally there is a need for more realistic portrayals of females in everyday life. Female qualities need to be valued and given status; it is not just a matter of giving females opportunities to enter 'male domains'. Pam Gilbert suggests:

The future must lie in the creation of new texts from old – in deliberate encouragement of alternative stories for women, by women, of the experience of being women; and it must also lie in the encouragement of critical, resistant reading practices which open closed gendered texts and display their ideology.[16]

There is a problem, too, in the fact that most popular children's fiction writers are men; 'girls learn about what girls are like, about their appearance and personality and behaviour and sexuality, through men's eyes'.[17]

Similarly, male characters would benefit from a more enlightened image, which accepts the fact that boys do not spend all their time having adventures and performing heroic deeds, but that sometimes they do feel sad, or frightened or lonely, and that is acceptable.

Too many children's stories focus on the male experience. Careful analysis of children's books by Glenys Lobban and Rosemary Stones showed up preoccupations with the male presence at the expense of girls and women. Bruner observes: 'texts produced for girls and young women serve the needs of a patriarchal society very well'.[11] There is a need for a more balanced representation of male and female characters. Even the language used in many books is male orientated. Hilary Minns comments that 'Only recently have we become aware that conventional English usage, including the generic use of masculine genderwords, often obscures the actions, the contributions, and sometimes the very presence of women.'[18] Minns worries that sexism is so deeply embedded in our language and literature, and has been left largely unchallenged for so long, that it is frequently invisible to pupils if they are not explicitly encouraged to read critically. It is important that children are made aware because it is partly through spoken and written language and through encounters with linguistic images that children learn how they are expected to behave.

An Emotional Matter

Throughout the investigation it became increasingly apparent that what the children had read exerted a strong influence on the writing they produced. The boys in the group seemed to feel that it was inappropriate to be emotional in the way they wrote, just as boys in stories do not show emotion. The children did their best to replicate in their writing the structures they knew. Indeed, they appeared to have reproduced in their writing the values they had imbibed from their reading.[12]

The 'softer' element was visible in the work produced by the girls, through their more sensitive approach. They felt at ease with feelings and were able to create more emotional narratives. This is apparent when comparing the level of emotion in Andrea's work and Paul's. A potentially emotional moment in Paul's story is when Keith manages to score a goal. The occasion is marked by the crowd shouting 'What a goal!' Paul does not choose to expand upon how Keith feels at his triumph, what it means to him. He does not even share his own pleasure as a spectator with the reader. This differs greatly from the style adopted by Andrea. Even though Andrea's story has a boy as its central character, it is still full of emotion. She builds up the boy's character and likewise our sympathy for him as she reveals that he is helpful and caring, but lonely, and has 'got no friends' in Malvern Road. Consequently we can feel his despair at being ignored as he tries to warn people away from the haunted house. The reader cannot help but feel sorry for him as he dejectedly laments 'As always no one listened to me.' Later we are able to experience his joy when someone finally takes notice of him, and we share in his exultation as he proclaims, 'She actually listened to me.'

Story or the Real World?

The investigation illuminated many differences between girls' and boys' writing. However, it would be naive to imagine that the literature the children had encountered was solely responsible for shaping their writing. The work produced by the children resounded with many influences; television was particularly predominant. The children demonstrated an acute awareness of the projection of stereotypical images by television and other media, and to varying degrees resisted these images. But they were less likely to challenge or even notice the stereotypical characters and notions presented in their literature. It was somewhat alarming that the children seemed to just absorb and accept the written word.

The children regarded the world of stories and the real world as two very separate entities. This was clearly demonstrated during the final session with the group. On this occasion we began by recapping the observations made over the previous weeks. This involved a detailed discussion of the portrayals of boys and girls with which they were regularly confronted. There was no doubt that the children were absolutely clear about what they were being presented with by society in general, including images related through the stories they read.

Bearing all this in mind, the children were given their final written task. It involved sketching a storyline and shaping a main character. I waited patiently for them to complete the task, sure in the knowledge that they were going to produce something very different from previous work. I anticipated sensitive portrayals of balanced male and female characters. I pondered on the sort of storylines they would produce where both males and females were valued and awarded equal significance.

Imagine my disbelief and dismay at the work handed to me. I was confronted by 'boisterous', 'adventurous', 'handsome', 'tough', 'strong' boys, who were having adventures in castles and rescuing damsels in distress, and by 'pretty', 'friendly', 'weepy', 'nice', 'dopey', 'sulky', 'giggly' girls who were being rescued and falling in love!

There was some attempt at resistance by a couple of the children: Andrea's heroine actually defends a boy who is caught in a fight, and Martin's rescues a boy from a swamp, even though she is totally confused by what is going on.

In general, the children had chosen to adhere to accepted forms and content of writing despite their enlightened discussions. When they were challenged about this, the reply was simple:

Jill: Well, 'cos that's what happens in stories.
Martin: It's not the same as the real world.

Despite Martin's comment, the ironic truth of the situation was that although the children did not regard what they read as real, their reading undoubtedly had a very profound effect on how they saw the 'real' world, and influenced their own writing. It seems bizarre that the children are willing to accept stereotypes in their literature when they openly reject them elsewhere. Two distinct systems seem to be in operation for children of this age: texts and reality. The relationship between children's reading and writing and the real world is perplexing.

A process of 'language socialization' appears to have taken place in the children's writing; it follows socially established rules, as in the books they read. Indeed, the children seemed to think that was how stories had to be, as otherwise adults would not find them acceptable. Jill declared, 'You've got to do it like that for the teachers and grown-ups to read.' They try to reproduce in their writing what they believe will satisfy our expectations. Children give us stories which are akin to those that we give to them.

It would seem that children do not actually write what they believe, only what they believe to be socially acceptable. Surely this must be discouraged; we must encourage children to take their own stances, and to write in their own voice. Teachers need to show children that they do not have to accept what is offered to them in their literature. However, reflecting on my own work with the children I cannot help but wonder if it is possible for the classroom to become a 'site of challenge'.

It is difficult for schools alone to overcome values imposed on children by society. However, much has been claimed for literature. Margaret Meek points out that 'From the stories we hear as children we inherit the ways in which we talk about how we feel, the values we hold to be important, and what we regard as the truth.'[19] It would therefore seem feasible that if schools provide a range of sources and resources which reflect positive images of both sexes, then gender bias and stereotyping can at least be challenged, if not eliminated from children's own writing.

The findings of this investigation illustrate how important it is for children to experience a range of texts, rather than constantly being allowed to make limiting 'gender appropriate' reading choices. The role of the school is an important one; teachers can take children beyond the limited choices they may make if left to their own devices, by offering a diverse range of texts, which cover a range of genres and topics.

The National Curriculum document for English does express concern about the narrowness of girls' and boys' choices in reading and writing. It stipulates:

Just as pupils need to be able to use spoken language effectively in different contexts, so they need to be able to cope with a variety of texts and to write in different ways for a variety of purposes and audiences in order to be considered 'effective' communicators in the written word.[20]

It also stresses the importance of 'breadth' and 'balance'. However, although the non-statutory guidance confidently asserts, 'breadth will be achieved by covering all that is identified within the attainment targets and the programmes of study', little guidance is actually given that refers specifically to gender.

Schools will need to make sure that children are presented with balanced images in the literature that they encounter in order that they can have a balanced outlook. It is therefore important that teachers should select reading material which counteracts gender imbalances: books which present non-stereotypical images; books which show females, as well as males, in a positive light. Furthermore, 'English teachers need to draw on a balance of literature written by male and female writers'.[15] They should encourage pupils to review the books they encounter, and their own writing, in terms of their reliance on gender stereotypes. As Mary Hilton urges, 'consciousness formation' must become part of literacy.[8]

Teachers also need to be more aware themselves of gender issues. The implementation of non-sexist language policies in schools would be beneficial. Even the discussions arising from the conception of these policies may be conducive to heightening awareness; for instance, one teacher discussing her criteria for selecting a class reader confessed, 'the girls will read anything so I always choose a book that will interest the boys'.[21]

Recent investigations by HMI revealed that few teachers monitored differences in girls' and boys' reading experience although they were aware that the boys had different tastes in reading compared with the girls. Indeed, 'It was assumed by teachers ... that boys would have different attitudes towards reading and that girls would, in general, do more reading than boys, particularly of fiction.'[22] It was also noted that 'There were few examples of schools, or even individual teachers, taking a coordinated approach to monitoring these differences in attitude and experience, and no examples of programmes designed specifically to improve boys' attitudes towards and involvement in reading.'[22]

To conclude, it would seem fair to say, from the evidence of this investigation, that what children read has a considerable influence on their writing. In terms of gender, at the present time many of the influences are negative, leaving children with stereotypical notions about gender. The way forward would seem to be towards more careful selection of reading material, so that the influence of children's reading on their writing can be a positive one.

Notes and References

1. Swann J. (1992) *Girls, Boys and Language*, p. 114. Oxford: Blackwell.

2. Gilbert, P. (1988) Stoning the romance: girls as reluctant readers and writers. *Curriculum Perspectives* 8 (2), 14.

3. White, J. (1991) On literacy and gender. In R. Carter (ed.) *Knowledge about Language and the Curriculum*. London: Hodder and Stoughton.

4. Meek, M. (1991) *On Being Literate*, p. 58. London: The Bodley Head.

5. Meek, M. (1991) *On Being Literate*, p. 210. London: The Bodley Head.

6. Sarland, C. (1991) *Young People Reading: Culture and Response*. Milton Keynes: Open University Press.

7. Minns, H. (1991) *Language, Literacy and Gender*, p. 17. London: Hodder and Stoughton.

8. Hilton, M. (1994) The blowing dust. In M. Styles, E. Bearne and V. Watson (eds) *The Prose and the Passion*, p. 18. London: Cassell.

9. Gilbert, P. (1988) Stoning the romance: girls as reluctant readers and writers. *Curriculum Perspectives* 8 (2), 16.

10. Moss, G. (1989) *Un-popular Fictions*, p. 56. London: Virago.

11. Bruner, J. (1987) Research currents: life as narrative. *Social Research* 54, 13.

12. Swann, J. (1992) *Girls, Boys and Language*, p. 15. Oxford: Blackwell.

13. Meek, M. (1991) *On Being Literate*, p. 43. Oxford: Blackwell.

14. Such 'non-sexist' literature is problematic and has its limitations. In attempting to portray females as independent and assertive, it can fall into the trap of simply 'dressing girls as boys'.

15. ILEA (1986) *The English Curriculum: Gender*, p. 38. The English Centre.

16. Gilbert, P. (1988) Stoning the romance: girls as reluctant readers and writers. *Curriculum Perspectives* 8 (2), 14.

17. Minns, H. (1986) In ILEA, *The English Curriculum: Gender*, p. 11. The English Centre.

18. Minns, H. (1986) In ILEA, *The English Curriculum: Gender*, p. 27. The English Centre.

19. Meek, M. (1991) *On Being Literate*, p. 103. London: The Bodley Head.

20. Department of Education and Science and the Welsh Office (1990) *English in the National Curriculum*. London: HMSO.

21. ILEA (1986) *The English Curriculum*, p. 11. The English Centre.

22. HMI (1993) *Boys and English 1988–1991*, p. 4. OFSTED.

Chapter 10

Love at First Sight?

Children Who Have Special Educational Needs Working on *Romeo and Juliet*

Peter Fifield

The bottom line in any debate about literacy is the question of how to help those children who find fluency in reading and writing a problem. What strategies, classroom approaches and theories of language development will provide supportive ways for them to make progress? A common educational truism is that it is important to start where the child is and then to move on. Trite though this may seem to be, it is worth considering just what that can mean to a teacher faced with the responsibility of providing access to as full a curriculum as possible for young people who are still grappling with some quite basic elements of literacy. In Peter Fifield's case it meant starting with his awareness of the pupils' oral abilities and knowledge of narratives drawn from their everyday television and film experience. It meant an assumption that their difficulties with reading and writing did not mean a lack of intellectual scope. Most importantly, it meant an open acknowledgement of their right to enjoy what began, after all, as mass entertainment. The fact that Shakespeare's plays are now part of the literature curriculum which is considered accessible only by older, more competent readers was no barrier to this teacher and this class. The account of the pupils' success and enjoyment in reading and writing about a text which had significance for their own lives is a moving witness to the importance of not accepting an exclusive view of literacy.

... less able pupils were too often asked to follow up what reading they had completed by trivial tasks.

pupils of low ability (and sometimes even average pupils) continued to be subjected to shallow and poorly written teenage fiction which did little to help them acquire any literary appreciation. . . [1]

I want to start by challenging several of the assumptions implicit in the most recent OFSTED Report (from which these quotations are taken). I teach in a Special School for pupils with medical, emotional, behavioural and associated learning difficulties. The children I work with are often described as 'less able' or of 'low ability' and so are in danger of being excluded from the full curriculum which is offered in mainstream schools. There are two reservations I should like to advance about this:

1. It is too easy to assume that lack of fluency in reading and writing indicates a general lack of intellectual capability.

2. The term 'poorly written teenage fiction' suggests a scale of literary value which deserves further thought: just what kinds of experiences are likely to help young people learn how to become readers in the widest sense?

Having said that, I certainly agree with the writers of this report that even if young learners are struggling to improve their literacy, they deserve opportunities to show what they can do beyond 'trivial tasks'. The National Curriculum has demanded that all teachers examine carefully what is being learned in their classrooms. Teachers like me, involved in Special Needs, are particularly conscious of providing a full and balanced curriculum for all pupils. This includes having access to the kinds of literary experiences that their peers in mainstream schools enjoy. What follows is a description of how I introduced Shakespeare to a Year 8 class by studying *Romeo and Juliet*. It was a learning experience for us all!

I knew this particular class very well. They had a variety of special needs ranging from cerebral palsy and hearing impairments to complex emotional and behavioural difficulties. Most of the pupils were lively and eager learners but only 3 out of 12 were confident writers and most were reluctant readers. Generally, however, they were able to express their ideas and opinions orally with confidence. I was aware that in the following year these pupils would be expected to participate in statutory tests and so one reason for studying this play was in preparation for this experience.

I decided to devote half of the spring term to a project on *Romeo and Juliet*. Although the class had not met anything as different as the language of Shakespeare in school before, I was confident that they would respond to the challenge. We were used to sharing and enjoying narratives together. We had read as a class many complex texts, including *Tom's Midnight Garden* by Philippa Pearce, with its intricate narrative structure, *Buddy* by Nigel Hinton, which tackles serious moral and emotional issues, and Tony Robinson's version of *The Odyssey*, which, although retold in a muscular and amusing way, still has the blood and guts of classical myth and the complexities of relationships between gods and humans. From these experiences of reading and talking about a wide range of serious issues, I knew that the plot of *Romeo and Juliet* would interest the class, but I was concerned before I started that there might be difficulties regarding the language of the text.

Taking Risks

I was trained as a history teacher and was just beginning to extend my own teaching into the area of English. This was my first experience of introducing Shakespeare in the classroom. The pupils had not read Shakespeare in school before, so we were trying things out for the first time together. However, I put my faith in the genius of the Bard and we began! I found that the first advantage that any teacher has when introducing Shakespeare is that it is likely that the class will all have heard of him. This is where we started. I found that all the pupils knew that he was a famous man who had written plays. Some could give me titles of plays written by Shakespeare and two of the pupils had watched the video with Mel Gibson as Hamlet. I found that a second advantage was the fact that Shakespeare has status in the pupils' minds; they felt it very grown up and serious to study *Romeo and Juliet*. A third advantage was that most of the pupils knew that the play was about falling in love and personal relationships. When they found that the central characters were about their age, then they became even more intrigued.

I decided that if my class was to gain as much as possible from the play, I had to build bridges between the text and the pupils' own experience. I knew that I had to begin with the familiar and to use their strengths as starting points. I planned to start by getting the class to talk about the play. I would tell them the story first and then gradually introduce the written text. On the way I would include visual texts in the form of the 'Animated Tales', both the television cartoon and the book versions.[2]

We first thought about a hot day in a hot city where temperatures and tempers were rising. I introduced them to the Capulets and Montagues as two families in conflict. We discussed families and family loyalties and talked about how fights start. We thought about how a quarrel could divide two families and be so important that it lasts for generations; a disagreement that so deeply divided the families that they were prepared to fight and die. The pupils were interested in the whole area of conflict, being familiar with such issues through their television and film watching, the comics they liked to read and their own everyday experience. In the play we are not given any reason why the feud began and so I asked the pupils to use their knowledge of people and life to think of a likely explanation. They all knew that it was possible to have family arguments and rows with the neighbours. Having discussed these issues, they wrote about some of the reasons they had discussed to account for the conflict between the Capulets and Montagues:[3]

A murder something stolen the house burent down by one of the families. (David)

Someone could steal something valuable and the other family want it back but the family resist and refuse to give it back and so starting a great big argument, which lasts a long time going on generation after generation. (Kate)

The child would steal an ornament and the family would find out and it would start into a big argument. (Dino)

These were all plausible explanations. The idea that something had been stolen and not given back was a common reason that the pupils gave as a likely cause of the feud and may reflect personal experiences of rows between friends and siblings. We went on to discuss how it only needs a small incident to set off a major argument and make everyone fall out. This again was a familiar experience and everyone knew someone who could lose their temper easily over a small thing. The pupils particularly enjoyed the thumb-biting incident at the beginning of the play. We talked about how gestures and manner of speaking can cause trouble. The Prince's intervention after the fight was again a familiar incident within a school or home context, with teacher or parent giving out dire warnings and threats to anyone caught misbehaving.

Making a Response

After following the story using the *Animated Tales* text and the linked video, I used the abbreviated text and the full text versions to have fun with quotable quotes. We discussed what quotations were and decided to have a quotable quotes notice board. The pupils chose quotations to write into speech bubbles and then stick them on to the board. There was one particularly enjoyable session with the pupils trying to say the quotations to each other seriously! The Language Advisory Support Teacher found a Turkish version of *Romeo and Juliet* to help Fatima participate; she is a Turkish speaker with little experience of reading and writing English, and the whole class enjoyed looking at versions of the quotable quotes in both languages.

We continued with the narrative. At the stage where Romeo was exiled after killing Tybalt, none of the pupils knew what was going to happen next in the play. They all believed that the story would have a happy ending. Their home experience of narrative – of fairy tales or stories from television or film – meant that they expected that Romeo would triumph and be able to ride back over the horizon on a white steed to rescue his Juliet. At this stage we watched a film version of the play which is full of action and very accessible. To my surprise the language did not put them off and they were able to follow the plot successfully. But because of their expectations drawn from romantic texts with happy endings, the tragic resolution to the story was a shock to them all.

Although it was clear that they had enjoyed the play, I was unsure about just how much of the complexity of the narrative they had understood. So in true teacherly fashion, I asked them to write about the ending of the play. As most were reluctant writers, the following extracts show that their responses were extremely impressive. They use an economy of words to achieve succinct and poignant summaries:

Romeo died because he drank all of the poison that he bought from an Apothecary. He drunk the poison because he thought that Juliet was dead, then Juliet woke up and found Romeo dead, she finds the empty poisoin bottle and kisses Romeo's lips but Romeo's lips are warm. Then she took Romeo's dagger and kills herself. The reason they thought that Juliet was dead was because she drank a potion that made her sleep for forty two hours so the family thought she was dead and she did not have to marry Paris and she could leave with Romeo. (Lewis)

Romeo thinks Juliet is dead so he buys some poison he goes to her tomb and sees her asleep but he thinks shes dead so he drinks the poison and dies then she wakes up and sees Romeo dead and stabs herself. (David)

Romeo drank some poison because he thought Juliet was dead in the Capulet tomb. Then Juliet saw Romeo was dead so she stabbed herself with a dagger. (Martin)

Keeping in mind the pupils' experience of 'everyday' texts, we talked about how the events of the play would have been reported in the news. I asked them to select a particular incident, one they thought would be newsworthy, and to

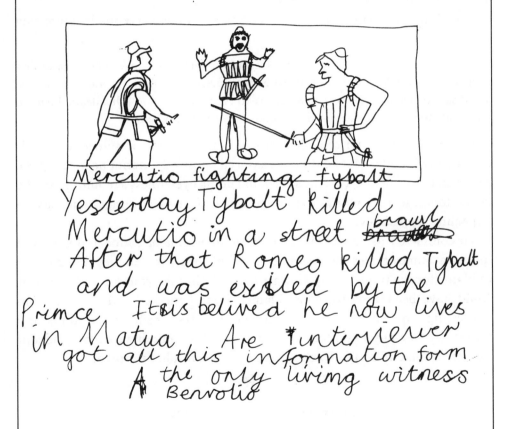

Figure 10.1 Ricky's news story: Dateline Verona, 9 December 1300.

write a newspaper article about it. The class had not done any writing based on newspapers before, so their responses were drawn entirely from their own experience of television and newspaper reportage. I gave each of them a blank sheet with 'Verona Times' at the top. Ricky put a headline 'Mercutio and Tybalt killed', and then wrote (Figure 10.1):

Yesterday Tybalt killed Mercutio in a street brawl. After that Romeo killed Tybalt and was exiled by the Prince. It is believed he now lives in Mantua. Our interviewer got all this information from the only living witness Benvolio. (Ricky)

This was an impressive achievement for Ricky. It shows that he has a good understanding not only of the text but also of the style of reporting that is expected in newspapers. His layout and the inclusion of the date 9 December 1300 show an eye for detail in visual text.

Colin's newspaper report 'Romeo and Juliet Tragedy' is equally interesting (Figure 10.2):

Last night two teenagers killed themselves and it was all for love. They met at first sight in the Capulet's Party when the Montagues gatecrashed. 'It was love at first sight' said Benvolio as he saw it. We spoke to Nurse who found Juliet dead. 'I had no idea that Romeo saw Juliet on the balcony' said Nurse. (Colin)

It is clear from his writing that this is not the work of someone who is confidently literate, yet Colin shows assured knowledge about how things are reported in the media. This interview, including eyewitness accounts from the characters, includes many familiar features of news coverage, and has an appealing immediacy.

To complete this project we focused on questions of blame and guilt and looked at some of the main characters. I asked the class who they thought was to blame for the tragedy and whether they felt that the young couple's deaths could have been avoided. Most blamed Friar Laurence and the nurse, an interesting way of reflecting the comparative responsibility of adults and teenagers. One pupil pointed out that the deaths could have been avoided if the servant had not told Romeo that he had seen Juliet's funeral.

Enjoying Literary Appreciation

I do not want to pretend that overnight this class became avid Shakespeare scholars, nor that those who found reading and writing difficult were immediately transformed into happy and fluent readers and writers. What I do

VERONA TIMES

1350 AD

ROMEO AND JULIET TRAGEDY

Last night a h two teenagers killed themselves and it was all for love they fit met in the capulets pub when the motagues satcraed. "It was love at firt sisth" said behrollo as he saw it. we spoke to NURSE who found JULIET Dies " I had on ese bear that Romeo saw Juliet on the Balcony" said NURse

Figure 10.1 Colin's news story: Dateline Verona 1350 AD.

want to stress is that it is all too easy to undervalue the ability of children with special needs. Rex Gibson makes the point aptly when he asserts the importance of Shakespeare to 'British social and cultural history', pointing out that 'every pupil is entitled to knowledge and understanding of his plays'.[4] He goes on to explain that Shakespeare is

a necessary part of the furniture of the mind of future citizens. His plays are regarded as a storehouse of value and values in British cultural life. Pupils are entitled to access to that storehouse, to enable them to make their own judgements of worth and commitment. To deny pupils that access is to condemn them, without choice, to a vacuum of disinheritance.[4]

I began this chapter by pointing out my own commitment to equal opportunities for pupils to gain access to the more 'prestigious' texts included in the school curriculum. That is one very good reason for having tackled Shakespeare with my class. However, the aim was not just a kind of curricular tokenism. I wanted the pupils to enjoy the play and to make connections between their existing knowledge of texts and this different kind of literary experience. I knew that they had experience of reading the visual and pictorial texts of comics and television. They also read newspapers and some (often brief) novels, but I wanted them to extend their confidence by recognizing that what they already knew could feed into what they saw as 'serious' literature. I wanted to see if I could widen their reading repertoire.

The most recent OFSTED report criticizes dull and reductive approaches to literary appreciation.[1] Rex Gibson puts it more forcefully. In attacking restrictive approaches to the plays, he warns against making Shakespeare 'a dull, joyless, arid, narrowly defined comprehension exercise'.[4] This class certainly found enjoyment. But more than this, they found that the dialogue structures of their preferred reading – of books, comics and television – gave them a way into dialogue of a more taxing kind. If I wanted to estimate the 'comprehension' of the play by this class, I need look no further than their reflective writing.

Kate's comments about her favourite characters provided more than the usual 'character sketch' of a traditional classroom approach to Shakespeare:

My favourite characters were Romeo, Juliet and the Prince. Romeo and Juliet because they got on so well in spite of their families continually arguing and battling and the Prince for trying to end the feud between the two families and making them see what they had done when Romeo and Juliet had committed suicide. (Kate)

This is not only a crisp summary of the plot and a justification for choosing particular characters as favourites, but engages with motivation and consequences – the larger matters of imaginative narrative. This grasp of the whole play, plot and characterization, was demonstrated even more forcibly when four months later I took the class to see a production at the Open Air Theatre in Regent's Park. I felt that I should take a 'revision' session beforehand to remind them about the events. This proved unnecessary. They did not need any revision; they knew the storyline and were able to quote parts of the play from memory – further proof of the fact that they had fully internalized what had been an important literary event. Not only that, but they had come to know a different kind of text about people in love – a more complex and less clearly cut set of relationships. Although, as I mentioned earlier, they knew a lot about stories of love and marriage, their experience of romantic texts was limited to more simple forms. By using this knowledge to gain entrance to *Romeo and Juliet* they had come to understand more about texts – and human relationships. Their discussions of the characters in the play stretched to include more subtle interpretations of motive and intention.

Close attention to an unfamiliar text, written in the unfamiliar dialect of Shakespeare's English, led not only to greater familiarity with larger units of text and how they are put together, but also to an awareness of the details of language. The thumb-biting insults, the delicate and amusing love exchanges between the young couple and the high temperature of the fights were carefully examined. Then they were translated into other forms of language – the language of news and analysis. From the pupils' cultural experience of visual texts – cartoons, videos, film and television – alongside their ability to discuss the social texts of spoken language and serious matters of relationships they moved into greater efforts in reading and writing.

They were able to make connections between the cultural experiences of school and their personal lives. One of the most rewarding moments, which demonstrated just how much one boy had taken the play into his own experience, came when he described a playground argument. David came and told me how he had stood between two of his friends who were at loggerheads 'just like Benvolio' and had said to them, 'a plague on both your houses'! I can only think that when literary experience feeds back into the social world of the playground, it really has taken root! The strong links between lived, social experience and the power of Shakespeare are perhaps best seen in the simple and elegant words of one of the pupils as he summarizes the full force of the tragedy. Ricky captures his sense that 'never was a story of such woe' when he writes:

Romeo drank some poison because he thought Juliet was dead and could not bare to live on without her.

This is mature understanding of loss from a child whose own emotions were often turbulent.

I began this chapter with an objection to OFSTED's references to pupils of 'low ability'. The class who read *Romeo and Juliet* may find literacy a slippery thing to hold on to, but they have shown emphatically that not only have they right of access to demanding texts but through their encounters with these texts they can acquire the habits of literary appreciation.

Notes

1. OFSTED (1993) *English Key Stages 1, 2, 3 and 4 Fourth year 1992–3: The Implementation of the Curricular Requirements of the Education Reform Act*, p. 11. London: OFSTED.

2. Garfield, L. (1992) Abridged version, *Shakespeare: The Animated Tales, Romeo and Juliet*, illustrated by Igor Makarov. London: Heinemann Young Books.

3. All the pupils' quotations in this chapter are as they were written; I have not altered the pupils' own spelling and punctuation.

4. Gibson, R. (1993) 'Shakespeare and schools'. In *The Politics of Reading*, a special issue of the *Cambridge Journal of Education* 23(1).

Chapter 11

Rhyme Time
the Naming of Experience

Sarah Theaker

It is easy to adopt slogans about empowerment. As the previous chapter suggested, it is not so easy to ensure that school approaches to reading and writing will authentically offer greater power over literacy to children in classrooms. This is not because of any lack of energy, will or attentiveness on the part of teachers, but because matters of power and texts stretch beyond schools. However, it would be equally easy to make slogans about how difficult it is for schools to operate within those large-scale institutional settings which define what counts as powerful literacy. Typically, what teachers do is duck under the slogan-emblazoned banners and get on with it! Sarah Theaker's chapter is an example of how a fully integrated approach to reading, writing, talk and texts, without slogans, can serve much wider learning. She locks into the social and cultural texts brought by the diverse population of her classroom and, by the way, teaches information-gathering and research techniques, selection of material, written justification and analysis, explanation, persuasion. Using the notion of 'wholegrain nourishment' for language she shows how the yeast of children's cultural experiences of all kinds can leaven learning.

Mary, Mary, quite contrary,
How does your garden grow?
With silver bells and cockleshells,
And pretty maids all in a row.

In language lies the most important difference between mankind and the rest of the animal kingdom. Language expresses identity, enables co-operation, and confers freedom. In language we create a symbolic model of the world, in which past and present are carried forward to the future. Language is the naming of experience, and what we name we have power over.[1]

I teach (and learn from) a class of twenty-eight 7 to 9-year-olds at St Andrew's Junior School, Chesterton. The school serves a mixed catchment area and my class includes two Bengali speakers, three Traveller boys and one statemented child. Although St Andrew's is an Anglican-aided school, it is enriched by the presence of Muslim, Hindu and Jewish children, who offer a wide variety of social and language backgrounds.

Over the past year I have worked with my class on sharing quality picture books and their effects on storywriting. Together we have delighted in *Old Bear*, *Mr Gumpy's Outing* and *Elmer*. We helped Little Bear to find his trousers and we wondered whether worms have a place in heaven. I hope that each of us made friends with at least one book.

As we began to talk about books and poems, to discuss characters, illustrations and language, I began to question the children's literary experience. Had they all shared nursery rhymes with a parent? Had they all received a copy of *Peter Rabbit* with their teething ring? Was the oral tradition still flourishing in the playground? Could I entice it into the classroom? I decided in the long, warm summer term to make time for rhyme.

Mary had a little lamb,
Its fleece was white as snow
And everywhere that Mary went
The lamb was sure to go.
It followed her to school, one day,
Which was against the rule . . .

When young children start school or nursery, they meet a new oral tradition in the classroom and the playground. In the sheltered world of the classroom they may be introduced to 'The Alphabet Song' and 'Five Little Speckled Frogs'. Outside they may be included in clapping games and elaborate 'counting-out' rituals.

However, they may already possess a repertoire of nursery rhymes inherited from parents and grandparents, from aunts and uncles and from a neighbour.

I thought that lower juniors would dismiss nursery rhymes as babyish and boring so I introduced the topic as 'research'. I suggested that we could make and illustrate collections of rhymes for the nursery class at a nearby infant school. Many of the children had younger brothers or sisters at the nursery school and looked forward to sharing their work with a known audience.

What did I hope to discover? I wanted to find out whether there was a link between knowledge of nursery rhymes and development in reading, writing, speaking and listening. I also wanted to take a sneaky peek into the oral culture and literary tradition of the school community.

We began by brainstorming our collective repertoire of nursery rhymes. This activity stimulated memories of childhood for me and of learning to talk for the children. The most commonly known nursery rhymes were 'Baa, Baa, Black Sheep', 'Humpty Dumpty', 'Hickory, Dickory Dock' and 'Twinkle, Twinkle'. Most children had a favourite nursery rhyme, often one that reflected their personal characteristics or appearance. As a child I suffered 'There Was a Little Girl and She Had a Little Curl' on more than one occasion, and I used to quote 'Here Am I, Little Jumping Joan' because I could not find my first name in any of my nursery rhyme collections. 'Twinkle, Twinkle' and 'Pat-a-Cake' were suggested by Karen's table, but were queried by Laura: 'They're not really nursery rhymes. One's a song and the other's a clapping game.' Natalie and Kelly had already decided that 'One, Two, Buckle My Shoe' and 'Solomon Grundy' were not nursery rhymes but that they remembered learning them before starting nursery. Graham wanted to include 'The Alphabet Song'. When he first started to use a dictionary he used to sing through the song in order to locate the position of a letter. He also taught it to his brother, Nathan, aged 3. Daniel asked if it 'counted' if the nursery rhyme was learned at school. His friends thought it did. Our grand total was fifty nursery rhymes, six counting rhymes and eight skipping/ clapping games.

I had assumed that each child would know about ten nursery rhymes. In practice, however, although four children could recite only one or two rhymes and two did not know any nursery rhymes at all, six children could each name and recite over thirty clapping and nursery rhymes.

This year we have embarked on a reading recovery programme loosely based on the pioneering work of Marie Clay in New Zealand. Each day Alex works with a special classroom assistant who hears him read a familiar and an unfamiliar text and helps to discover patterns and sounds in his reading and writing. This intense activity and personal attention have increased his knowledge of spelling and word-families. Do we need a nursery rhyme recovery programme, visiting readers prepared to devote half an hour each day to 'Ding, Dong, Bell' and 'Round and Round the Garden'? Perhaps so, but we certainly needed anthologies of nursery rhymes quickly! The local cheap bookshop yielded an Oxford collection illustrated by Brian Wildsmith, and one of the town bookshops offered *Inky, Pinky, Ponky* and *This Little Puffin* by Michael Rosen and Elizabeth Matterson respectively. A kind assistant in the Early Learning Centre pointed me towards *Oranges and Lemons* and *Pudding and Pie*, both of which were accompanied by tapes.

Back at school these were pored over and discussed by all the children. Slight variations in the text were examined and debated and familiar rhymes were greeted by shouts of 'I know that one!' It was like meeting old friends in new surroundings or wearing different clothes.

Some of the children brought in their own anthologies and I expected irate parents to charge through the door demanding that we study Shakespeare rather than nursery rhymes. However, the message about 'research' must have reached home because Laura's father brought in a beautifully illustrated book of rhymes with their original musical setting, and Nanette Barnard, Alex's special assistant, brought him an article about the history and meaning of well-known rhymes such as 'Ring o' Roses' and 'Lucy Locket'. A boy in Year 6 had 'heard that we were doing nursery rhymes in language work' and let us borrow his little sister's video – with permission, of course.

Each child in the class then chose one rhyme to copy out and illustrate for a class anthology. This involved using the index to find their rhyme and thinking carefully about the content and characters after reading their rhyme to a friend or neighbour. Sima was captivated by 'Pussycat, Pussycat' and Tommy drew squirrels for the narrator and the King of Spain's daughter in 'I Had a Little Nut-Tree'. Tommy is a most accomplished artist who loves drawing squirrels. Making squirrels the subject of a nursery rhyme was his way of accommodating a new literary experience.

All these old chants and verses that we seem to dredge up from early memories to pass on to our children are the rags and bones of a once flourishing oral tradition ... children are guardians of the oral culture in a way that makes them the inheritors of a literary tradition that is older than books. The enchantment of this lore is what early readers know they can find in stories that they read for themselves.[2]

After sharing some of our work in assembly, we received nursery rhymes with intricate borders from Mr Sharpe's and Mr Henaby's classes (Years 5 and 6). This prompted a decision to present our anthology on the word processor, and photocopy our finished product for each class in our school and for the nursery. Natalie and Vicky took turns with Oliver and Owen as typists, and Clare and Carolyn marbled sugar paper for the softback covers. Tommy designed the layout and Jake had the privileged position of editor. These tasks required co-operation and collaboration. Here was collating, recording and publishing for a real purpose and a real audience. The class-room was buzzing with the three Rs – rhyme, reason and 'rgument!

When we had amassed our anthology, I asked small groups of children to sort the rhymes into sections or chapters. Vicky suggested nursery rhymes, playground rhymes and classroom rhymes. Sebastian made lists of rhymes for babies, clapping rhymes and rhymes that 'teach you something'.

When we had finished our class anthology, the work on rhymes became more diversified. As part of our term's topic on the Victorians we had all played with a diabolo, a cup and ball game, and with a skipping rope. A few of the girls owned skipping ropes, but I had not heard any skipping rhymes in the playground. This did not mean that they were not known – many games belong to a small circle of intimate friends, no adults being allowed. However, one Thursday PE session saw a slightly plump teacher turning the handles of a skipping rope and chanting, 'Mother's in the kitchen, doing all the stitching, how many stitches can she do? 1, 2, 3, 4, 5, 6 ... ' to the great delight of twenty-eight giggling children. Undaunted, I also managed 'I'm a Little Bumper Car' and 'Nebuchadnezzar' with doubles (two turns of the rope during one jump). Graham and Wayne had difficulty in co-ordinating their jumps with the rope but Sarah and Alayna managed to sing, dance and skip.

Later that week I observed Alayna sharing a skipping rhyme with her older sister, Charlene. Charlene and her friends were also keen to show me their clapping rhymes. I watched 'A Sailor Went to Sea, Sea, Sea' and 'When Suzie Was a Baby', and invited the players to add their rhymes to our collection.

Back inside the classroom, in the cushioned comfort of the reading corner, we were learning two more rhymes from the oral tradition. 'Cecil is a Caterpillar' and 'Little Rabbit Foo Foo' were great favourites around the campfire when I was a Guide. They have to be said aloud or 'performed' with appropriate gestures and facial expressions. A greedy caterpillar who eats all the cabbages in the universe and is then sick is almost as attractive a role model as a cheeky rabbit who persists in 'scooping up the wriggly worms and bopping them on the head' despite repeated warnings from the Good Fairy. Imagine our delight when 'Little Rabbit Foo Foo' was immortalized by Michael Rosen and published by Walker Books. 'Don't Forget the Bacon' by Pat Hutchins soon moved off the printed page and was absorbed into Class

3/4T's shared oral tradition. 'I know that one' was replaced by 'We know that one'.

These activities had been very teacher-led and I felt it was time for the children to take control whilst I designed and evaluated a questionnaire to complete my own investigations into language acquisition and development.

Naturally, everyone in the class wanted to visit the nursery and read with the pre-school children. How could we choose a small group of children to deliver a copy of *Rhyme Time* and the slightly thumbed copies of *Oranges and Lemons* and *Pudding and Pie*? (We had decided to keep *Inky Pinky Ponky* with its playground rhymes and graffiti.) Eventually it was agreed that anyone with a younger brother or sister in the nursery could accompany the precious gifts. Graham then wanted to know if we could visit all the local playschools – sadly I had to refuse.

The nursery teachers suggested that we visit during story time and share some rhymes with the children in an informal setting. Trying to look older than their 8-year average, and scanning the room for relatives, Joe, Jake, Daniel, Clare, Samantha and Alex took their seats in the circle. Each was introduced and welcomed as a 'real' visitor before leading the group in saying a well-known rhyme. Alex acquitted himself very well but turned bright red when he had finished 'Humpty Dumpty'. After the nursery children had marched up and down to 'The Grand Old Duke of York' it was time to say our goodbyes and return to the 'big school'.

Thus far we had been collectors and recorders of rhymes. We had said them, read them, mimed them and listened to them. We had even added cautionary tales by Hilaire Belloc, and Michael Rosen's *Hairy Tales and Nursery Crimes* to our traditional favourites, but we had not created our own nursery rhymes. Now it was time to start playing with rhyming words, repetition and situation comedy. Kerry had already informed the class that after Humpty Dumpty's fall 'all the king's horses and all the king's men had scrambled eggs for breakfast again'.

Rewriting nursery rhymes is like adding your own blend of herbs to your favourite tinned soup, a familiar flavour with that personal touch. I adapted:

Ickle, ockle, blue bottle, fishes in the sea,
If you want a pretty maid please choose me.

to

Ickle, ockle, cola bottle, icing on the cake.
If you want a clever boy, please choose JAKE.

Later versions included 'tail on the cat ... please choose NAT' and 'bowl of jelly ... please choose KELLY'. The chosen children enjoyed hearing their names in a rhyme and reading their names in personal anthologies. Jake created 'Jack be simple, Jack be thick. Jack burn yourself on the candlestick.' Sima and Carolyn wrote, 'Ring a ring of pansies', and Karen and Rachel penned '1, 2, 3, Mother caught a bee, put it in the frying pan and ate it for her tea'. These alternative rhymes were written out and decorated with a border or an illustration before being added to the class anthology, which now occupied pride of place on the bookshelf next to *Little Bear's Trousers* by Class 3/4T and Class 3/4T's *Book of Songs and Poems*.

Familiar Literacy

Monday's child is fair of face,
Tuesday's child is full of grace,
Wednesday's child is full of woe,
Thursday's child has far to go ... '

Most learning in most settings is a communal activity, a sharing of the culture. It is not just that the child must make his knowledge his own, but that he must make it his own in a community of those who share his sense of belonging to a culture.[3]

Before starting school the young child has assimilated the social, behavioural and linguistic patterns of the family and community. Parents and carers feed, clothe and nurture their developing progeny according to their own theories and experience of childcare. Margaret Meek says that 'the lucky children are those who are read to. If they know stories or rhymes by heart, they bring the words to the page when they read to themselves.'[4]

But it is not enough to provide a selection of board books and a cuddly Jemima Puddleduck. Learning to speak and to listen requires interaction and positive reinforcement. Nursery rhymes and lullabies are not ends in themselves but means of establishing interpersonal relationships and opening the door to literacy.

Familiar literacy events for mainstream pre-schoolers are bedtime stories, reading cereal boxes, stop signs and television advertisements, and interpreting instructions for commercial games and toys. In such literacy events, participants follow socially established rules for verbalizing what they know from and about the written material.[2]

As a 10-year-old, I used to watch my mother playing 'Down at the bottom of the deep blue sea, catching fishes, one, two, three' with my youngest sister, who had just started to talk. On the words 'Dead or alive-oh!' she dropped my sister off her knees before lifting her high into the air and giving her a happy little shake. This game would be repeated five or six times and then they might start on 'Horsey, Horsey, Don't You Stop' or 'This Little Piggy Went to Market'.

Before each rhyme, mother and baby would establish eye-contact. During the rhyme their eyes focused on the other's facial expressions and mouth movements. 'More' was the cue for a repeat performance. At this stage, the rhymes were appreciated for their rhythmic properties and the predictable inflections and accompanying gestures.

When the child begins to join in, the simple vocabulary and repetition of key words or sounds in nursery rhymes such as 'Three Blind Mice' and 'Baa, Baa, Black Sheep' help them to be said, or sung. This experience of oral culture paves the way to speaking, reading and writing.

Children's ordinary discourse does not display the same degree of disciplined formal patterning, control of rhythm, metre, rhyme, stanzaic forms, metaphor, simile, syntactic repetition and morphophonological patterns. These are, however, all features of effective adult oral discourse and writing.[5]

Did the parents of the children in my class view nursery rhymes and action songs as contributory factors in language acquisition and development? I wrote to each child's parents asking them if they were prepared to fill in a questionnaire about their reading habits and history. Twenty families requested one or more questionnaires, and four families even said that their grandparents would like to contribute their ideas, thereby building up a picture of three generations of readers/writers/speakers/listeners.

By the end of term I had received 40 completed questionnaires; four from grandparents, 27 from parents/guardians and nine from children. All the respondents knew and could say more than 20 nursery rhymes, although three admitted that they did not enjoy reading or writing. When asked whether they thought nursery rhymes were instrumental in the process of acquiring language, replies varied:

Yes, they teach us to learn words. (Alayna, 8)

Yes, nursery rhymes are an introduction to books. (Mrs McKenzie, Kelly's mother)

When a child follows a rhyme in a book, she will see that the reader is going from left to right. (Mrs Wick, Emily's mother)

Children can match up words on a page with the words they know in their heads. (Mrs Tipple, Oliver's mother)

In his introduction to *Reading for Real*, Barrie Wade reinforces the links between speaking, listening and learning to read:[4] 'Interaction and sharing with others are fundamental to the process of becoming a reader at home at school, in the workplace and in society at large.[6]

Nursery rhymes can also be seen as 'little histories'. 'Ring a Ring o' Roses' is said to be a macabre parody on the horrors of the plague, and 'Goosey, Goosey, Gander' may describe Cromwell's soldiers hunting for Royalist fugitives after the Civil War. Iona and Peter Opie have interpreted many traditional rhymes, but Mrs Wick, Emily's mother and nursery nurse, suggests:

A lot of old rhymes have political or historical undercurrents which are not known by the speaker but the rhymes are taken as fun and are enjoyed.

The music of the Italian opera and the thrill of listening to soaring arias can be appreciated without understanding every word. In opera, however, cows do not jump over the moon, but in Mother Goose's queendom teddies walk unaided, bells talk and dishes run away with smiling spoons! In *The Child and the Book*, Nicholas Tucker explains that

the static objects of picture books may now sometimes be treated as animated characters in their own right, whether they be steam-shovels, motor-cars, household goods or toys. Children can easily accept this type of fantasy since the idea of universal animism seems fundamental to all human imagination.[7]

Which train can be relied on in a crisis, Thomas the Tank Engine or the 14.50 to Peterborough? Ask the Fat Controller or any 3-year-old.

One potato, two potato, three potato, four,
Five potato, six potato, seven potato, more.
You-are-not-IT.

As the name suggests, counting-out rhymes (or dipping rhymes as they are usually called by children themselves) display a relationship between the format, i.e. rhyming, and function, i.e. counting, characteristics.[8]

In the school playground, putting up your fists for potatoes heralds inclusion, belonging. When children start school they will meet a new oral tradition consisting of skipping games, songs about school dinners and counting-out rhymes. This oral culture is transmitted through simple or more developed narratives. It is passed on to apprentice skippers or hand-clappers, but rarely written down.

Playground rhymes contribute to the process of socialization in three distinct ways. First, they offer the delight of sharing intricate gestures and clapping rhythms with a close friend, solidarity against the potential violence of the football game or the insults of older children. Second, they allocate roles in a non-threatening group situation. Faced with a difficult task, a group of adults might draw straws or pull pieces of paper out of a hat. Children have developed this game of chance into an extended, formal ritual, the counting-out game.

The literary texts children employ in this case allow possibilities for dealing with forms of social power, for learning about structural modes of membership allocation to either dominant or subordinate positions, i.e. mechanisms of exclusion, while at the same time enhancing group cohesion and offering the possibility of experiencing delight.[8]

Third, playground rhymes and chants offer an opportunity to question or parody social conventions. In the rhyme 'When Suzie Was a Baby' the subject progresses rapidly from childhood to motherhood, into the rocking chair and into the grave. Opie and Opie call this 'mimicry', since the players mimic an outdated expectation of development.

Many rhymes are rude or subversive. 'My Friend Billy' and 'Popeye the Sailor-Man' are traditional favourites, but recent additions include 'I Should Be So Potty, Going Out With Scotty' and 'A Mars a Day Makes You Fat and Ug-lay'. These show children challenging the bland diet offered by the music and confectionery industries.

Despite nonsensical rhymes and elaborate gestures, all playground rhymes are meaningful to their owners. They are initiated and guarded by children. Adults have no part in this world of role experimentation and repetition. So how can the structure and rhythm of rhymes such as 'A Sailor Went to Sea, Sea, Sea' be reinforced in the classroom? I have already mentioned *Don't Forget the Bacon* by Pat Hutchins. Other favourites in my classroom are *Chicken Soup with Rice* by Maurice Sendak, and *The Little Red Hen* and *Not Now Bernard* by David McKee.

Strong pattern will carry young readers through a book when they could not actually tackle a text of such complexity without it. Pattern encourages prediction, phrasing, word recognition, and it gives the same security as nursery rhymes or skipping rhymes.[9]

The man in the wilderness asked of me,
How many strawberries grow in the sea?
I answered him as I thought good,
As many red herrings as grow in the wood.

At the end of the summer term, I had to ask myself several questions. How had my view of the importance of nursery rhymes changed? Had the children in my class benefited from making time for rhyme? Where should we go from here?

As a class teacher, my role is to provide a stimulating environment complete with richly illustrated texts to facilitate the development of reading, writing, speaking and listening. I have to provide resources which invite the receptive skills of reading, for meaning and enjoyment, and listening. These skills provide wholegrain nourishment for the productive skills of speaking, to convey information and to entertain, and writing, to extend reality through story and to experiment with words for the sake of playing with language.

I began my classroom investigation with the assumption that all the children would be familiar with nursery rhymes. Margaret Meek also believes that many young readers bring their own knowledge of nursery rhyme and their characters to the text:

As a writer you could count on children knowing, say, Humpty Dumpty or Old Mother Hubbard, Jack and Jill, Cinderella perhaps. That's what Janet and Allan Ahlberg do in *Each Peach Pear Plum*. The young reader doesn't have to know about Tom Thumb to be able to read the words 'I spy Tom Thumb'; the invitation from the artist is to find him in the picture. But if the beginner has heard of him before, in a rhyme or in another book, there are two kinds of finding; one of the boy hiding in the picture, the other of the fact that Tom Thumb is also known to the Ahlbergs in the way that we all say we know Jane Eyre or Billy Bunter.[4]

Members of my class say they 'know' Paddington, Mary Poppins, Winnie the Pooh and Bramudl Brown. Certainly, familiarity with these literary characters has been aided by television, but they can be rediscovered on the printed page with the help of the imagination. Frank Smith describes readers (of any age) with this knowledge as belonging to 'a literacy club'.[10] But what about those readers who do not belong, those readers who decode the Griffin

Pirates and the Puffin paperbacks but who have yet to be introduced to Humpty Dumpty and Tom Thumb? It is never too late to join.

For the teacher this means reviewing collections of nursely rhymes and displaying them alongside *Each Peach Pear Plum* as parallel texts.

In order to capture the reader's attention, books have to invite close investigation. Pictures should be extensions of meaning which enhance each rhyme. I have invested in Prue Theobalds' *For Teddy and Me*. All her teddies are drawn from 'life' in the Bethnal Green Museum of Childhood. Another find was *No Hickory, No Dickory, No Dock* by John Agard and Grace Nichols. These Caribbean rhymes seem to sing themselves off the page!

Sharing rhymes, both in the classroom and the playground, requires active listening. I had to listen carefully to Kelly when she taught me Solomon Grundy; she has to listen to my voice all day. Tapes and radio programmes encourage careful listening and provide a change of voice.

There are many reasons for using rhymes with young children. The first and most important is that adults enjoy it enormously. If we need more justification than that, then it provides excellent speech practice and voice control. Although many rhymes and songs are simple in content, they increase vocabulary and the repeated patterns and sequences of words and rhythms are good memory exercises. The ritual of taking turns and conforming to the 'rules' and the communication there can be in sharing an experience which crosses both age and cultural gaps are useful factors in social development.[11]

Reciting rhymes, telling a story with gestures, chanting a football song and sharing a joke are examples of communication and socialization within a group. Although I respect the fact that talk in the playground may be 'private', I want to welcome the child's own linguistic experience into the classroom. Sylvia Ashton Warner describes language as 'organic' and 'inorganic'.[12] 'Organic' language grows out of the child's own emotions and needs. 'Inorganic' language is foisted upon the learner by teachers and other adults and is essentially meaningless. The oral tradition is a living, breathing mass of songs, rhymes, proverbs and mnemonics – truly organic. Is there a place for this in the curriculum?

My answer is an unequivocal 'yes'. Dipping my big toe into the sea of nursery rhymes, counting rhymes and playground rhymes has opened my eyes to neglected, forgotten favourites lying on the shore. What easier way is there to learn the length of the months than 'Thirty Days Hath September'? Which artist, or scientist for that matter, can ignore the fact that Richard of York gave battle in vain?

I will have to make time for rhymes in my classroom – time to read aloud, to speak and listen, to discuss and debate, to create; time for nursery rhymes, haiku, sonnets and songs.

If all the world were paper,
And all the sea were ink . . .

If we want to see what lessons have been learned from the texts children read, we have to look for them in what they write. Of course, they draw on the whole of their culture if we let them. We have to be alert to what comes from books as well as from life.[4]

Many writers draw on the literary tradition of intertextuality and the oral tradition of life. Natalie Eaton composed the following rhyme in response to Environment Week and the enchanting book, *Dear Greenpeace*.

Freddie is a whale, Freddie is my friend,
The last time I saw Freddie he was this big!
I said, Freddie what have you been doing?
I've eaten all the krill in the sea.

The rhythm and metre are taken from 'Cecil Is a Caterpillar' but Natalie, as a speaker, a reader and a writer, can create a powerful model of her world. Freddie eats all the krill in the ocean, in the world and in the universe, until in the final verse:

Freddie is a whale, Freddie is my friend,
The last time I saw Freddie,
It was being towed away for oil.

References

1. Department of Education and Science (1988) Report of the Committee of Inquiry into the Teaching of the English Language, p. 7. London: HMSO.

2. Meek, M. (1982) *Learning to Read*. London: The Bodley Head.

3. Bruner, J. (1986) *Actual Minds, Possible Worlds*, p. 132. London: Harvard Educational Press.

4. Meek, M. (1988) *How Texts Teach What Readers Learn*. Stroud: Thimble Press.

5. Grugeon, E. (1988) Children's oral culture: a transitional experience. In M. Maclure, J. Phillips and A. Wilkinson (eds) *Oracy Matters*, p. 171. Milton Keynes: Open University Press.

6. Wade, B. (ed.) (1990) *Reading for Real*. Milton Keynes: Open University Press.

7. Tucker, N. (1981) *The Child and the Book*, p. 47. Cambridge: Cambridge University Press.

8. Van Peer, W. (1988) Counting out: form and function in children's counting out rhymes. In M. Maclure, J. Phillips and A. Wilkinson (eds) *Oracy Matters*. Milton Keynes: Open University Press.

9. Waterland, L. (1988) *Read With Me*. Stroud: Thimble Press.

10. Smith, F. (1978) *Reading*. Cambridge: Cambridge University Press.

11. Matterson, E. (1991) *This Little Puffin*. Harmondsworth: Puffin Books.

12. Ashton-Warner, S. (1980) *Teacher*, p. 33. London: Virago.

Postscript
Teaching Reading and Writing:
Interventions for Success

The varied strands of classroom enquiry in this book represent differences in ages, schools, social contexts and focus of investigation. What binds them together is the commitment to seeing reading and writing (and talking and listening as well) as necessarily linked. Another common link takes this interrelatedness further by suggesting that the wholeness of language, rather than its fragmentation, makes it possible to stretch the boundaries of what might be expected of developing reader-writers. In turn, extending the scope of what is possible tends to make for greater success. In reading the varied accounts in this book for guidance about how best to teach reading and writing, a pattern emerges. This is not a formula – 'Do it like this and you will succeed' – but there are important practical, as well as principled, elements which can be identified. Many of these cluster around *intervening* for learning. However, in locating the ways in which this book depicts classroom intervention, I want to suggest a rather different interpretation than is often give to the term.

For many years, and no doubt still around and about educational thinking now, there has been a view that teachers can get better at teaching if a few enlightened people explain what they are doing wrong. Those 'experts' then provide a particular programme of work, special materials or prescribed methods to 'intervene' in the process of learning, and magically the teacher's classroom practice improves with the concomitant raising of children's standards. If only it were that easy! What is very clear from the accounts in this book is that intervening for progress in literacy is a highly complex matter which cannot be reduced to slick formulae or naive rhetoric. Intervention to raise standards of literacy is not a matter of a straightforward link between cause and effect; it is not like 'prescribing a cure'. And it does not just happen in the classroom. It helps, perhaps, to shift the perspective about what teacher intervention can mean by first making another shift in thinking: seeing 'teaching' as 'making it possible for children to learn'. This signals a much broader and positive view of intervention, one which starts before the teacher and children even reach the classroom.

The chapters in this book provide practical examples of positive intervention. The classroom examples given suggest that raising standards of reading and writing means setting up an environment in which learning can be most effective, rather than adhering to particular methods or materials. When this notion of organizing an effective learning environment is related to the curriculum for English, it means providing *contexts* for the study and production of texts. The context for any classroom activity will frame what it is possible for children to achieve. But it is not just the physical setting of the classroom which contributes to an effective context; there needs also to be a context of possibility, that intangible area of a teacher's expertise which feeds into planning for activities which will both challenge and support literacy.

The first interventions that can be made, then, are those which a teacher makes 'in the head'. When planning for children's progress in reading or writing, a teacher will keep in mind both the larger scale types or genres, forms and formats of text (for writing or reading) which she or he wants the children to experience as well as the close focus on details of text construction or interpretation – the 'big shapes' and smaller units which contribute to the literacy curriculum. The specific approaches which are to be used will depend on the particular aims for that programme of work – the context of expectation into which the teacher will introduce selected reading or writing activities. Part of this stage of intervention will be the teacher's consideration of what *resources* to use. It is easy to think that resources, also, are those familiar ones which are regularly brought into the classroom in the physical form of books, artefacts, videos and all the other carefully selected (and important) materials for engaging children in learning. However, as has become clear from many of the accounts in this book, one of the most fruitful resources resides in the children themselves and their existing knowledge of texts. Awareness of pupils' competence with texts of all kinds means saving much valuable time and effort which might otherwise be squandered in the assumption that the teacher has to start on a blank sheet to develop a child's literacy.

Finding out what children know about reading, writing, talking and listening not only establishes an essential knowledge base, but helps the children themselves move their implicit knowledge into the conscious light of careful scrutiny. This helps them to recognize what they already know so that they can extend this knowledge. They have a hold on those systems of thought which are important to later learning. Hilary Minns, in her detailed study of children's pre-school and schooled literacy experience, emphasizes that:

Children become part of a new social group when they enter school, and bring with them views of themselves as learners. It is crucial that the school helps to build on that view by showing children that their pre-school experience is valid and significant, and finding ways of reflecting it back to them.[1]

As many of the chapters in this book show, it is not only pre-school literacy experience which is worthy of attention in the classroom. Asking pupils what they think about reading and writing can yield surprising, and often salutary, results! A significant point in the quotation from Hilary Minns highlights another important part of language teaching and learning: deliberate, *conscious attention* to the texts which children know about or can produce. It is not enough just to find out what children know and can do; this needs to form the basis for planned and systematic future learning. However, *systematic planning* need not signal inflexibility. It is like a meticulous route-planner who insists on sitting in a traffic jam in order to adhere to the plan and so misses a lot of interesting scenery as well as losing the chance to find new ways of reaching the destination. Teaching to prescribed and inflexible language schemes – whether commercially produced or provided in school for all the best reasons – runs exactly the same risks. It is just not worth missing the scenery to stick to the route, and sitting in a traffic jam enhances nobody's life or learning!

Planning for Progress

In order to be able to plan for flexibility and changes of direction, a teacher will have some idea of where the learners should be at the end of a series of activities or period of time. This means that there will be a way of *recording and measuring progress*. In CLPE's splendid *Reading Book* the authors put it like this:

Any kind of record-keeping system needs to be based on sound educational principles and the collection of different kinds of evidence. It should be cumulative in nature, building up a picture of a child's learning, and clear in the way it communicates, not only to teachers but also to parents and children.[2]

What is of particular importance here is the point about 'different kinds of evidence'. As so many of the children represented in this book demonstrate, their knowledge about texts is shown not only through the texts they can read or write, but also through conversation and, significantly, behaviour. A child's ability to select preferred reading, whether deliberately or with quick enthusiasm, tells us something about that child's literacy. Similarly, a decision to write in a particular form – or even a choice not to write at the time – can indicate positive new literacy behaviours which are significant markers of progress.

These observed features can only be noted as progress if they form part of a continuing careful system of record-keeping about literacy. Assessment of development needs to be capable of capturing detailed knowledge reservoir of different kinds of texts; their increasing ability to become independent in working with texts; and the gradual development of discrimination and choice.

If young reader-writers are to develop discrimination, then part of the literacy environment must include *opportunities for choice*. Apart from the need for children to rehearse making decisions about what to read or write, how to do it, when, and what might help, it is clear from everyday classroom experience, as well as the accounts in this book, that different children (and adults!) have different styles of learning. To adopt a single approach to learning runs the risk of excluding some of the learners. Similarly, it is becoming more evident that there are no necessary age barriers to learning how to discriminate. Traditional views about 'ages and stages' and the materials which are produced according to these theories of 'building block' stages of progress suggest that the more complex thought processes which may be needed to make literary choices based on clear criteria or to analyse literary texts belong in the later stages of school learning. Several of the chapters which give accounts of work in infant classrooms strenuously counter such assumptions. Given opportunities for *reflection and evaluation*, even very young children can be confident literary critics of their own, as well as other people's, texts. When this reflection and evaluation is directed towards their own reading and writing, children themselves can become involved in the process of tracking their own progress, giving them not only responsibility but a framework for future development.

But, as is also acknowledged in this book, there are still those for whom reading and writing are major hurdles. Evidence offered in this book shows that often their knowledge of a wider range of texts can be used to help them take on the mysteries of schooled literacy. What seems important is to keep alive an awareness of just how richly the range of popular texts can feed teachers' proper interventions (including those which are less obvious) towards confident literacy. A key to how this might be made possible lies within the very kinds of textual knowledge which come from home communities and cultures. This very often depends upon dialogue forms of texts – spoken, media, comic and magazine – and it is through *dialogue and response* that literacy can be developed further. Talking about texts, responding carefully to those which the pupils produce, offering *models and examples* not only of the range of available texts, but also of what it is like to be a developed reader and writer, all contribute to the context of possibilities outlined earlier.

Since much literacy experience takes place as part of the shared culture of a community, whether it is the home, school or classroom community, *collaboration and partnerships* become important ingredients of intervention for literacy. Many of the classroom accounts, particularly in the third part of this book, examine just how important the cultural and community elements of literacy can be in promoting progress. In the variety of texts, ages, approaches and aspects of learning, there is no doubt about the importance of offering *challenge and support* if young people are to have access to a fuller version of literacy. The results of bold experiments by teachers and children lead to the dynamic of *further challenge* as the continuing form of positive intervention for improving standards of literacy.

A Curriculum for Diversity

Diversity emerges as an important strand of this book. Recent debates about literacy have tended to talk about 'opposing' theoretical positions and so to shift attention towards contrasts. This is to be expected, perhaps. To win an argument you do not find areas of agreement with your opponent. Or perhaps you do. It depends a great deal on the consequences of the debate; the area over which contention is raging. In the case of schooled (and home) literacy, the territory under dispute is peopled with children – and their futures. On the one hand, that means that the debate must be all the more passionately continued, since children's literacy matters so much. On the other hand, it might mean that some settlement of the dispute is urgent, *because* literacy matters so much. As always with educational matters, there are no easy answers. What the work in this book suggests is that it is time to ask some sharp questions about the nature of recent arguments over literacy – about the most effective ways to help children become successful readers and writers. It is time, perhaps, to set aside differences in favour of a diversity of approach.

One important question might be: *how far are arguments about literacy to do with differences in theoretical principles or is there an element of power-point scoring?* Another is: *how much is done to make clear what children already know or is there more emphasis on describing failure?* Even more critical might be: *how far does any viewpoint about reading and writing inform teachers about the range and diversity of children, their language communities and language use, or are there significant gaps and silences when it comes to variety and difference?* There is great emphasis at the moment on providing a 'differentiated' curriculum so as to promote children's learning more effectively. This may well have grown from a proper concern to make sure that the variety and range of children's styles of learning and existing experience are taken into account in providing variety and range in classroom approaches.

When it comes to teaching reading and writing, however, the emphasis on differentiation can lead to a restricted curriculum for some – the 'trivial tasks' or underexpectation identified by OFSTED in some classrooms.[3] As every chapter in this book reiterates, overtly or implicitly, low expectations will inevitably hold back children's literacy. What is equally repeated is that it is critically important to offer equal opportunities for learning by adopting an assumption of diversity in:

- the value given to children's varied literacy experiences

- the full range of texts which can be included in the reading and writing curriculum

- the varieties of literacy experiences on offer

- 'ways in' to literacy

There is then no need to create spurious ways of differentiating further in the teaching of reading and writing.

Conclusion: a Full Literacy Curriculum

This book begins with a promise to place educational theory in the practical context of classroom approaches to literacy. All the contributors to the work captured in these pages – children and teachers alike – provide the evidence and examples for both a practical framework for a full literacy curriculum and the operation of well-grounded theory. As traced in the earlier sections of this Postscript, patterns of practice reflecting a particular theory of literacy development have emerged. This suggests that effective teaching to promote successful learning in reading and writing involves the following:

- setting up a stimulating physical context in the classroom

- creating a 'context of possibility'

- using a range of resources, starting with the children's own language experience

- paying conscious attention to the texts children read and write

- planning systematically

- observing, recording and measuring progress cumulatively

- offering opportunities for choice and discrimination, reflection and evaluation, dialogue and response

- providing models and examples, including the teacher's own literacy practice and experience

- organizing for a range of collaborations and partnerships, both within and outside the classroom and school

- presenting challenges, support and further challenge to push forward the boundaries of literacy

All of these elements of the literacy curriculum signal a strong sense of underlying theory about what development means. If children are to be helped to extend their literacy, then it is essential to understand the inter-relatedness of reading, writing, speaking and listening. This acceptance of the integrity of language leads to acceptance of how language in all its forms is the central means by which children make sense of experience and create new knowledge. A developmental theory like this necessarily sees the growth of literacy as recursive and dynamic – a steady upward spiral of achievement, revisiting old knowledge and experience in the light of the new and so extending even further. Rather than a linear progression through clearly defined stages, this more complex theoretical view makes literacy a living experienced matter, not something to be got from 'out there' but the result of a combination of the diverse possibilities of all the literacies on offer and the rich diversity of children's potential. These are critical times for literacy but there is hope for the future in the energy that such a dynamic theory-in-practice can release for children's literacy development.

References

1. Minns, H. (1990) *Read It to Me Now!* p. 114. London: Virago Education.

2. Barrs, M. and Thomas, A. (eds) (1991) *The Reading Book*, p. 102. London: Centre for Language in Primary Education.

3. OFSTED (1993) *English Key Stages 1, 2, 3 and 4 Fourth Year 1992–3: the Implementation of the Curricular Requirements of the Education Reform Act*, p. 11. London: Office for Standards in Education.

Index